THE POLICE FOUNDATION

Motorcycle Roadcraft

The Police Rider's Handbook

Did you know that Motorcycle Roadcraft is also available as an e-learning course with a certificate?

The Stationery Office
London

Contributing authors: Penny Mares, Philip Coyne, Barbara MacDonald.
Current author: Mark Rylander.
Design: Adam Ray, Adam Kimberley.
Illustration: Original illustrations created by Nick Moxsom.
Front cover photography: Rob Brown and Adam Kimberley. Motorcycle courtesy of Norfolk Constabulary.
Project manager: Catherine Saunders, The Police Foundation.
Project advisor: Daniel Whittle, TSO.

The Police Foundation

The Police Foundation is an independent charity that researches, understands and works to improve policing.

For further details of the Police Foundation's work and other related *Roadcraft* publications, contact:

Email: roadcraft@police-foundation.org.uk
Website: www.roadcraft.co.uk

Charity Registration Number: 278257

Other essential guides to safe driving and riding also published by The Stationery Office include:

Roadcraft – The Police Driver's Handbook (2025)
ISBN 978 0 11 709504 5

Motorcycle Roadcraft e-learning platform
https://www.safedrivingforlife.info/shop/motorcycle-roadcraft-elearning/

To order or find out more about these or any other riding titles, please refer to the contact details printed inside the front cover of this book.

New edition 2025

Second impression 2026

ISBN 978 0 11 709505 2

SD000401

WORLD LAND TRUST™
www.carbonbalancedprint.com
CBP2223

Acknowledgements

This edition of *Motorcycle Roadcraft* has been approved by the National Police Chiefs' Council (NPCC) and Police Scotland, which are satisfied that it reflects current best practice in police rider instruction and takes into account the relevant views of civilian experts.

The Police Foundation would like to thank the many individuals and organisations who gave so freely of their time and expertise in the preparation of this new edition of *Motorcycle Roadcraft*. Particular thanks go to Craig Arnold, Technical Lead at the Transport Research Laboratory; Dr Helen Wells, Director, Roads Policing Academic Network; Dr Graham Hole, Honorary Senior Lecturer in Psychology, University of Sussex; and Jason Powell, Fleet Lead, National Police Chiefs' Council. Some sections of material in Chapters 1 and 4 are adapted from *Human Aspects of Police Driving* by kind permission of Dr Gordon Sharp and Police Scotland.

The Police Foundation would also like to thank Norfolk Constabulary for their kind assistance in arranging the cover photography.

The Police Foundation would like to thank Drivetech for providing a financial contribution towards the cost of producing the handbook.

drivetech from the AA

This new edition of *Motorcycle Roadcraft* was produced with the strategic oversight of a Standing Advisory Board with representatives from major police and civilian riding organisations, to whom we are most grateful.

Standing Advisory Board

Mark Bull, Regional Senior Examiner, Royal Society for the Prevention of Accidents (RoSPA)

Jon Curtis, Roads Policing Business Manager, College of Policing

Roger Gardner, Chairman, National Police Chiefs' Council National Driver Training (Practitioners) Group

Richard Gladman, Chief Examiner, IAM Roadsmart

Bob McNay, Head of Road Policing and Driver Training, Scottish Police College, Police Scotland

Rick Muir, former Director, The Police Foundation (Chair)

Stuart O'Neill, Metropolitan Police Driver Training Academy

Colin Stewart, Assistant Chief Driving Examiner and Driver Training Policy Manager, Driver and Vehicle Standards Agency (DVSA)

It was undertaken with the dedicated help of a Reflective Practitioners group of senior police, fire, ambulance and civilian instructors, whose contribution to the detailed editorial and updating process has been invaluable.

Reflective Practitioners

Byron Chandler, Specialist Skills Manager and Chief Driving Instructor, Gloucestershire Constabulary

Iain Cook, Driver Training and Development, West Yorkshire Police

Kevin Dell, Emergency Response Driver Specialist, National Fire Chiefs Council

Donna Kidd, Road Policing and Driver Training, Scottish Police College, Police Scotland

Nick Lambert, Head of Education, East Midlands Ambulance Service.

Peter Mosdell, Head of Specialist Skills, Education and Training, Babcock International Group

Peter Rodger, former Inspector, Metropolitan Police Driving School and former Chief Examiner, IAM RoadSmart

Colin Stewart, Assistant Chief Driving Examiner and Driver Training Policy Manager, DVSA

Matthew Thomas, Head of Driver Training, Dyfed-Powys Police

Editorial and Project Management Board

Lisa Daniels, Account Director, TSO

Mark Rylander, Editor and Technical Writer

Catherine Saunders, Communications and Publications Manager, The Police Foundation

Daniel Whittle, Content Development Manager, TSO

Foreword

In its 60th year, *Motorcycle Roadcraft* remains the backbone of police riding, providing a valuable reference and learning tool for police riders.

The first edition of *Motorcycle Roadcraft* was published in 1965. Over the years, it has been used more widely by the emergency services and members of the public who acknowledge its benefits in providing a system of safe riding. UK police riding is held in very high regard and seen as the best across the policing world. The skills and standards of police riders are extensively used and tested daily, demonstrating the value of quality training. I am confident that the experience and qualifications of our trainers using the curriculum supplied by the College of Policing, and supported by *Motorcycle Roadcraft*, will continue to enable police officers and emergency response riders to meet the challenges they face.

Each year sees a growth in the number of road users and advancements in vehicle technology, which create new challenges for rider safety. The reduction of road casualties and the safety of all road users remains paramount. Given that riders face very specific safety challenges, raising the standard of awareness of vulnerable road users amongst drivers is as important as becoming a better, safer rider. For this reason, I would encourage all road users to read and understand the principles outlined in this publication to further enhance their skills and safety on the road.

Deputy Chief Constable Terry Woods,
NPCC Lead Police Driving

Motorcycle Roadcraft is endorsed by the following organisations:

College of Policing

NPCC National Police Chiefs' Council

Police Scotland Poileas Alba

IAM RoadSmart

NFCC National Fire Chiefs Council

RoSPA accidents don't have to happen

Association of Ambulance Chief Executives

Contents

Preface to the new edition

This new and fully updated edition of *Motorcycle Roadcraft* is the result of sustained consultation with experts in the theory and practice of advanced riding.

The last edition of *Motorcycle Roadcraft* was published in 2020 and featured major updates to the overtaking and limit point sections, as well as other significant changes designed to reflect the changing state of advanced riding practice.

The 2025 edition seeks to maintain this tradition by explaining the purpose of advanced rider-assistance systems (ARAS). As well as a general introduction to the core concepts, the text features clear explanations of common types of ARAS and their functions.

This emphasis on technology is due, in no small part, to the way that police vehicles have changed since the last edition went to press. With the rapid increase in assistance technologies, it's become essential to deal with the fundamentals of these systems and recognise their primary role as a tool to assist riders, not a replacement for good judgement.

To support the development of advanced observation skills, this edition also contains a new section on using cross views to take information on bends. This forms part of a series of complementary techniques, including understanding zones of visibility and using observation links to gather information about the road environment.

As in previous editions, *Motorcycle Roadcraft* specifically focuses on addressing human factors in police riding. Central to this theme has been the work of psychologist Dr Robert West (1997 edition), occupational physician Dr Gordon Sharp (2007 edition) and psychologist Dr Lisa Dorn (2007 and 2013 editions) with additional contributions made by Dr Gemma Briggs and Dr Julie Gandolfi (2020 edition) and Dr Helen Wells, Dr Graham Hole and Craig Arnold for the current edition. Each has contributed a range of insights to equip students to recognise, manage and reduce risks arising from these human aspects. And, as understanding of the psychological factors that influence riding behaviour evolves, new developments in this field – including the way that vehicle technology affects the relationship between the rider, the machine, and the environment – will continue to inform future editions of *Motorcycle Roadcraft*.

This edition of *Motorcycle Roadcraft* includes an updated emergency response chapter that demonstrates nationally formalised response advice. As well as its value in an operational context, it is considered to be useful for the public to be informed about response driving and riding so they are better prepared to react when they encounter an emergency vehicle.

About *Motorcycle Roadcraft*

How can *Motorcycle Roadcraft* help you become a better rider?

Motorcycle Roadcraft is the handbook for police and other emergency services riders undertaking rider training. In rider training, *Motorcycle Roadcraft* is combined with practical instruction. This edition is designed so that it can be used for self-study either before or during a course, and for ready reference afterwards.

The aim of *Motorcycle Roadcraft* is to improve your riding ability. Your safety and that of other road users depends on your awareness of what's happening around you and your ability to control the position and speed of your machine relative to everything else on the road. A collision or even a near miss can be the result of a lapse in riding skill. *Motorcycle Roadcraft* aims to help you become a better rider by increasing your awareness of all the factors that affect your riding – your own capabilities, the characteristics of your machine, and the road and traffic conditions, including the actions of other road users that can put you at risk.

The system of motorcycle control explained in *Motorcycle Roadcraft* is a methodical approach to hazards which increases your safety by giving you more time to react in complex situations.

What machines does *Motorcycle Roadcraft* cover?

You can apply the principles of *Motorcycle Roadcraft* to any machine you ride, large or small, modern or old.

The basic design and the supplementary features built into a machine all affect its capabilities. As motorcycle design and safety technology become more sophisticated, it would be impossible in a book of this size to cover the range of variations in, for example, transmission systems, adaptive suspension and active safety features. You should always get to know your machine's characteristics and adapt your riding to them, and have a good grasp of the manufacturer's guidance for every bike that you ride.

What *Motorcycle Roadcraft* does not include

Motorcycle Roadcraft assumes that you're thoroughly familiar with the current edition of the Highway Code and is intended to be used in conjunction with that publication.

Certain techniques that require a high level of instruction to ensure their safety, such as those used in pursuit and other specialist situations, aren't included. Your instructor will introduce you to these when appropriate.

Using *Motorcycle Roadcraft* for self-study

These are the features that will help you to get the most out of *Motorcycle Roadcraft*, whether you're studying independently or using it as part of formal instruction:

- The main learning points are listed at the start of each chapter. These lists will help you choose the chapters or sections that you need to concentrate on.
- The self-assessment questions in the text are designed to help you develop your awareness of the human factors (for example, personality, mood, stress) that could affect your riding safety, and help you to manage them. These and the practical questions will enable you to transfer the advice in *Motorcycle Roadcraft* to your everyday riding.
- Illustrations and diagrams are used to explain complex ideas. Read them along with the text as they often expand on this or provide a different level of information. Bear in mind that all illustrations are only a guide to the real world – don't rely on them alone.
- Important points are highlighted in coloured boxes.
- The learning points are repeated at the end of each chapter to help you check your understanding.

Working through the chapters

Chapters 1, 2 and 3 are the foundations on which later chapters build so you should ideally read these in order first. If you're using *Motorcycle Roadcraft* as part of a riding course, your instructor may suggest you study certain sections of the book in a different order.

Personal risks, practice and self-assessment

Just reading *Motorcycle Roadcraft* won't make you a better rider. Awareness of your personal risks, practice and self-assessment are an essential part of developing competence. What matters is not how well you can recall what's in this book but how well you can apply what you've learnt to your riding.

Aim to develop your awareness of the human factors that can affect your riding behaviour even before you get on your machine. Your personality, state of mind, attitudes to other road users, stress and operational distractions can all affect your performance. In order to achieve the highest levels of riding competence and safety, *Motorcycle Roadcraft* encourages you to develop your self-assessment skills, so that you learn to recognise and safely manage the human factors that can put you at risk.

Many of the practical competences explained here are fairly simple in themselves. A sophisticated riding ability comes from applying them consistently. All competences depend on judgement and this only comes with practice. Aim to apply the techniques in *Motorcycle Roadcraft* systematically so that they become an everyday part of your riding.

You can't absorb all the information in *Motorcycle Roadcraft* in one reading, so we suggest that you read a section, select a technique, practise it, assess your progress, and then refer to *Motorcycle Roadcraft* to refine the technique further.

Using *Motorcycle Roadcraft* for reference

The contents pages at the front of the book list all the main headings and a selective list of the most useful sub-headings. Cross references throughout the book will help you find linked information in other chapters. There's also a comprehensive index on page 306.

Learning is a continual process

Being a good rider means that you never stop learning. *Motorcycle Roadcraft* offers advice on the principles of better riding but can't be a definitive guide to all riding situations and techniques. Machines and riding conditions are constantly changing, and your riding competences need to keep pace with this change, otherwise they could become outdated and even dangerous. Aim to constantly self-evaluate and, where necessary, adapt your riding so that you maintain high standards and continually improve your performance. Every time you ride, use the journey as an opportunity to develop your riding ability.

Chapter 1
Becoming a better rider

Learning outcomes

The learning in this chapter, along with rider training, should enable you to:

- explain the competences required for police riding
- identify the human factors that may increase your vulnerability as a rider
- explain the Goals for Driver Education and how these can help you manage risks and assess your own riding
- show that you give priority to safety at all times
- show that you can recognise and manage the human factors that may affect your decision-making and riding performance
- show that you can honestly and critically assess your own riding behaviour to achieve continuous improvement.

Becoming a better rider

This chapter is about how you can become a better rider. Many people say they enjoy riding a bike because it gives them a strong sense of freedom – but it's even more satisfying when you know you have the necessary competences to keep yourself safe. This chapter focuses on the personal qualities that are essential for safe and competent riding. Understanding your personal risks and knowing how to increase your safety will lay the foundations for a long, enjoyable and rewarding riding career.

Across the UK and the European Union, driver and rider training at all levels now encourages learners to consider the effects of human factors – personality, attitudes, state of mind and emotions – on their riding or driving abilities. Research shows that all these factors have a strong influence on an individual's risk of crashing.

This is because your personal characteristics affect how you approach technical skills, use your machine, respond to traffic conditions and to other road users, and deal with the demands of a particular journey and the job of riding. This chapter introduces the main elements of the European Goals for Driver Education. It also explains how these can support your awareness of personal risks and your self-assessment abilities.

See Appendix 4, page 300.

Your ability to honestly self-assess your own riding performance accurately and learn from experience is the most important skill of all. Without this, you can't become a better rider.

As self-assessment is so important, each chapter in *Motorcycle Roadcraft* includes questions to help you check your understanding of police riding competences and assess your own riding behaviour. Questions are highlighted like this in a coloured panel with a self-assessment symbol.

What makes a good rider?

The qualities of a safe and competent rider are:

- critical and honest self-awareness and understanding of your personal characteristics, attitudes and behaviour that are necessary for safe riding
- taking action to keep identified risks to a minimum
- awareness of your own limitations and those of the machine and the road
- awareness of the risks inherent in particular road and traffic situations
- concentration and good observation
- continuously matching the machine's direction and speed to the changing conditions
- skilful use of machine controls.

Police and other emergency services riders should be exemplary riders. The attitude of police riders towards their riding is noticed by members of the public and influences other riders. Always be aware that you're seen as a role model and can influence the behaviour of other riders for the better. If other riders see you with a courteous attitude and an obvious concern for safety, they're more likely to behave in the same way.

The hierarchy of road users

Drivers of larger or less vulnerable vehicles are expected to allow for those who are more vulnerable, such as pedestrians and cyclists; this is known as the 'hierarchy of road users'. By extension, riders of emergency vehicles are expected to take account of others when responding to emergencies. You should always be aware of the potential presence of more vulnerable road users, and be ready to take account of that vulnerability. However, it would be unwise to assume that you will be given the same consideration by others; you should always be prepared for the potential actions of others not to conform to this principle.

Competences for police riders

Competence is the ability to do the job – the knowledge, skills and behaviour required for police riding.

There are three core competences that are the foundation of all riding. Police and other emergency services riders need to develop these competences to the highest possible standards:

- the knowledge and skills to ride safely
- an understanding of factors that increase your risk of a collision
- the ability to accurately assess your riding behaviour.

See Appendix 4, Goals for Driver Education, page 300.

As an emergency services rider, your working life is characterised by the number and variety of different tasks that you must carry out, often within a single shift. For a police rider, a day that starts with a routine patrol might end up at the scene of a multi-vehicle collision. Whatever the riding task, you're expected to maintain the highest possible standard of riding and to complete the task in hand calmly and efficiently.

As well as the core competences above, there are task-specific competences that are particularly important for the operational police rider. These are:

- multi-tasking – being able to carry out complex riding tasks at the same time as monitoring incoming information from various sources: this is a demanding competence for new police riders

  See Chapter 1, page 17, Distraction due to multi-tasking.

- alertness – being vigilant and remaining focused so as to spot potential hazards early and leave nothing to chance
- attention distribution – sharing your attention across all aspects of a riding task
- situational awareness – using your senses to build and maintain an accurate mental picture of the operational environment

- anticipation – using your observational skills and riding experience to spot actual and potential hazards and predict how the situation is likely to unfold
- planning – planning precisely and making rapid and accurate decisions throughout the task
- making judgements – judging situations accurately and taking safe and appropriate action.

See Chapter 4, Information, observation and anticipation, for a full discussion of alertness, anticipation and planning.

Situational awareness is essential for everyone on the road, but it's particularly expected of police and other emergency services riders and drivers.

This involves gathering, interpreting and using any relevant information to make sense of what's going on around you and what's likely to happen next, so that you can make intelligent decisions and stay in control.

Developing these multiple and complex abilities begins with training but is a process of continuous improvement. It needs constant practice and accurate self-assessment throughout your professional riding career.

How good is your situational awareness?

Your vulnerability as a rider

Motorcycle miles make up only 1% of annual vehicle miles in the UK. Yet riders accounted for 22% of all those killed or seriously injured on UK roads in the year to June 2018.

Riding a motorcycle doesn't increase your chances of a collision compared to driving a car, but for riders the outcomes tend to be more severe.

Riders are far more exposed in a collision than car drivers are because they don't have a protective shell around them. Even in a relatively minor collision, a rider is far more likely to suffer serious or fatal injuries, especially of the head and neck, or of vital organs in the thorax and abdomen.

According to Road Safety Observatory figures, motorcycle riders are more than 65 times more likely to be killed in a collision than car drivers.

Most riders think they're both safer and more skilful than the average rider – but we can't all be right. In around 2 out of 3 collisions, human error is the principal cause. Riders are most vulnerable to the actions of other road users.

This is why understanding your vulnerability and learning to reduce your risks, especially the risks from the errors of other road users, is so vital. Riding safety is not an add-on extra – it must be built into the way you ride on every journey without exception.

Those who ride in poor weather, all year round, have an increased risk of collision, even after other exposure and experience have been taken into account. As a regular rider, you will be on the road when drivers may take greater risks, for example, on weekday evenings.

Experienced riders who stop riding and take it up again in middle age also have a higher than average risk of crashing, possibly because they ride more powerful bikes than they did when younger. Formal training can help to refresh or maintain rusty skills and reduce the risk.

What are the commonest causes of motorcycle crashes?

In the majority of collisions, inappropriate speed for the circumstances is a factor.

The commonest causes of all motorcycle collisions in the UK are:

- Driver/rider failed to look properly. The commonest cause of a motorcycle collision is when a driver looks but fails to see a motorcyclist approaching a junction and pulls out across their path, mainly on urban roads at low speeds.
- Driver/rider failed to judge the other person's path or speed.

Nearly half of drivers involved in a daylight collision with a motorcyclist fail to look properly and don't see the rider before the crash. (This is often referred to as SMIDSY, which means 'Sorry, mate, I didn't see you'.)

Even a small mistake at the wrong speed can result in loss of control.

An inappropriate speed could be 20 mph in a narrow street crowded with pedestrians moving in and out of the road ...

... or 60 mph on a straight open road if you are tired and your attention is split between several tasks.

- Loss of control. Collisions on bends are often the rider's fault. They're more likely to be fatal because of the speeds involved, as even a small mistake can result in loss of control. Around a third of collisions in which a motorcyclist is killed or seriously injured happen on bends in rural roads; only 1 in 12 happen on bends in urban roads, of which half are at or near a junction.
- Driver/rider careless, reckless or in a hurry.
- Poor turn or manoeuvre.

In addition, for police and other emergency services riders, riding a motorcycle in an operational environment involves multi-tasking. This can distract attention from the riding task.

Critical learning from experience

Many riders involved in a collision don't accept that they contributed to it. If you think that you didn't help to cause a collision, you'll also think that you have nothing to learn from it and so your riding behaviour won't change.

To become a better rider, the first step is to recognise the resistance in ourselves to accepting responsibility. The second step is to accept every near miss and collision as a learning opportunity to assess how you can avoid the same mistake in future.

For example, collision statistics show that all riders are at risk from the actions of other road users who fail to see them. If you have a 'look but failed to see' crash, you can choose how to view it. Is it all the responsibility of the careless driver? Or can you take action to reduce your own vulnerability? You can choose to reduce your chances of a 'look but failed to see' collision by anticipating this potential hazard whenever you ride.

See Defensive riding, page 13.

1

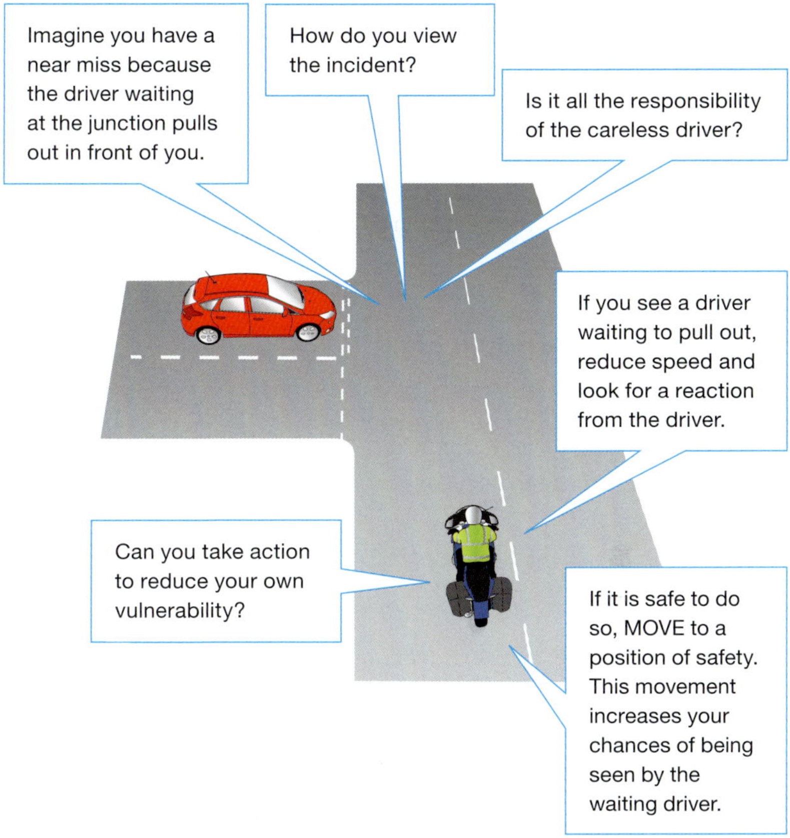

Have you ever had a near miss?

☐ yes ☐ no

Have you ever felt threatened or alarmed by another road user's actions?

☐ yes ☐ no

What did you learn about your own actions from this experience?

Develop awareness of your personal vulnerability

To develop your awareness of risks and your ability to honestly assess your own riding, it can be helpful to think about the riding task in terms of four different levels. It's useful to think about these separately at the start of the learning process, but the goal of learning and practice is to integrate them.

Four levels of the riding task

The four levels set out in the European Goals for Driver Education (GDE) are:

- human factors that affect your riding
- the purpose and context of your journey
- traffic situations
- machine and machine control.

See Appendix 4, Goals for Driver Education, page 300.

When you first learned to drive or ride, you started with the basic skills of vehicle control. With practice, you gradually combined smaller skill elements until they became automatic. Once you had mastered the basic controls and manoeuvring skills, you were able to concentrate on traffic situations, learning to anticipate and respond to hazards. Eventually you built up and integrated these complex skills and competences until you were able to drive or ride safely in traffic and plan and make journeys independently.

But the most important point about the learning process is that we're not a blank canvas when we learn to drive or ride. We bring to the task our personality, our life experiences, our beliefs about the world and our own attitudes to riding based on what we've seen as pedestrians, passengers or drivers. These factors all have a strong influence on how we learn to ride, how we make decisions on the road and our chances of being involved in a collision.

Let's consider the four levels in more depth:

- **Human factors** – your personal characteristics can increase or reduce your risk of a collision compared to other riders. Your attitude to your own vulnerability and to other road users, confidence, emotions, mood and stress all affect your riding behaviour. Learn to recognise personal tendencies that increase your risk and find ways to manage them.

If there is heavy fog, ice or snow, ask yourself: 'Is my journey really necessary?'

See Appendix 1, I AM SAFE checklist, page 292, to make sure you are fit to ride.

- **The journey** – each journey you make has a purpose and involves decisions and judgements: what preparation is needed, which route is best, what distractions there are and how to minimise them. The ability to deal with operational distractions is vital for police riders. Assess the risks of the journey and your own fitness to ride. Take account of these in the way you manage each journey.
- **The traffic** – training will increase your hazard perception skills and your ability to negotiate your way safely through traffic. It will develop your competence at scanning the road and anticipating hazards, and increase your awareness of the risks that riders face in traffic. Situational awareness is essential for all riders. Allow your senses to provide you with information and help you maintain an accurate picture of your environment.
- **The machine** – a vital part of knowing your own limitations as a rider is knowing exactly what the machine you're riding can and cannot do. Take time to familiarise yourself with a machine before you ride it. Check the machine is fit to ride. Check its condition (for example, lights, tyre tread depth, brakes), its capabilities, its safety features, and how to use the controls correctly. Make the mental adjustments necessary if you regularly ride another machine.

See Appendix 2, POWDDERSS checklist, page 294, to make sure your machine is fit to ride.

The table below shows how you can use these four levels of the GDE matrix to consider your personal risks and assess your riding in a structured way.

	Potential risks	Possible self-assessment questions
Human factors	Personal tendencies, motives or attitudes that might affect your riding. Risks might include risk-taking or an impulsive personality, operational stress, competitiveness, overconfidence in riding ability, justifying risk-taking for a noble cause, or distraction caused by deeper stresses such as family or financial problems.	How easy is it to detach yourself from wider problems or stresses when you get on your bike? Do you tend to react to or disengage from other road users' aggressive behaviour? Do you know how operational stress affects your riding?
Journey	Risks could include an unfamiliar route, time pressure, peer pressure, distraction due to multi-tasking, tunnel vision ('red mist'), fatigue or the wrong clothing.	Is this journey necessary? Are you fit to ride? Are you wearing the right clothing and protective equipment? What can you do to reduce the risk of general distractions and of distractions from operational tasks?
Traffic	Maintain a high level of alertness in traffic, scanning the road so you can anticipate what's likely to happen next. Risks could include loss of concentration, failure to anticipate the actions of drivers who don't see you, or weather conditions.	What are the traffic, road and weather conditions? How should you adjust your riding for the conditions?
Machine	Always ride within your machine's capabilities. An unfamiliar bike increases your risk.	Is the machine fit to ride? Can you ride it slowly? Is it adjusted for best position and comfort? Do you know how its safety features behave?

Defensive riding

As a rider you're extremely vulnerable. You have no protective shell, your stability can be affected by the condition of the road surface (for example, potholes, ironwork, debris, surface spills), you're not very conspicuous, and drivers either don't see you or take greater risks when pulling out in front of you.

Set against this, you have the advantages of height, positioning flexibility and the acceleration that your machine provides. Make the most of these advantages.

Whenever you ride, your safety depends on your actions and your ability to anticipate and avoid the actions of other vehicles. You need a high level of attention, good hazard perception and excellent situational awareness.

The ability to sense danger in a situation increases with experience, so you should always ride well within your capabilities.

Conspicuity – ride to be seen

Many drivers have a blind spot when it comes to seeing riders. This is in part because it's harder to spot a bike than a car when it's some distance away and in part because drivers are expecting to see cars and lorries, not motorcycles. When drivers do see you, the head-on view of a rider and machine is a small image from which to assess speed. There's also evidence that smaller vehicles appear to travel more slowly. At night or in bad weather, your headlight may become lost among the confusion of other headlights and may fail to attract attention. And a single light provides a poor cue for assessing speed and distance.

In making your riding plan you should always think about how to make yourself conspicuous: how well do you stand out against the background? This can change rapidly: a white machine against black tarmac is fairly easy to see but the same bike against a white lorry isn't.

See Chapter 4, page 64, Planning.

How well do you stand out against the background?

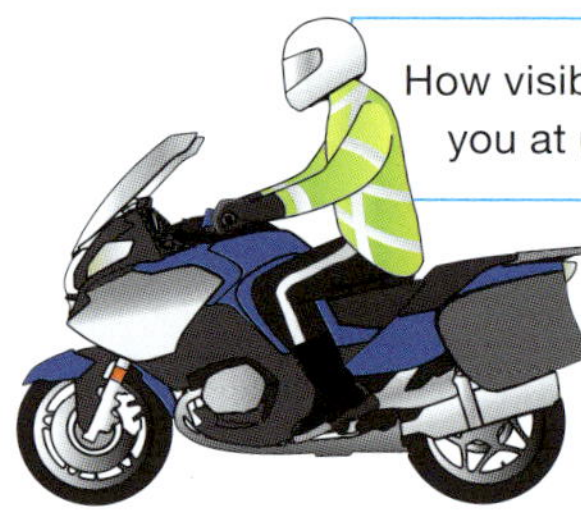

How visible are you at night?

Don't assume that because you're conspicuous you're safe. Your safety depends on the quality of your observation and planning.

You are especially vulnerable at junctions

Approach junctions where there's a vehicle waiting or approaching with great caution. Reduce speed and look for a clear sign that the driver has seen you. The fact that a driver appears to be looking straight at you isn't a good enough indication that they've seen you. If it's safe to do so, move to a position of safety. This movement increases your chances of being seen by a driver waiting to pull out. Follow the advice in the chapters on observation and positioning.

See Chapter 4, Information, observation and anticipation and Chapter 10, Positioning.

Remember that even in daylight other road users may not realise you're there. It's safest to assume that you are invisible to other road users.

The right clothing and protective equipment

Before any journey, you should ask yourself: 'Am I fit to ride?' For a bike rider, what you wear is as important as your state of mind.

Your main physical protection on a bike is what you wear. Clothing, gloves, helmet and boots protect you from the weather but, above all, they can give you some protection if you crash, particularly when fitted with approved body armour or airbag technology. Check all protective clothing regularly and replace worn equipment immediately. Make sure that all clothing is well maintained and always use it according to the manufacturer's guidelines.

Clothing should be flexible, resistant to abrasion, conspicuous and provide a degree of support. It should have padding on key areas such as elbows, knees and shoulders. Wear approved boots to protect the foot, ankle and lower leg.

Weather

Always ensure your equipment is suitable for the weather. In warm weather, be aware of the risk of dehydration. In wet weather, wear fully waterproof outer garments, gloves and boots. Wet clothes remove heat from the body very quickly in the airflow of a moving bike.

Cold weather is dangerous. As your body's core cools, you become sluggish and lose attention. Being cold can reduce your ability to process information and your reaction times will be slower. The extremities cool more quickly than the body and in cold weather the average temperature of a rider's hands is around 14 to 15°C. At this point your hands lose most of their sensitivity.

To prevent chilling:

- wear multiple layers – the more layers you wear, the warmer you will be
- close all fasteners to prevent the suit from ballooning – movement of air inside a suit causes chilling
- avoid clothes which make you sweat – sweat removes heat when it evaporates
- keep your head, hands and feet well insulated.

Wear as many thin layers as possible but you must be able to maintain enough movement for effective control and observation, especially rear observation.

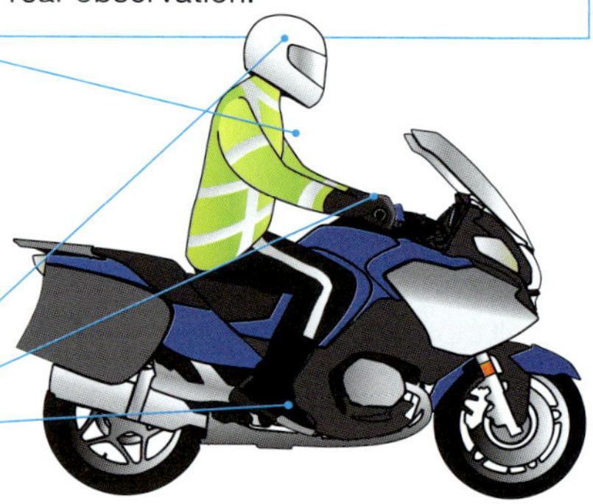

Your helmet

Head injuries are a major cause of rider death. Your helmet must be in good condition, as even the slightest damage can seriously reduce its strength. Consult the manufacturer's guidelines and replace your helmet at the end of its lifespan. It should be correctly fitted and properly fastened –adjust the padding and straps so that it doesn't move once it's on your head. Make full use of features such as the sun visor and air vents in warm weather.

Noise from a bike causes fatigue in the short term and damages your hearing in the long term. Wearing ear-plugs or ear defenders helps to reduce these harmful effects.

Human factor risks for emergency services riders

Police and other emergency services riders have to deal with demanding and difficult situations in the course of their work. Certain human factors linked to the nature of the job can put you at risk:

- distraction due to multi-tasking
- riding stress
- operational stressors
- time pressure and the purpose of the journey
- 'noble cause' risk-taking
- 'red mist'.

Distraction due to multi-tasking

Operational riding requires police and other emergency services riders to deal with multiple tasks. The demands on your attention from a radio and other technologies inside your helmet and the operational tasks can be intrusive. Be aware that your vulnerability increases if you fail to focus on the primary task of riding safely. Even minor distractions can severely impair your ability to anticipate hazards.

Riding stress

All riders are vulnerable to riding stress, especially police and other emergency services riders who regularly deal with difficult and hazardous situations. During a demanding or difficult ride where brain processing is already stretched to the limit, operational stressors can overload the system and impair your decisions and judgement. Training aims to increase your information-processing and problem-solving effectiveness. This gives you more time to think and complete the riding task efficiently, which helps reduce the effects of riding stress.

Deeper stresses can also affect your riding. For example, a rider may be dealing with heavy demands in their personal life. Family problems, financial difficulties or even a new baby can increase chronic stress and fatigue, and impair concentration and riding performance.

> We each respond differently, so what you find stressful may not be stressful for a colleague, and vice versa. Learn to recognise your personal stressors – the things that you believe could impair your riding.

Operational stressors

Emergency services riders are also exposed to several types of operational stress:

- the anticipatory stress of facing a difficult or demanding task (for example, anxiety about what you'll find on arrival at an incident)
- the 'adrenaline rush' arising from a sudden event such as an emergency call-out: a degree of arousal enhances performance but, beyond this optimum level, alertness and concentration tend to fall away
- stress related to aspects of the task: difficult traffic or weather conditions, navigation problems, lack of advance detail about an incident, time pressures and the length of time you spend exposed to risk
- the stress of being in a situation in which you or others may be exposed to extreme hazards
- stress arising from repeated exposure to distressing incidents in the past; aspects of a current situation may 'prompt' recall of distressing memories and the effect may impair current decision-making and judgement
- preoccupation with a previous error of judgement
- stress from other work factors: working long shifts or night shifts, peer pressure or difficult working relationships can affect riding performance.

Under pressure, in difficult and demanding conditions, stress and tiredness can cause the release of powerful negative feelings. Learn to recognise these reactions and manage them:

- impatience – through a desire to get to the incident quickly
- intolerance – a belief that the importance of the task automatically gives the emergency services rider priority over other road users
- impulsiveness – rushing decisions because time is short
- anger or frustration – for example, at other road users getting in your way
- personalisation – getting into personal conflict with another road user.

There's more about dealing with tiredness in Chapter 4, Information, observation and anticipation.

Practical steps to combat stress

Be aware that stress is cumulative. Research shows that repeated exposure to stress can increase the chances of a collision and, in more severe cases, susceptibility to a stress-related illness. Look after your health – getting regular exercise and learning to relax can help reduce chronic stress.

- Adjust your machine and clothing so that you're not physically tense or uncomfortable.
- Use the techniques you learn in training and practise them continually – well-learned techniques are less likely to break down under stressful conditions. This is an advantage of using the system of motorcycle control (Chapter 3).
- Maintain a calm, professional approach to your riding – especially in an emergency situation.

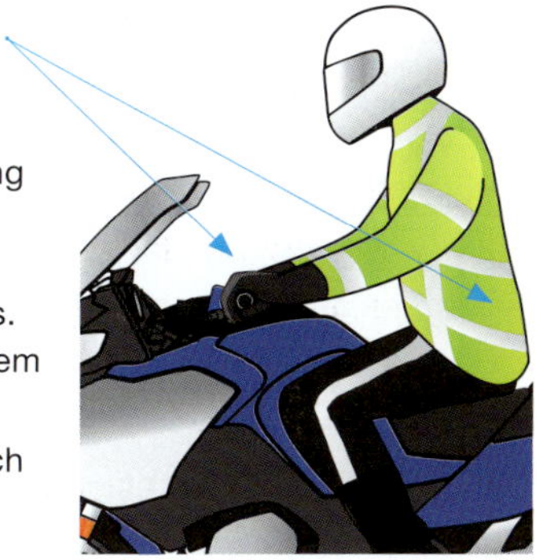

- Learn techniques to help you focus on your riding and switch off other problems when you get on your bike.
- After a journey, reflect on any stressful experiences or errors of judgement, but don't dwell on them.

Time pressure and the purpose of your journey

Emergency services riders are trained to respond to urgent calls without taking undue risks. But it's a fact that riders who feel their journey is urgent, because of organisational time pressure or the purpose of the journey, tend to respond less safely to hazards and take more risks. A sense of urgency doesn't give the right to take risks.

> No emergency is so great that it justifies the possibility of injuring or killing someone. It is better to arrive later than not at all. A sense of urgency doesn't give you the right to take risks or to use a lack of proportionality in judgements.

'Noble cause' risk-taking

Never justify risk-taking by telling yourself that the risk is for a noble cause – to help someone else, or to catch a person suspected of a crime.

If you're tempted to take risks in an emergency, **STOP**. Think about the consequences for yourself and other people if you crash and fail to arrive. You will be of no help to the people in need. If you injure yourself or someone else on the way, you will have turned an emergency into two emergencies and a possible tragedy. You will have to live with the consequences of what you've done.

'Red mist'

'Red mist' is a colloquial term used to describe the state of mind of riders who become determined to achieve some objective on the journey – catching the vehicle in front, or getting to an incident in the shortest possible time. Fixed attention on a particular goal (sometimes referred to as 'target fixation') can lead to blindness to other potential hazards, such as pedestrians or other vehicles at intersections. This means a rider is at best less able and at worst no longer capable of realistically assessing riding risks.

The key to preventing 'red mist' is to concentrate on the riding task in hand rather than on the incident. You'll need to develop your own strategy for achieving this, but there are some key steps you can take:

- Don't get into a personality conflict with another road user.
- Be dispassionate and concentrate on your riding – use neutral, non-aggressive language to describe other road users (to yourself and others).
- Don't try and imagine what you'll find at the incident – assess the situation when you get there.
- Concentrate on riding – talking yourself through the hazards you identify can help you to focus on the riding task and keep negative emotions under control.

'Red mist' means your attention is not on your riding but on some specific goal; you've become emotionally and physiologically caught up in the incident.

How you learn

You'll find it easier to improve your riding ability and safety if you understand how you learn and apply new competences. The basic requirements are training, practice, feedback and experience.

Training, practice and feedback

Motorcycle Roadcraft training mirrors the process by which you learnt the basic driving or riding skills to pass your test. At first, manoeuvres such as changing gear or turning round in the road demand all your attention. But when you've mastered the basic controls and skills, you can give more of your attention to the road and traffic conditions. You'll improve your ability to anticipate and respond to hazards, and learn to use the system of motorcycle control and other routines so that you can respond rapidly, safely and flexibly to the demands of police riding.

Rider training can accelerate your learning, enabling you to develop your critical awareness and competences that you might otherwise never possess. It can draw your attention to risky riding behaviour and to parts of a task or ways of doing things that you were unaware of. But practice is the only way in which new competences become integrated, automatic and readily available when you need them. With practice, you'll steadily develop and enhance your core riding competences at all levels.

See Appendix 4, Goals for Driver Education, page 300.

To develop these competences to a high standard, you also need continuous feedback on the effects of your actions. At first you'll need feedback from your instructor, but from the outset you should critically review all your actions. You'll be expected to continuously assess your own riding behaviour and performance. Your aim is to develop your own internal feedback – your ability to question, honestly self-assess and modify your actions – whenever you ride.

Overconfidence after training

Overconfidence in the period after training is a risk you should be aware of. It's important not to underestimate the amount of practice that's required to become a fully competent rider. You'll encounter many new traffic and operational situations as an emergency services rider and lack of experience in dealing with these situations means that you're vulnerable.

Overconfidence can take you into situations you can't handle and will increase your risk of a collision. Riders can overestimate their abilities in various ways:

- Moving on to ride a different machine after training – manoeuvring a more powerful bike with different handling characteristics and safety features requires additional practice.
- With increased training comes the feeling that the task of riding is automatic and relatively easy, but the operational demands of the job mean increased demands on your attention from radios, etc. This can lead to attention overload, making you less likely to notice hazards and more likely to crash.
- Less experienced riders tend to believe their hazard perception is better than it actually is, when measured objectively.

Is your hazard perception as good as you think it is?

- Bike safety technology and equipment have advanced at such a rapid pace that they can give riders a false sense of security, leading them to take more risks. This is especially true for riders who return to riding after a break. Riding a machine that has many more safety features than the one you learned on can lead you to take risks that you would not have taken before.

See Chapter 4, page 66, Anticipate hazards.

This is why critical and honest self-awareness is so important. It will help you to keep your actual riding ability and your perceived ability in balance.

Self-assessment will help you continually improve

People who develop a high level of ability in any field have better than average self-assessment skills. They're continually reviewing their performance, analysing their mistakes, and working out how they can improve.

Aim for a cycle of continuous improvement in your riding competence.

People who aren't very good at assessing themselves find it difficult to develop a higher level of competence as they fail to reflect on what they can do to improve.

Self-assessment is only possible through reflective practice. Monitor your actions as they are actually happening, and review your performance after a ride. Ask yourself:

- What's my aim?
- What went well and why?
- What went less well and why?
- How could I do better next time?
- Have I been honest with myself?

Be honest

The first thing you should focus on when you review a ride is your own safety and that of other road users. Being honest with yourself about what didn't go so well is vital if you want to continue to improve. For example, you might look back on a ride to consider:

- how you controlled the machine
- how you managed traffic situations, and anticipated and planned for hazards
- what aspects of the journey you found challenging
- what personal characteristics affected your riding behaviour.

See Appendix 4, Goals for Driver Education, page 300.

Reviewing things that went well and analysing why you handled them well is also important. It will help you to transfer your competence in one particular situation to other situations. This will broaden your ability to make accurate decisions and judgements.

But in the end, you'll only become a better rider if you understand your own vulnerability, know the limits of your riding capabilities and recognise the human factors that affect your safety. Riding a bike gives a satisfying sense of freedom. Studying *Motorcycle Roadcraft* and practising continually to develop your riding ability will increase your satisfaction, enjoyment and safety. It will lay the foundations for a long and rewarding riding career.

Check your understanding

You should now be able to apply learning from this chapter in your rider training so that you can:

- ☐ explain the competences required for police riding
- ☐ identify the human factors that may increase your vulnerability as a rider
- ☐ explain the Goals for Driver Education and how these can help you manage risks and assess your own riding
- ☐ show that you give priority to safety at all times
- ☐ show that you can recognise and manage the human factors that may affect your decision-making and riding performance
- ☐ show that you can honestly and critically assess your own riding behaviour to achieve continuous improvement.

Chapter 2

Advanced rider-assistance systems

Learning outcomes

The learning in this chapter, along with rider training, should enable you to:

- explain the purpose of advanced rider-assistance systems (ARAS)
- explain in general terms how ARAS work on a motorcycle
- explain how ARAS help the rider
- identify the types of ARAS technologies that may be fitted to your motorcycle.

What are ARAS?

Advanced rider-assistance systems (ARAS) are technologies that assist you with riding. The various features can help you avoid collisions by alerting you to potential dangers and, in some cases, intervening to take evasive action.

How do ARAS work?

Motorcycles with ARAS fitted use cameras, radar and other sensors that combine to monitor your surroundings. When the system perceives a danger, it may send you a visual or audio signal, or even a vibration. In some cases, it may intervene and make adjustments to rider inputs to maximise your bike's stability.

You can think of ARAS as your motorcycle's senses; they help your bike detect things around it, whether they're other vehicles, pedestrians or obstacles like potholes or rubbish bins. Sensors can quickly spot objects around your bike and figure out where they are, how fast they're moving, and in which direction. This may help your machine react faster than you could, especially in complex traffic situations.

The systems can also provide information in poor riding conditions. Whether it's raining, foggy or dark outside, these sensors don't get tired or distracted, giving your bike the ability to gather information even in low visibility situations, which can help you spot a hidden obstacle that might be difficult to see on your own.

ARAS do, however, have limitations. They may struggle in extreme weather conditions or give off false alarms. They may not anticipate unpredictable behaviours, such as a child darting onto the road or another road user making an erratic move. ARAS features might feel advanced, but they still require constant rider oversight.

Why do ARAS matter?

ARAS matter because you can expect them to be a feature of your toolkit as a rider. Many bikes are already fitted with them, and the number and types of features are expanding. Additionally, these systems are increasingly being developed to interact with each other to further enhance the range of tools available to you as a rider.

The kind of help these systems can give you includes:

- putting safety first – by tracking the movements of other vehicles, people and objects around your motorcycle, the sensors can alert you to potential dangers before you even notice them; this could be as simple as warning you about a car in your blind spot, or braking automatically if someone steps into the road
- heightened awareness – the system can tell the difference between something small, like a bicycle, and something bigger, like a car or lorry; this extra awareness helps your machine react better in a variety of riding scenarios.

Think of ARAS as a co-pilot, not a replacement

Imagine ARAS as a helpful co-pilot; they give you extra information and assistance, like monitoring your blind spots or helping with braking.

Don't assume they can make judgement calls or replace the need for a fully attentive rider.

Maintain a proactive approach to riding to be better equipped to handle any situation, whether ARAS work flawlessly or encounter a limitation.

ARAS features at a glance

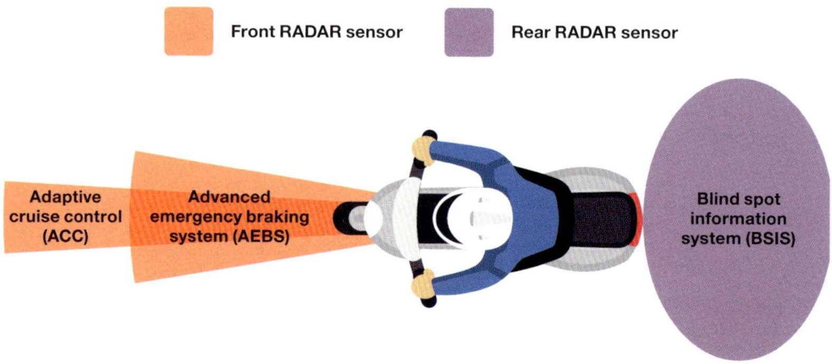

This table summarises many of the ARAS features and how they can help you. They are explained in more detail on the pages following this table. However, be sure to refer to your motorcycle's handbook.

Remember that ARAS are evolving technologies and the list will continue to grow.

Feature	How it helps you
Adaptive cruise control (ACC)	Intelligently controls your cruise speed by monitoring the traffic ahead of you.
Advanced/autonomous emergency braking system (AEBS)	Warns you and automatically brakes if a frontal collision is imminent.
Blind spot information system (BSIS)	Uses sensors to let you know there is another vehicle in your blind spot.
Cornering ABS	Adjusts the braking force according to the bike's lean angle and speed.
Electronic stability programmes (ESP)	Helps improve stability and directional control by adjusting power and braking inputs, with various levels of sophistication.
Emergency brake assist (EBA)	Helps avoid a collision by automatically adding pressure to the brakes.
Emergency stop signal (ESS)	Activates your bike's brake light or rear indicators to flash at a high frequency.
Group-ride assist (GRA)	Helps to keep riders travelling together at a safe distance from each other.
Hill-start assist (HSA)	Helps prevent your bike rolling backwards when starting on an incline.
Intelligent speed assistance/intelligent speed adaption (ISA)	Helps you stay below the speed limit.
Rear-end warnings	Warns you, or activates your hazard lights, if a vehicle gets too close behind you.
Tyre-pressure monitoring system (TPMS)	Alerts to you a change in tyre pressure.
Vehicle-to-everything (V2X)	Allows vehicles to share information with their surroundings.

ARAS features in more detail

The following is a description of many of the constantly evolving ARAS features. While they are listed as separate systems here, remember that they may communicate and work with each other in various riding situations.

There will be differences in how each feature behaves from manufacturer to manufacturer, machine to machine. Refer to your motorcycle's handbook.

Adaptive cruise control

Adaptive cruise control (ACC) is a development of earlier cruise control systems. It lets you know or takes action when a hazard is detected by monitoring the traffic around you when your bike is in 'cruise' mode.

ACC has other names such as active cruise control, radar cruise control, autonomous cruise control and intelligent cruise control.

Advanced/autonomous emergency braking system

The advanced/autonomous emergency braking system (AEBS) senses when a collision is imminent (for example, with a vehicle ahead or with a pedestrian or cyclist crossing the road) and automatically brakes if you take no action.

The speed at which AEBS operates may differ from manufacturer to manufacturer. Always consult your motorcycle's manual.

Blind spot information system

The blind spot information system (BSIS) aims to let you know there are other vehicles like cycles, motorcycles and cars in your blind spot. The alerts may be visual, audible or vibrational.

You should note that BSIS:

- should not be used in place of using your mirrors, or a lifesaver check before changing lanes

- may not work properly in severe weather conditions
- is not designed to detect parked vehicles, pedestrians, animals or infrastructure.

Cornering ABS

When you brake during a cornering manoeuvre, the cornering anti-lock braking system adjusts the braking force according to many things, including the bike's lean angle and speed, helping to optimise braking performance and maintain stability.

Electronic stability programmes

Electronic stability programmes (ESP) are active safety systems that incorporate anti-lock braking and traction control systems, which are designed to help improve stability and directional control. ESP are becoming more sophisticated and are likely to incorporate more variables as the technology develops.

See Chapter 8, page 185, Traction control systems.

Emergency brake assist

Emergency brake assist (EBA) increases braking pressure in an emergency situation.

See Chapter 6, page 134, Emergency brake assist.

Emergency stop signal

Emergency stop signal (ESS) is a safety feature that activates your machine's brake light and/or rear indicators to flash at a high frequency if you brake hard, or brake suddenly at a higher speed, or if the ABS is activated.

You should be prepared to act if ever you notice this on another vehicle.

Group-ride assist

Group-ride assist (GRA) builds on adaptive cruise-control (ACC) to regulate speed and distance in group-riding situations. It helps to keep riders travelling together at a safe distance from each other, particularly when positioned in a staggered formation.

Hill-start assist

Hill-start assist (HSA), also known as hill hold or hill control, helps prevent bikes rolling backwards when starting on an incline. After you release the brakes, it maintains brake pressure for a few seconds, allowing you time to accelerate without rolling back.

Intelligent speed assistance

Intelligent speed assistance (ISA) helps you manage your speed by notifying you of the current speed limit. Some systems will warn you if you exceed that limit.

Rear-end warnings

A rear-end warning system monitors the situation behind your bike and, if another vehicle gets too close, the system may:

- activate your bike's hazard lights (known as a 'rear collision warning'), or
- flash a warning on your bike's display (known as a 'rear-distance warning').

Based on these, you may be able to take mitigating action.

Tyre-pressure monitoring system

The tyre-pressure monitoring system (TPMS) helps you keep track of the air pressure in your tyres. If the TPMS warning appears, use a tyre-pressure gauge to measure the tyre indicated and adjust the air pressure to the appropriate level.

Even with TPMS, check the condition of your tyres and your tyre pressure regularly.

See Chapter 6, page 115, The tyre grip trade-off.

Vehicle-to-everything

Vehicle-to-everything (V2X) is a technology that can give vehicles the ability to communicate with the world around them. It can be used, for example, to communicate with traffic lights, to operate bus priority systems or to take account of approaching emergency vehicles.

Check your understanding

You should now be able to apply learning from this chapter in your rider training so that you can:

- [ ] explain the purpose of advanced rider-assistance systems (ARAS)
- [ ] explain in general terms how ARAS work on a motorcycle
- [ ] explain how ARAS help the rider
- [ ] identify the types of ARAS technologies that may be fitted to your motorcycle.

Chapter 3

The system of motorcycle control

Learning outcomes

The learning in this chapter, along with rider training, should enable you to:

- explain the system of motorcycle control
- demonstrate how to apply the system to any hazards.

The need for a system of motorcycle control

This chapter explains the system of motorcycle control used in police rider training. It outlines the competences that will enhance your ability to master a wide range of traffic situations.

Chapter 1 explains that riders are more vulnerable than drivers. If a rider makes an error of judgement the outcome is more serious, because there's no protective shell as in a car, but riders are also vulnerable to the mistakes of other road users who fail to see them. The system of motorcycle control aims to prevent collisions by providing a systematic approach to hazards, including the potential misjudgements of other road users. It's a decision-making process that enables you to efficiently assess and act on information that is continuously changing as you ride. Using the system gives you more time to react, which is vital in complex and demanding riding situations.

If you use the system consistently with the information-processing, observation and anticipation skills discussed in Chapters 4 and 5, it will help you anticipate dangers caused by other road users and avoid collisions. Your progress will be steady and unobtrusive – the sign of a safe and competent rider.

Integrating a range of competences

As described in Chapter 1, riding to police standards requires more than just the ability to control your machine. It's essential to develop honest self-assessment of your own capabilities, understanding of traffic situations and 'situational awareness' – your ability to read the road. Many hazards that riders meet are unpredictable. The system gives you a methodical way of processing information, and applying observation and anticipation so that you recognise and negotiate hazards safely.

Human factors/ the purpose of the journey

Take into account personal factors and attitudes and the goals of the journey that might influence your riding behaviour.

- Are you aware of your own riding abilities and limitations?

The traffic situation

Scan the environment, recognise, anticipate and prioritise hazards, and form an achievable riding plan.

- What are the prevailing weather and road conditions?
- How are other road users likely to behave?

Machine control

Translate intentions and thoughts into physical action – manoeuvre your machine accurately and smoothly.

- Are you familiar with the capabilities of your machine?

What is the system of motorcycle control?

The system of motorcycle control increases your safety in a constantly changing riding environment by giving you time to react to hazards.

A hazard is anything that is an actual or potential danger.

See Chapter 4, page 63, What is a hazard?

The system of motorcycle control is a way of approaching and negotiating hazards that is methodical, safe and leaves nothing to chance. It involves careful observation, early anticipation and planning, and a systematic use of the controls to maintain your machine's stability in all situations.

Riding hazards fluctuate: they come singly and in clusters, they overlap and change all the time. The system takes account of this continual flux because:

- it has a centrally flexible element – you, the rider
- it draws together all levels of riding competence into a logical sequence of actions to help you deal with hazards and respond to new ones safely and efficiently.

How the system works

The system of motorcycle control consists of processing information and four phases – **position**, **speed**, **gear** and **acceleration**. Each phase develops out of the one before.

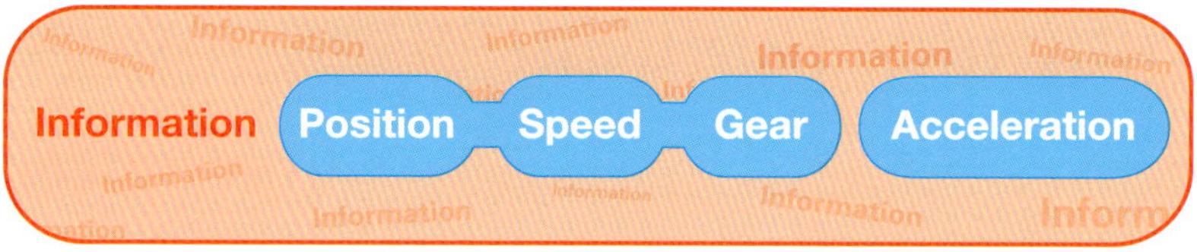

Processing information is central to the system – it runs through and feeds into all the phases. Start by asking yourself:

- What information do I need to gather about the road conditions, the behaviour of other road users, and actual and potential dangers?
- Which actual or potential dangers are the greatest risks to me as a rider?
- What do other road users need to know about my intentions?

Then work through each of the phases in turn. As road conditions change, you'll need to process new information and this will mean re-entering the system at an appropriate point, then continuing through it in sequence. If a new hazard arises, re-apply the system and consider all the phases in sequence.

The importance of information

Your ability to process complex information is essential to becoming a better rider.

Processing information (taking, using and giving information) introduces the system and continues throughout. Because of your vulnerability as a motorcyclist, your safety, and at times your survival, depend on your ability to take, use and give information.

Remember **TUG** – **t**ake, **u**se and **g**ive information.

See Chapter 4, Information, observation and anticipation.

You need to:

- **take** and **use** information to plan your riding
- **give** information whenever other road users could benefit from it.

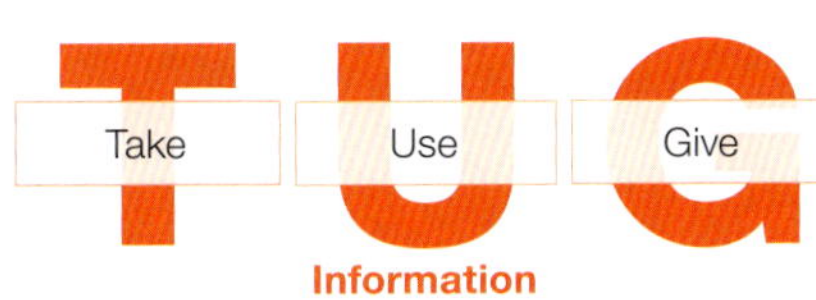

Develop your competence at assessing the continuous flow of information. This competence underpins the entire system and enables you to adapt it to changes in road circumstances.

See Chapter 9, Rider's signals.

Mirrors, rear observation and signals

Use your mirrors and/or look behind as often as is necessary to be fully aware of what's happening behind you.

Whenever you consider changing position or speed, always check first what is happening to the front, sides and behind you. You must check your mirrors and/or look behind at this point.

Give a signal whenever it could benefit another road user. Sound your horn when you think another road user could benefit but remember its purpose is to tell other people you are there – not to rebuke them.

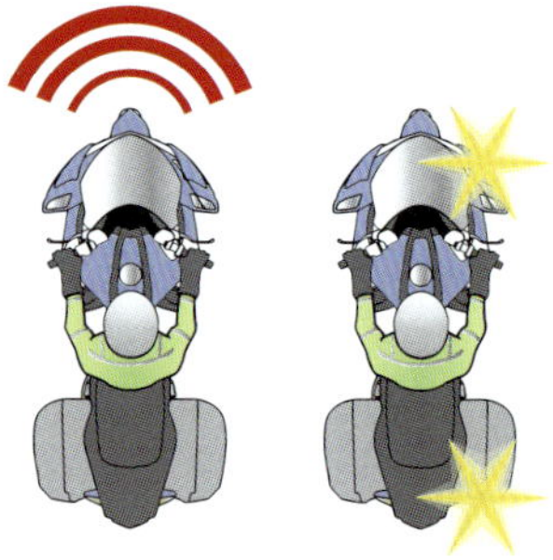

The lifesaver check

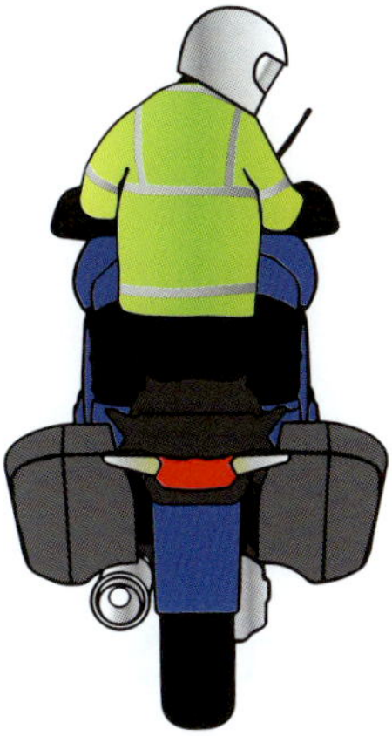

The lifesaver is a last check to the side into the blind spots before you commit yourself to a manoeuvre. If you're turning, use it to check the blind spot on the side to which you intend to turn.

The place for the lifesaver is just before the action. Do it early enough to allow you to adopt an alternative plan. It's too late to do it as you start to turn the machine.

Use your judgement about when to use the lifesaver. In congested urban situations it's usually essential, especially when turning right into a minor road. During high-speed overtaking, when you're certain what's happening behind, it's often safer to keep your eyes on what's happening ahead.

See Chapter 4, page 69, Improving your observation. See also Chapter 9, Rider's signals.

With practice, the system will become second nature and form a sound basis for developing the finer points of your riding competence. It will help you process information, make decisions and plan your approach to hazards so that you're able to avoid, or give yourself plenty of time to react to, potential dangers.

See Chapter 4, page 58, Processing complex information.

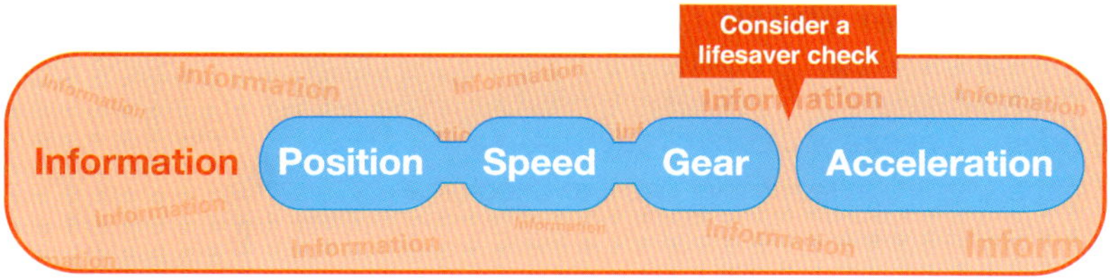

The system of motorcycle control

The system of motorcycle control is set out in detail here. Use this information in conjunction with the other chapters for a complete understanding of the system. When and how you read each chapter depends on your own study plan. If you're using *Motorcycle Roadcraft* as part of a course, ask your instructor for advice.

Information

Processing information runs throughout all phases of the system.

Take information

Look all round you. Scan to the front and sides. Check what's happening behind you – use your mirrors and/or look behind – at appropriate points in the system. Always check behind you before you change speed or direction.

Carefully observe the quality of the road surface as you approach and go through the hazard.

Take information through your other senses as well as your eyes. Sounds such as a horn or siren can warn you of other road users. Smells such as diesel or a bonfire can alert you to hazards such as spills or smoke.

Use information

Use information to plan how to deal with the hazards you identify. Use the system to decide on your next action. If new hazards arise, consider whether to rerun the system from an earlier phase.

See Chapter 4, page 64, Planning.

Give information

Give a signal if it could help other road users, including pedestrians and cyclists. You could use indicators, your brake light, arm signals, the horn or flash your headlight. For maximum benefit, give your warning signal in plenty of time.

Be aware that the position of your machine also gives valuable information to other road users.

See Chapter 9, Rider's signals.

Position

Position yourself so that you can negotiate the hazard(s) safely and smoothly.

See Chapter 10, Positioning.

Take account of the road surface and other road users, including pedestrians, cyclists and children.

Speed

Adjust your speed as necessary. Take into account visibility, the road surface, the degree of cornering required, the actions of other road users and the possibility of unseen hazards. Use acceleration sense or brakes as appropriate to give you the correct speed on approach to the hazard, and then select the correct gear for the road speed achieved. It's preferable to separate braking and gear-changing but it may be necessary to overlap them towards the end of the speed loss in some circumstances – for example, on a downhill slope.

See Chapter 6, page 120, Acceleration sense, and Brake/gear overlap in this chapter, page 53.

Use your anticipation skills so that you make all adjustments in speed smoothly and steadily.

Gear

Select the appropriate gear for the speed at which you intend to negotiate the hazard.

Pass through intermediate gears during the later stages of braking by the block-changing method or by systematically working through the gears, engaging each appropriate gear as speed is lost. Avoid using your gears as brakes. Always avoid late braking and snatched gear changes.

See Chapter 6, page 123, Using the gears.

Acceleration

Apply the correct degree of throttle to negotiate and leave the hazard safely.

Taking account of your speed, other road users, and the road and traffic conditions ahead, choose an appropriate point to accelerate safely and smoothly away from the hazard. Adjust acceleration to the circumstances.

See Chapter 6, page 118, Using the throttle.

Continuously assessing information runs through every phase of the system.

Use the system flexibly

The system works if you use it intelligently and proactively and adapt it to circumstances as they arise:

- Consider all phases of the system on the approach to every hazard, but you may not need to use every phase in a particular situation.
- Take, use and give information throughout to constantly reassess your plans.
- Be ready to return to an earlier phase of the system as new hazards arise.

Applying the system of motorcycle control

When you begin using the system, it may help to name each phase out loud as you enter it. After you practise using the system, review your performance:

- Do you take, use and give information throughout all phases? If not, what can you do to improve?
- What can you do to ensure you consider each phase systematically?
- Do you think about all aspects of each phase?

Where you've identified problems in using the system, work through them one by one, solving the first before you go on to the next.

Also think about human factors that might create difficulties in using the system, such as work pressure, stress or tiredness. If you're distracted or preoccupied, consider giving a running commentary in your head to help you focus on working through the system as you approach each hazard.

We now look at how you can apply the system to four common hazards: a left-hand turn, a right-hand turn, a roundabout, and a potential hazard – in this case, children on the pavement. Before you look at these examples, make sure you know the *Highway Code* advice on road junctions and roundabouts.

Applying the system to a left-hand turn

Information

Take information and identify hazards. What can you see in the junction? What's the current traffic flow? What hazards can you anticipate? Throughout the manoeuvre, scan to the front sides and use rear observation to know the position of other road users and anticipate their intentions. Give a signal at any point where this could help other road users, including pedestrians and cyclists.

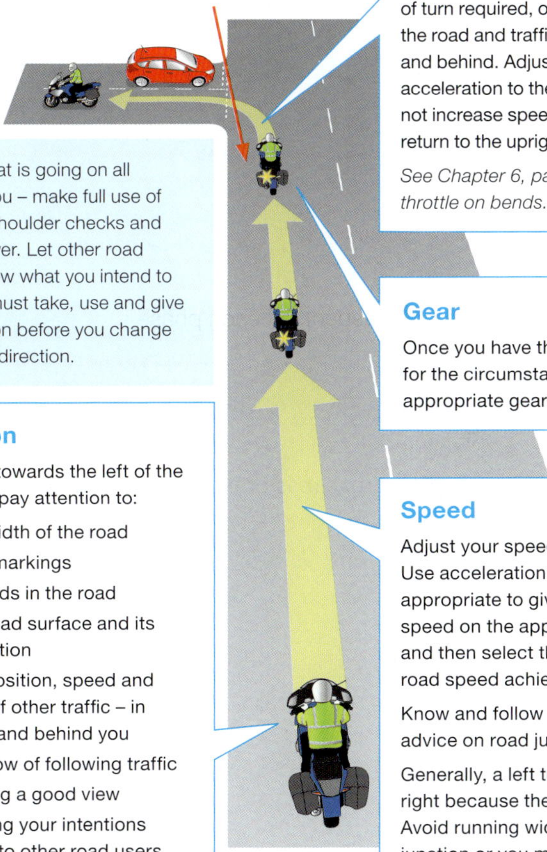

Know what is going on all around you – make full use of mirrors, shoulder checks and the lifesaver. Let other road users know what you intend to do. You must take, use and give information before you change speed or direction.

Position

Position towards the left of the road but pay attention to:

- the width of the road
- lane markings
- hazards in the road
- the road surface and its condition
- the position, speed and size of other traffic – in front and behind you
- the flow of following traffic
- getting a good view
- making your intentions clear to other road users
- positioning to be seen.

Acceleration

Be aware of the possibility of cyclists and other motorcycles moving up quickly on your inside.

Use the throttle to maintain your speed and stability round the corner. Open the throttle sufficiently to offset any loss of speed due to cornering forces.

Choose the appropriate point to accelerate safely and smoothly away from the hazard, paying attention to your speed, the road surface, the amount of turn required, other road users, and the road and traffic conditions ahead and behind. Adjust the amount of acceleration to the circumstances. Do not increase speed before you start to return to the upright position.

See Chapter 6, page 121, Using the throttle on bends.

Gear

Once you have the correct speed for the circumstances, engage the appropriate gear for that speed.

Speed

Adjust your speed to the conditions. Use acceleration sense or brakes as appropriate to give you the correct speed on the approach to the hazard, and then select the correct gear for the road speed achieved.

Know and follow the *Highway Code* advice on road junctions.

Generally, a left turn is slower than a right because the turning arc is tighter. Avoid running wide as you enter the junction or you may come into conflict with other traffic.

Applying the system to a right-hand turn

Information

Take information and identify hazards. How far ahead is the junction? What can you see in the junction? Use rear observation throughout. Look to the front, sides and rear, and check your blind spot to know the position of other road users and anticipate their intentions. Give a signal at any point where this could help other road users, including pedestrians and cyclists.

Acceleration

Use the throttle to maintain your speed and stability round the corner. Open the throttle sufficiently to offset any loss of speed due to cornering forces.

After you start to return to the upright position, choose the appropriate point to accelerate safely and smoothly away from the hazard, paying attention to your speed, the road surface, the amount of turn required, other road users, and the road and traffic conditions ahead and behind.

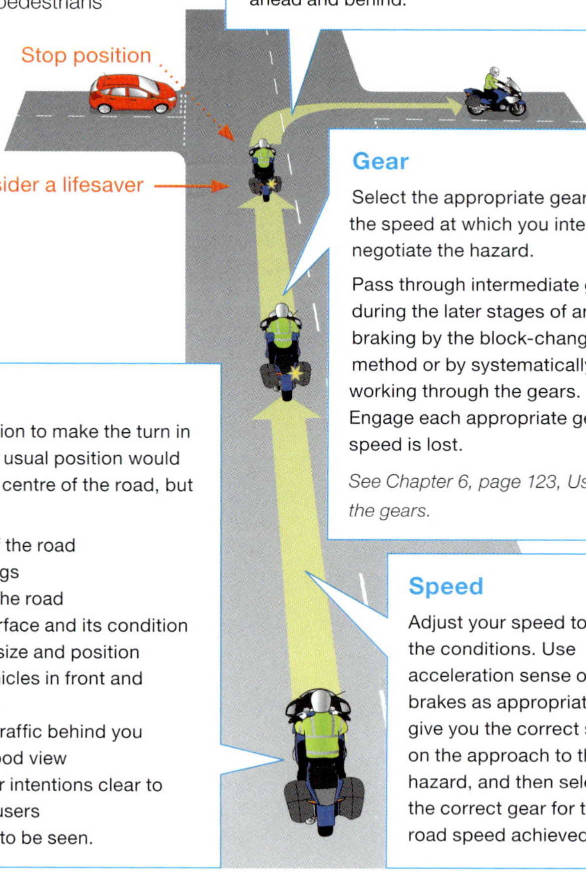

Gear

Select the appropriate gear for the speed at which you intend to negotiate the hazard.

Pass through intermediate gears during the later stages of any braking by the block-changing method or by systematically working through the gears. Engage each appropriate gear as speed is lost.

See Chapter 6, page 123, Using the gears.

Position

Alter your position to make the turn in good time. The usual position would be towards the centre of the road, but think about:

- the width of the road
- lane markings
- hazards in the road
- the road surface and its condition
- the speed, size and position of other vehicles in front and behind you
- the flow of traffic behind you
- getting a good view
- making your intentions clear to other road users
- positioning to be seen.

Speed

Adjust your speed to the conditions. Use acceleration sense or brakes as appropriate to give you the correct speed on the approach to the hazard, and then select the correct gear for the road speed achieved.

Applying the system to a roundabout

Information

Take information and identify hazards. Scan to the front, sides and rear. Use rear observation before you change speed or direction.

Decide early which exit to take and in which lane to approach the roundabout. Examine the road surface for anything that could reduce tyre grip: road paint, smooth bitumen, oil, petrol or diesel spills, dust or loose gravel. Be flexible: adjust your riding plan to take account of new hazards.

Give a signal when it could help other road users.

Take an early view of traffic on the roundabout and traffic approaching it from other entrances.

As you approach the roundabout, be prepared to stop but look for your opportunity to go.

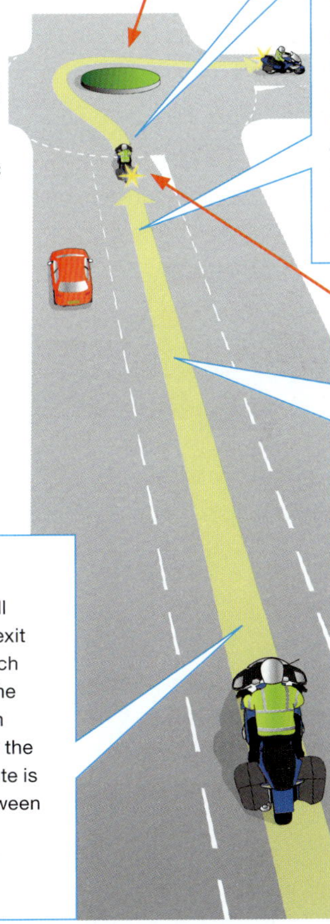

Position

Your approach position will depend on your intended exit and the number of approach lanes. The route through the roundabout will depend on the presence of traffic and the road surface. The best route is generally the shortest between entry and exit. Before you change position, consider rear observation.

Speed

Adjust your approach speed according to your view of the roundabout and the traffic using it. Lose speed smoothly, using deceleration or brakes. Either work through the gears systematically as you slow down or block change to the appropriate gear just before the end of braking.

Plan to stop, but look to go.

Gear

Choose the appropriate gear to move forward onto the roundabout. This will depend on your speed, the traffic conditions and your machine's characteristics.

Acceleration

Choose an appropriate gap in the traffic to accelerate safely and smoothly onto the roundabout without disrupting traffic already using it. When you are on the roundabout, deal with any new hazards using the appropriate phases of the system.

Consider rear observation to both sides as you leave the roundabout.

Re-applying the system to leave the roundabout

Information

As you leave the roundabout, re-apply the system. Take information about the new road: its physical features, hazards on the road surface and other road users. Plan the appropriate lane for your exit. If you need to move into the left-hand lane, check that your nearside road space is clear. Use your nearside mirror and check your blind spot. Signal left if it could benefit other road users.

Exit position

If there is more than one exit lane, choose the most appropriate taking into account nearside and offside hazards including the position of other exiting and oncoming vehicles, debris on the road and roadside furniture such as metal covers. Move over in plenty of time for your exit. If you move to the nearside lane, consider a signal and/or lifesaver before you move.

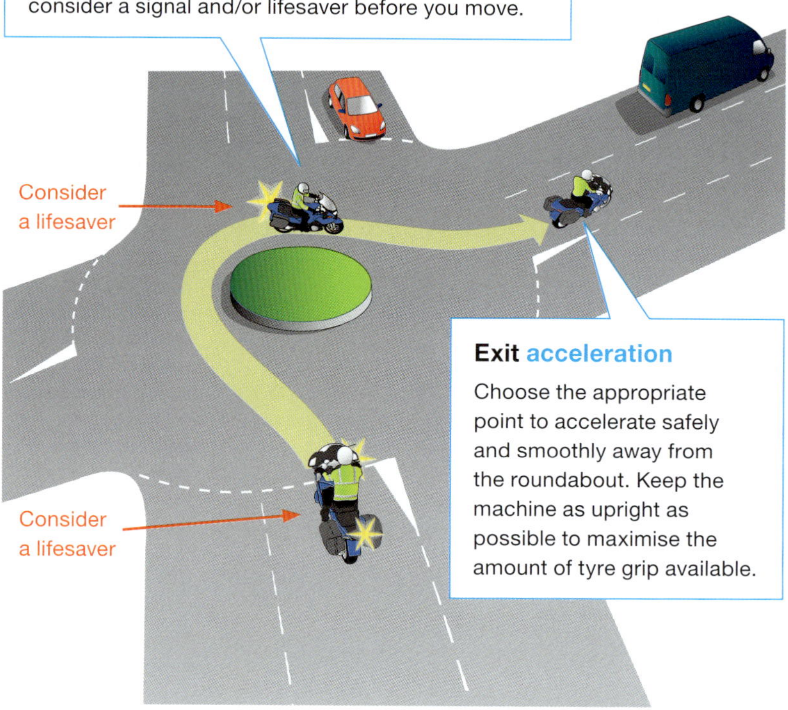

Exit acceleration

Choose the appropriate point to accelerate safely and smoothly away from the roundabout. Keep the machine as upright as possible to maximise the amount of tyre grip available.

Applying the system to a potential hazard

Information

Use your mirrors throughout. Look to the front and sides to know the position of other road users and anticipate their intentions. Give a signal at any point where this could help other road users, including pedestrians and cyclists.

Acceleration

Accelerate safely and smoothly away once you have passed the hazard.

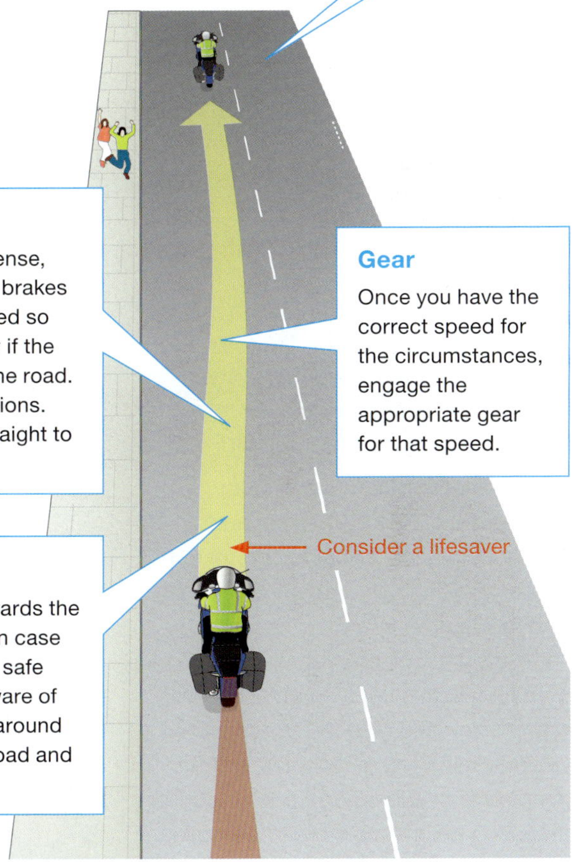

Speed

Use acceleration sense, deceleration or the brakes to reduce your speed so you can stop safely if the children step into the road. Adapt to the conditions. Don't always go straight to the brakes.

Gear

Once you have the correct speed for the circumstances, engage the appropriate gear for that speed.

Position

Take a position towards the centre of the road in case a child steps out, if safe to do so. But be aware of any other hazards around you. Adapt to the road and traffic conditions.

Overlapping braking and gear changing

The individual phases of the system of motorcycle control are usually applied separately. The principle is that brakes are to **slow**, gears are to **go**.

In some circumstances, it may be helpful to overlap braking with the gear change by braking normally but changing the gear towards the end of braking.

> If you use this technique, it must be part of a planned approach to a hazard. *Begin applying the system at the same time and in the same place as you would normally.* The system isn't compressed.

When riders first learn the system of motorcycle control, they separate braking and gear changing and try not to overlap. With tight turns, the problem with this approach is that if you brake some distance before the turn to avoid an overlap, you can confuse other drivers, with unexpected results. Drivers following you may think you're stopping and be tempted to overtake. Approaching drivers preparing to turn into the same junction may think you've slowed to leave space for them to turn ahead of you.

Situations where brake/gear overlap would be appropriate:

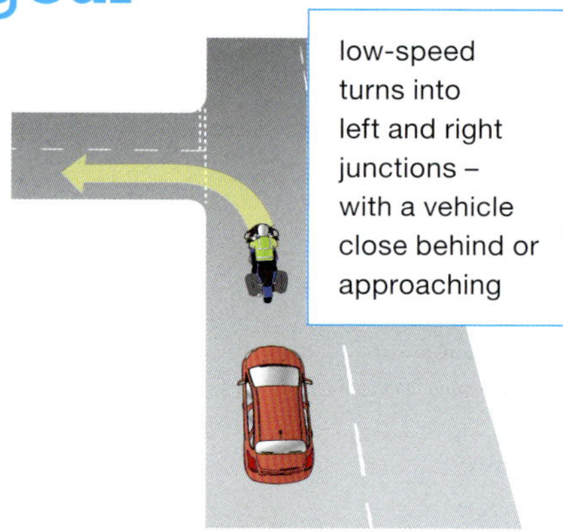

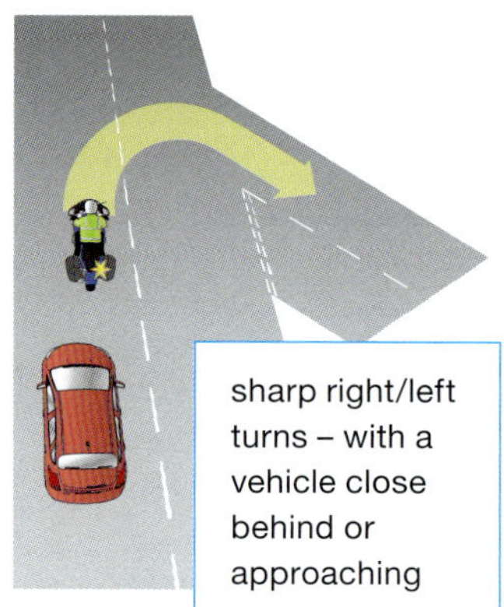

Brake/gear overlap – an example

Here's an example of using brake/gear overlap as a planned approach to a hazard, in order to maintain the correct speed.

If you turn left into a side road that's part of the way down a hill, the bike will start to accelerate when you release the brake. Instead, apply the system as normal up to and including the speed phase.

Incorrect use of brake/gear overlap

Brake/gear overlap has had a bad reputation because it's frequently misused by riders who approach a hazard too quickly:

- Overlap that isn't properly planned results in late, excessive braking and rushed gear changes.
- Braking late and rushing a gear change can destabilise your bike at exactly the point where you need greatest stability to negotiate the hazard.

But applied carefully in certain circumstances, brake/gear overlap takes less time.

Check your understanding

You should now be able to apply learning from this chapter in your rider training so that you can:

- ☐ explain the system of motorcycle control
- ☐ demonstrate how to apply the system to any hazards.

Chapter 4

Information, observation and anticipation

Learning outcomes

The learning in this chapter, along with rider training, should enable you to:

- explain how your brain processes information and how you can improve your ability to process complex information when riding
- explain the three main types of hazard you will meet on the road
- show how to use the information you gather from observation to plan your riding actions
- demonstrate good observation and anticipation skills
- identify human and physiological factors that can affect observation and anticipation, and show how you manage these.

Processing complex information

To develop your riding to police operational standards, you'll need to expand your ability to process complex information. Practice will help you to do this.

The diagram below is a simple model that explains how your brain processes the information that you receive through your senses when you ride. Your brain uses this information and past experience to understand the situation and decide what to do. It then continually monitors and, if necessary, adjusts the action as you carry it out.

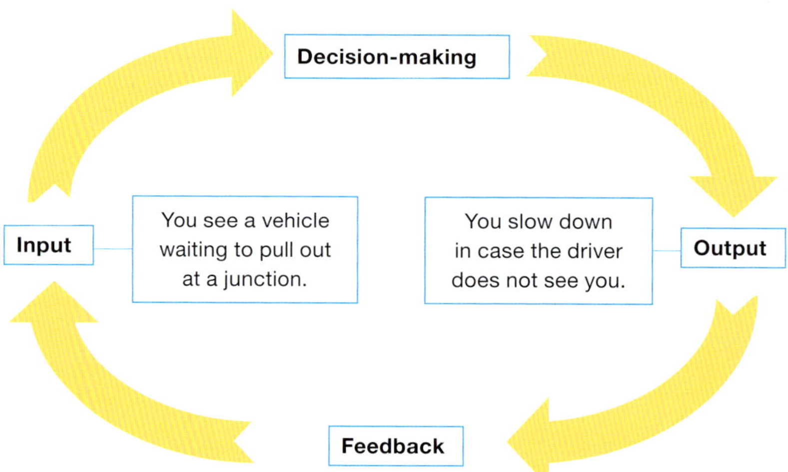

Input

Vision is the most important sense for riding but you should learn to use all your senses to build up the fullest possible picture of yourself, your surroundings and your situation. Your brain uses your observations – and information from your previous knowledge and experience that's stored in your long-term memory – to build up a detailed mental map or 'picture' of your situation.

Decision-making

Your brain compares this mental picture with situations from your experience, identifies what actions you took in the past and chooses a plan of action for the current situation.

Your brain assesses the suitability of the proposed plan of action by comparing it with actions that you've carried out safely in similar circumstances before. You use several types of judgement:

- anticipating how events are likely to unfold
- assessing the proposed plan for risk, noting hazards and grading them based on previous experience
- assessing your space, position, speed and gear.

4

Output

Take action – make an appropriate response.

Feedback

As you put your plan into action, your brain takes in new information and continuously checks it so that you can modify your actions at any time. Developing this ability to a high standard takes experience, practice, alertness and full concentration.

The ability to judge a situation, grade risks and anticipate how things are likely to unfold is essential to safe riding, especially at high speeds.

Improving your information processing

The highly demanding nature of police riding means that the brain's information-processing capacity can become overstretched, reducing riding performance and compromising safety. When information-processing capacity is stretched, it can lead to:

- increased reaction time
- errors of perception

- a decreased focus of attention
- issues with memory storage.

If you understand these, you can take steps to improve your information-processing ability.

Reaction time

Your reaction time is the time between gathering new information about a hazard and responding to it.

Reaction time = decision time + response time

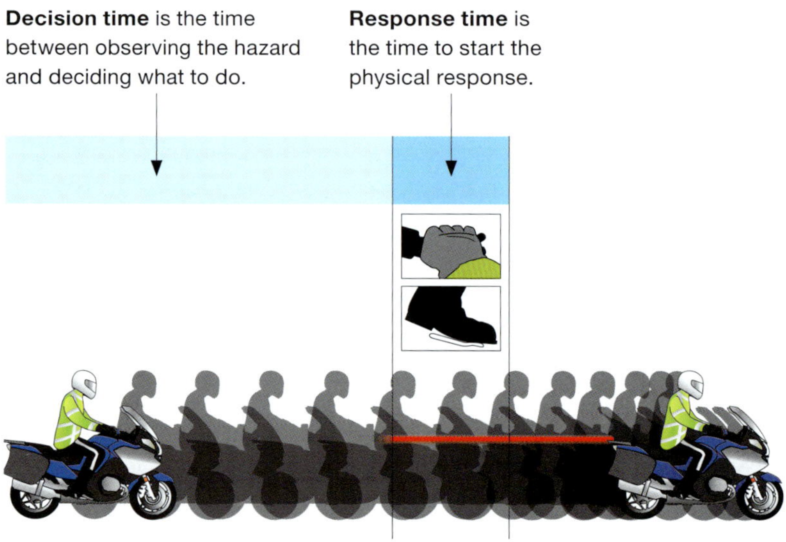

Most riders have a similar response time **but they vary greatly in the amount of time they need to decide what to do**.

As situations become more complicated, you need more decision time and so your overall reaction time is also longer. As a police rider, you may be dealing with situations requiring many complex decisions and judgements – often under pressure and at high speed – where a delayed reaction can have catastrophic results. The system of motorcycle control gives you a structured method for rapid decision-making. This reduces decision time and gives you more overall time to react in complex situations.

If you're using operational technology, you'll have longer reaction times for spotting hazards due to greater demands on your attention. Take steps to reduce these demands wherever possible if you're also facing a particularly challenging riding situation.

Errors of perception

In demanding situations like high-speed riding, it's sometimes possible to misinterpret the information that you receive through your senses.

Common errors of perception are:

- **Errors of judgement** – for example, less experienced riders often perceive a bend as being less sharp than it actually is so they negotiate it too quickly and risk loss of control or collision.

  See Chapter 8, Cornering, balance and avoiding skids.

- **Errors of hazard perception** – riders using operational technology make perceptual errors such as looking directly at hazards but not seeing them because their attention is directed elsewhere.
- **Habit and expectancy** – when you ride regularly on familiar roads, habit can prevent you from spotting a hazard that you don't expect, such as a vehicle emerging from a disused garage forecourt.
- **Regression effects** – riders who switch bikes regularly can, when under a lot of pressure, revert to previously learnt routines – for example, confusing the position of the controls. Do a pre-riding check to get to know the differences in the controls on an unfamiliar machine.
- **Sound and speed** – riders of electric vehicles may perceive speed differently due to less noise being generated.

Focus of attention

Emergency services riders have to process information from several different sources through different senses at the same time: road conditions, radio traffic, navigation, the nature of the operation, and so on. Processing complex information can affect your perception and slow your reaction times. Distractions such as the radio may divert attention from more important information. While training and practice can help you learn to filter complex information and concentrate on the priorities, it will not make you immune to distraction. Part of riding safely is having an understanding of how these distractions can compromise safety, and taking steps to mitigate this wherever possible.

Memory storage

The brain can't always deal with all the information it receives. In complex and demanding situations, your brain may fail to process adequately the information your senses are bringing in. This means that the information may not pass into your long-term memory, meaning that you cannot recall it later.

Tips to improve information processing

- Regularly practise riding techniques and manoeuvres so that you can do them accurately and efficiently.
- Sharpen your observation and perception, and develop your situational awareness.
- Use the system of motorcycle control whenever you ride so that you make decisions methodically and quickly.
- Learn to hold on to important pieces of information until you need them by repeating them, relating them to things you know well, or using other memory techniques.
- Try to avoid distraction so that you're focusing your full attention on the task in hand.

Why observation and anticipation are essential for better riding

The ability to process complex information will give you more time to anticipate hazards accurately when under pressure. An important goal of police rider training is to develop sophisticated anticipation skills.

Anticipation is the ability to identify hazards at the earliest possible opportunity. For the motorcyclist, this can mean the difference between life and death.

ECO Looking well ahead and anticipating potential hazards reduces fuel consumption by cutting down on unnecessary acceleration and braking.

See Appendix 3, Fuel-efficient riding, page 298.

What is a hazard?

A hazard is anything that is an actual or potential danger. It's useful to think in terms of three types of hazard:

- physical features (for example, junctions, bends, road surface)
- the position or movement of other road users (for example, riders, cyclists, pedestrians)
- weather conditions (for example, icy road, poor visibility).

A hazard may be immediate and obvious, such as a car approaching you on the wrong side of the road. Or it might be something less obvious but just as dangerous – for example, a blind bend could conceal an obstacle in your path. Failing to recognise hazardous situations is a major cause of collisions.

Observation is a key component of anticipation. Careful observation allows you to spot hazards and give yourself extra time to think, anticipate and react. You can then deal with unfolding hazards before they develop into dangerous situations.

Sight is the most important sense for observation when riding. But also make full use of your other senses:

hearing (horn sounds, children)

smell (especially helpful for riders: the smell of diesel could mean a slippery surface from a spill and new-mown grass could mean a slow-moving grass-cutting vehicle round the corner)

physical sensations such as vibration (e.g. juddering from road surface irregularities).

Good anticipation involves more than just good observation. It means 'reading' the road and extracting the fullest meaning from your observations. Remember that distraction can affect observation and hazard perception, making the anticipation of hazards much harder.

Planning

Safer riding depends on systematically using the information you gather from observation to plan your riding actions:

- anticipate hazards
- prioritise
- decide what to do.

Generally, things don't just happen; there's often enough time to anticipate how a hazard might unfold. Good planning depends on early observation and early anticipation of risk.

The purpose of the plan is to put you:

- in the correct position
- at the correct speed
- with the correct gear engaged
- at the correct time

to negotiate hazards safely and efficiently.

As soon as conditions change, a new riding plan is required; so effective planning is a continual process of forming and re-forming plans.

The diagram shows how the key stages of planning encourage you to interpret and act on your observations.

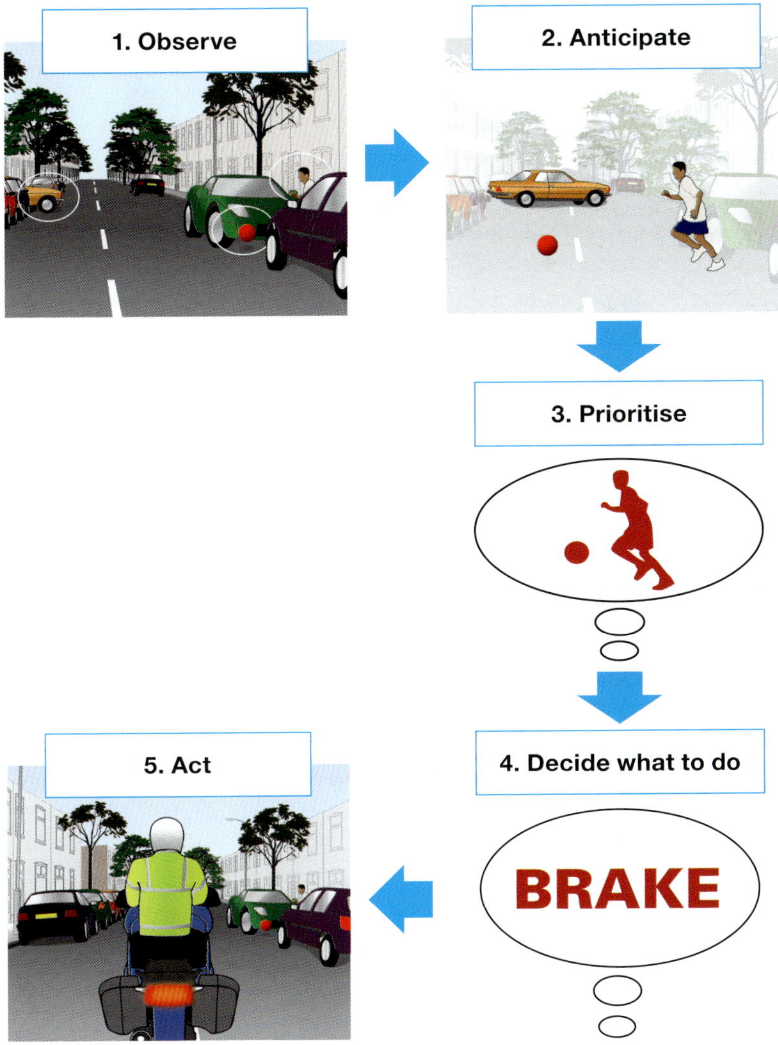

Anticipate hazards

You can develop your ability to anticipate hazards through specific training in hazard perception. But you can also learn to anticipate through experience, if you honestly assess your own performance and that of other road users each time you ride.

Young, inexperienced riders tend to react very quickly to simple hazards but react more slowly to complex traffic hazards. This is because they lack experience of the kinds of hazardous events that can lead to a collision. As they're not aware of the risks, they fail to anticipate them. Trained riders spot the early signs of possible trouble and anticipate what might happen, so they react quickly and appropriately. They're constantly monitoring risks at a subconscious level so that they're ready to respond quickly if the situation develops.

Observation and anticipation reinforce each other. On a familiar route, for example, you may know from experience where there are likely to be hazards, even if your view of the road is blocked by vehicles. Anticipating hazards means that you search the road for visual clues. From this careful observation you gather new visual clues that increase your ability to anticipate.

You can develop your competence at anticipating the actions of drivers by carefully observing their progress and behaviour, and their head, hand and eye movements. Even careful drivers can make mistakes, so learning to anticipate other road users' intentions can give you and them an extra safety margin.

Anticipating hazards gives you extra time. The more time you have to react to a hazard, the more likely it is that you can deal with it safely.

A useful technique to help develop your anticipation is to do a running commentary in your head as you ride. Describe what hazards you can observe and how you plan to deal with them. Remember to observe other drivers as well as their vehicles.

Ask yourself 'What if …?' when you observe a hazard. For example:

'What if the driver waiting at the junction looks but doesn't see me and pulls out?'

'What if there's a parked vehicle just round this bend?'

With practice you should find that you observe more hazards, earlier and in more detail, and gain more time to react.

Prioritise hazards

Where there are multiple hazards, deal with them in order of importance. The level of danger associated with particular hazards varies with:

- the hazard itself
- how close it is to you
- road layout
- whether the hazard is stationary or moving
- how fast you're approaching it.

The greater the danger, the higher the priority, but be ready to re-adjust your priorities as the situation develops.

Practise applying the three stages of planning during every journey until you do it automatically, even when you're riding under pressure.

Decide what to do

The purpose of your plan is to decide on and adopt a course of action that ensures the safety of yourself and other road users at all times, taking account of:

- what you can see
- what you can't see
- what you might reasonably expect to happen
- which hazards represent the greatest risk
- what to do if things turn out differently from expected (contingency plans).

If you plan your riding, you should be able to make decisions in a methodical way at any point and without hesitation.

While you're riding, you should be continuously anticipating, prioritising hazards and deciding what to do. At first, you might find it difficult to consciously work through these three stages all the time but, with practice, this will become second nature and prove a quick and reliable guide to action.

Forward planning beyond the next hazard

Dealing with the hazard immediately ahead is only the start to the process of managing hazards effectively, particularly when travelling in urgent situations. Look beyond the next hazard and consider what other hazards you can see. It's no help to identify the first bend as a relatively minor hazard in isolation if the result is that you're travelling too fast for the hazard beyond it. Similarly, an opportunity to overtake may appear to be available, but if you adopt the speed necessary to overtake safely, it may mean you're travelling too fast for the approaching bend beyond it. The process of identifying and prioritising hazards is an ongoing one. Continually make adjustments in your planning to allow for how an upcoming hazard may affect how you deal with a closer one. Be prepared to re-visit the system of motorcycle control if priorities change.

Planning through a series of hazards – sometimes effectively treating them as one complex hazard – can help you make progress, as well as prevent unsafe riding. Quickly observing the road ahead from the furthest you can see back towards where you're now, rather than working away from yourself towards the horizon, can help with this. Use as much information as you can gather to help you plan effectively.

Improving your observation

Observation and anticipation depend both on visual skills – how you use your eyes to observe the environment – and on mental skills, such as information processing and concentration. These vital skills are interlinked. As a rider, you have some advantages over most car drivers. A rider sits higher and has more flexibility in positioning the machine to get the best view.

Use these advantages to the full, but always be prepared to sacrifice a better view in favour of safety.

Scanning the environment

Our ability to handle information about the environment is limited so we tend to cope with this by concentrating on one part of it at a time. But riders who rapidly scan the whole environment looking for different kinds of hazards have a much lower risk of incident than riders who concentrate on one area.

Imagine your field of view as a picture – you can see the whole picture but you can only concentrate on one part of it at a time. This is why you need to develop the habit of scanning repeatedly and regularly.

When you use a radio, you largely focus your visual attention on one point – usually directly ahead – and fail to look across the scene to peripheral areas, as in the following image.

If you concentrate your vision on a small area, you are less aware of the whole picture.

Continually scan different areas of the environment in turn so that you build up a whole picture.

Routine scanning enables you to process information, spot hazards and monitor the situation as it changes.

Learn to use your eyes in a scanning motion which sweeps the whole environment – the far distance, the middle distance, the foreground, the sides and rear – to build up a picture of what's happening all around you, as far as you can see, in every direction.

Scanning is a continuous process. When a new view opens out in front of you, quickly scan the new scene. By scanning the whole of the environment, you'll know where the areas of risk are. Check and re-check these risk areas in your visual sweeps. Avoid fixing on particular risk areas because this stops you placing them in the broader context. Use your mirrors frequently, and consider a shoulder check when it's not safe to rely on your mirrors alone – for example, to check your blind spots when moving off from the kerb, turning into a junction, joining a motorway, changing lanes or leaving a roundabout.

Look where you want to go

A bike tends to go where the rider is looking, so when you become aware of a specific hazard, it's vital to keep your head and eyes up and continue scanning the whole scene. If you focus on the pothole or the patch of mud that you want to avoid, your bike is likely to head straight for it. This is known as 'target fixation'.

Keep your eyes on the furthest point to which you want to go. Your vision will take in the hazard as well as everything else, and this will allow you to negotiate it safely without being drawn towards it.

> You go where you look, so remember to look where you want to go. Don't focus on the hazard that you want to avoid.

Drivers who look but fail to see you

What we see largely depends on what we expect to see. Remember that drivers tend to see larger objects such as cars or lorries but can miss solo road users such as cyclists or motorcyclists. At a distance, your machine is a small point in a driver's overall field of vision. It remains a relatively small object until it gets quite close.

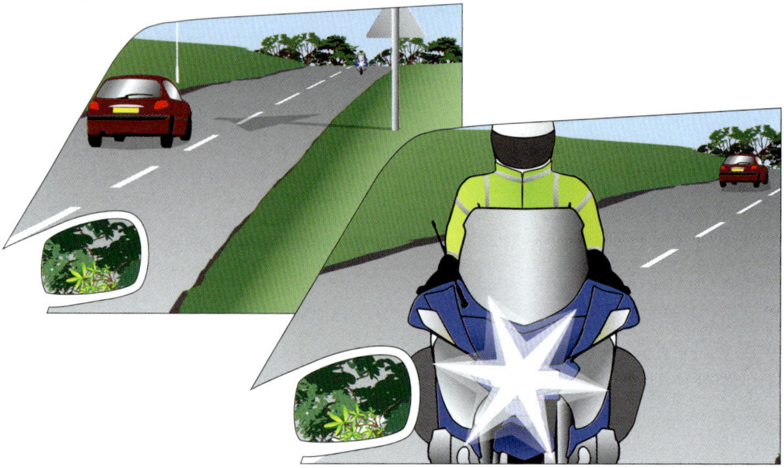

When we concentrate we don't just look at a particular part of a scene, we look for particular types of objects in that scene. We more easily detect and react to objects that we expect to see. Cycles or motorcycles represent a small proportion of vehicles on the road so are much less common than cars, lorries, etc. Drivers build their expectations on what they commonly see and this affects how they process visual information. This is why drivers sometimes fail to see a cyclist or motorcyclist until it's too late.

Be vigilant for drivers who may not have seen you. Anticipating the actions of a driver who may fail to see you helps to reduce your vulnerability. Be prepared to change your course and/or sound the horn.

See Chapter 1, page 6, Your vulnerability as a rider.

You see what you expect to see

Don't relax your concentration when riding in familiar situations, or you may not see the unexpected hazard. Give as much attention to observation and anticipation on routes you use every day as on journeys you're making for the first time. Also, take extra care when manoeuvring in familiar places at low speeds, such as when parking your machine at the end of a shift.

In looking for cars and lorries, riders too can become blind to smaller, less expected road users.

Rear observation

Use a combination of mirror checks and looking behind to make sure you're always fully aware of what's happening behind you. Rear observation is important because the view through the mirrors on some motorcycles is restricted, leaving significant blind spots. You need to look into these blind spots to make sure you know what's happening there.

Rear observation can be any head movement, from a quick glance to the side to a full backwards twist of the head. How you look depends on the circumstances, but the purpose is always to make sure that your intended course and speed will be safe.

Use your judgement in deciding when to look behind. There are situations when it's dangerous not to do so, such as a right turn into a minor road. But when you're looking behind you're not looking ahead. This could be risky if you're close to the vehicle in front or overtaking at speed.

There's an element of risk in taking your eyes off the road ahead, so learn to check behind quickly and don't do it twice when once is enough.

Consider rear observation when you're about to change position or speed as you approach and negotiate a hazard. Use the system of motorcycle control to decide when to do lifesaver checks.

See Chapter 3, page 43, The lifesaver check.

Use rear observation to help you decide where and when to position yourself so that you are visible from the front and not lost in the visual clutter of what's behind you, including large vehicles.

How well do you stand out against the background?

How visible are you at night?

Do you know exactly where the offside and nearside blind spots are on the machines you ride? Sit in your normal riding position on the stationary bike and look in the mirrors. Where are the nearside and offside areas that you can't see? Turn your head over your right shoulder until you can see into the blind spots to the right and behind you. Then do the same to the left.

Peripheral vision

Peripheral vision is the area of eyesight surrounding the central area of sharply defined vision. The eye's receptors in this area are different from the central receptors and are particularly good at sensing movement.

Peripheral vision:

- gives you your sense of speed and your position on the road
- registers the movement of other road users
- acts as a cue for central vision, warning of areas to examine more closely.

Learn to react to your peripheral vision as well as your central vision. Move your head and eyes so that you also scan the areas in your peripheral vision.

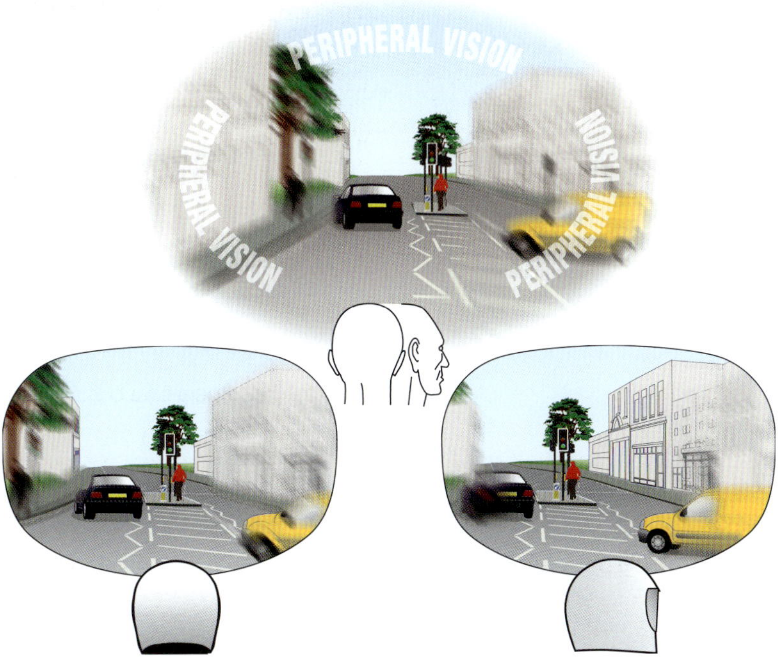

Your helmet cuts down what you can see in your peripheral vision, so move your head to each side so that you can better detect and react to movement at the edges of your vision.

Helmets and visors

Your helmet or visor may restrict your peripheral vision. Compare what you can see with your helmet on and off. Be aware of how and where your helmet restricts your vision. To compensate, move your head slightly from side to side regularly so you know what's happening alongside you.

Keep your visor free from water droplets, mist or scratches. Consider using 'anti-mist' or water-repellent sprays or compounds on both surfaces of your visor. Check the product manufacturer's instructions for correct use.

If you wear glasses, keep the lenses clean, mist-free and protect them from scratches. If the lenses become scratched, replace them. Some tinted lenses may reduce vision at night and in poor visibility.

Zones of visibility

The road around you is made up of different zones of visibility. In some areas, you'll have a good view and, in others, you'll only be able to see what's directly in front of you – for example, at junctions in towns or in winding country lanes.

The rider is approaching a crossroads where the view is restricted. For most of the approach the view improves very little and the rider needs to approach the hazard with great care. From point **X**, the view into the crossroads improves rapidly so the rider can see the position and behaviour of other road users. The rider now has enough information to decide what to do.

On the approach to a hazard where the view is restricted, position your bike to get the best view that is consistent with safety. It's often possible to assess the severity of a bend or gradient using lateral information such as the position of trees, hedges or lamp posts.

Use every opportunity to get more information about the road ahead:

open spaces and breaks in hedges, fences and walls on the approach to a blind junction

a curving row of trees or lamp posts

reflections in shop windows

the angle of approaching headlights

the shadow of an approaching vehicle.

Next time you ride along a familiar route, look for additional sources of information. Look for glimpses of wider views and information from lights and shadows.

Your choice of speed

Speed affects your perception and judgement, so your choice of speed has a major impact on your ability to anticipate hazards.

Adjust your speed to how well you can see, the complexity of the situation and the distance it will take you to stop.

At 70 mph, you would typically need to allow a safe stopping distance of about 100 metres (328 feet). This is the distance between motorway marker posts.

See Chapter 6, page 135, The safe stopping distance rule.

How speed affects observation and anticipation

The faster you go, the further ahead you need to look. This is because as you ride faster, the nearest point at which you can accurately focus moves away from you. Foreground detail becomes blurred and observation becomes more difficult because you have to process a lot more information in less time. The only way to cope with this is to scan further ahead, beyond the point where your eyes naturally come to rest, to give yourself more time to assess, plan and react.

At higher speeds, you'll travel further before you can react to what you've seen and you need to build this into your safe stopping distance.

Remember the safe stopping distance rule:

Always ride so you can stop safely within the distance you can see to be clear on your own side of the road.

When you're riding at high speed, remember the following:

- At speed, vibration can distort your vision.
- Riding at high speed requires a high level of attention and judgement, which you can't sustain if you're tired. Plan regular rest periods to help you to stay alert and get some fresh air. Rest for longer when tired.

  See this chapter, page 85, Practical steps to combat tiredness.
- Your ability to take in foreground detail decreases with speed and increases as you slow down. In areas of high traffic density, such as town centres, you must slow down so that you're able to take in as much foreground information as possible.

- Statutory speed limits set the maximum permissible speed, but this isn't the same thing as a safe speed. The safe speed for a particular stretch of road depends on the conditions at the time. It's your responsibility to select a speed appropriate for the conditions so that you maximise your ability to observe and anticipate hazards.

Know your limits and keep within the speed at which you feel safe and comfortable – resist the pressures that might encourage you to ride faster.

The statutory maximum speed limit is not the same as a safe speed.

Speed and safety

A central aim of *Motorcycle Roadcraft* is to equip you with the attitude and practical abilities to use speed safely. For this you need to understand how speed affects your perception and judgement and to always stay within the limits of your competence.

Accurate assessment of your own riding competence is essential. If you don't choose a safe speed for the circumstances, you won't have enough time to anticipate hazards.

Your safety and that of other road users depends on you being able to accurately assess what is a safe speed. This depends on:

- your riding capability
- your awareness of human factors, such as tiredness, stress or peer pressure, which may affect your capability on any given journey
- your machine's capabilities
- the road and weather conditions.

At 30 mph a minor misjudgement might be corrected but at 70 mph the same mistake could be disastrous.

Underestimating speed

Some common errors of perception are described earlier in this chapter. It's easy to underestimate the speed at which you're riding. This is because your perception of speed depends on several factors:

- the difference in detail perceived by your forward and side vision
- engine, road and wind noise
- the evenness of the ride
- your idea of 'normal' speed
- the road – its width and whether it's enclosed or open
- your height off the ground.

Underestimating your speed means you'll have less time to observe and anticipate hazards. Your speed perception can be distorted in many situations:

- When you come off a motorway or other fast road onto a road where speeds below 30 or 40 mph are appropriate, you'll feel as if you're travelling much more slowly than you really are. Allow time for normal speed perception to return.
- Low visibility can distort your perception of speed (for example, in fog, sleet, heavy rain and darkness), so you find yourself riding faster than you realise.
- If you ride a machine that's smoother, quieter or more powerful than your usual machine, you may go faster than you realise because you use road noise, engine noise and vibration, as well as sight and balance, to assess your speed.
- On wide open roads, speeds will seem slower than on narrow or winding roads.

Always keep a check on your speedometer. Take particular care when you leave a motorway or fast road, especially at roundabouts.

Assess yourself honestly – do you always keep to the safe stopping distance rule at higher speeds? The next time you make a journey involving higher speeds, monitor whether you can always stop within the distance you can see to be clear.

Keep your distance

The closer you are to the vehicle in front, the less you'll be able to see beyond it, especially if it's a van or lorry. In slow-moving traffic, it's better to drop back slightly so that you can see what's happening two to three vehicles in front.

You particularly need a good view of the road ahead on motorways and other fast-moving roads. Your view will depend on the curvature and gradient of the carriageway, the lane that you're in, the size and position of other vehicles and the height of your machine. Allowing for these, keep back far enough from the vehicle in front to maintain a safe following distance. Don't sit in the blind spot of other vehicles – either overtake briskly or drop back. Always check your own blind spot before you change lanes.

See also Chapter 10, page 207, Following position.

Have you ever had a near-miss or collision from riding too close:

- on a fast-moving road?
- in slow-moving traffic?

How did you react to this experience? Did it change the way you ride?

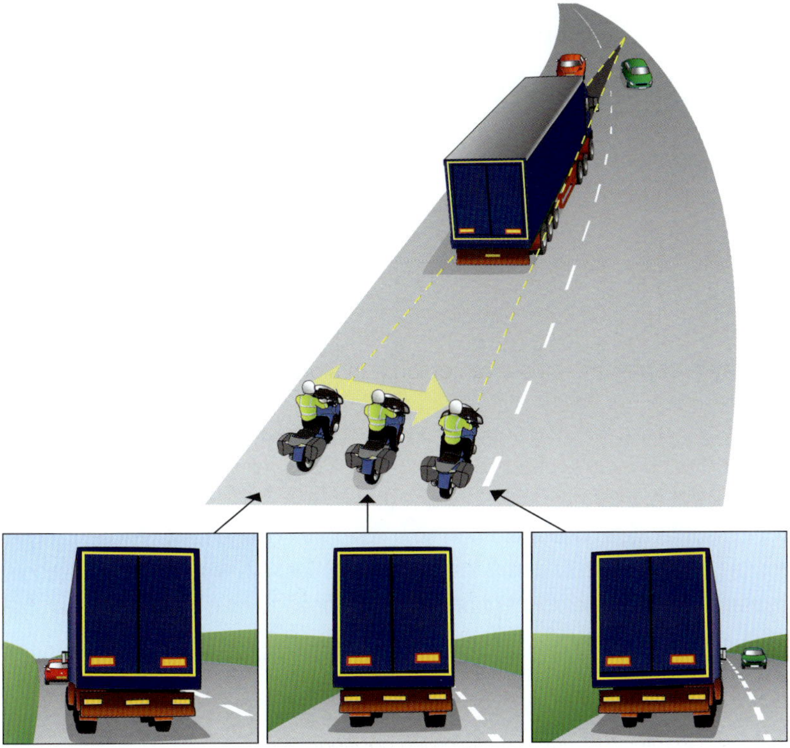

When you're following a large lorry, keep well back and take views to both sides of it.

Can you see both mirrors on a high-sided vehicle? If you can't, the driver may not be able to see you.

Look at the driver's face in the mirror. It gives you a lot of information. If the driver turns their head, it's more likely that they've seen you.

Human factors that affect observation and anticipation

Safe riding is about more than handling your machine and the immediate traffic situation. We look at human factors that can affect emergency services riders in Chapter 1. Here we look at factors that can affect alertness, observation and anticipation.

Alertness

To anticipate hazards we need to remain alert – ready to identify and respond to constantly changing riding conditions. Alertness determines the amount of information your brain can process. It depends on many things but tends to decrease with time spent on routine tasks. Most riding is routine and places few demands on your abilities. A low level of stimulation makes it easy to lose concentration, so you need to take active steps to stay alert, especially on long journeys on motorways or rural roads.

Tiredness

Alertness is reduced if you ride at times when you would normally be asleep, if you've not had enough sleep, or your sleep has been disturbed. It also varies with the time of day:

- Your reactions tend to be slightly slower in the morning than in the early evening.
- There's a dip in alertness after the midday meal.
- The greatest risk of tiredness-related collisions is between the hours of 11.00 pm and 6.00 am.

The risk of tiredness also increases with:

- Irregular work and shift patterns, which disrupt the body's biorhythms or 'biological clock'. This equips your body to perform most tasks by day. At night, many brain functions are normally damped down to allow recuperation and renewal of the body's reserves.
- Disturbed sleep patterns, which can reduce the brain's ability to process information during complex riding tasks.
- The total time spent at work and not just the time spent on your bike. If you're tired from other duties before you start a journey, you're much more at risk from tiredness during the journey. Tiredness is a particular problem for the emergency services and other professional riders because the demands of the job may mean that they have to ride beyond their safety limit.
- Riding for long periods of time in monotonous conditions, such as:
  - in low-density traffic
  - in fog
  - at night
  - on a motorway.
- Riding for longer than about four hours, whatever the conditions.

Practical steps to combat tiredness

The demands of the job and shift work mean that emergency services riders have to learn to deal with tiredness. Watch out for the warning signs such as blinking, yawning or loss of concentration and take steps to manage tiredness well before it becomes dangerous:

- Make available adjustments so that your riding position is comfortable. Find a comfortable position on the machine with your instep resting on the foot rests.
- Bad posture causes muscular tiredness, which in turn causes mental tiredness. This can be a problem during emergency riding, when some riders become physically tense. Learn to recognise physical tension and how to relax your posture, if possible.

- Noise and vibration cause tiredness. Wear earplugs to reduce noise. (Not wearing them causes a degeneration of your hearing range and may cause permanent damage and hearing loss.)
- Being too hot or too cold causes tiredness. Wear clothing that provides physical protection and is appropriate for the weather.

See Chapter 1, page 15, The right clothing and protective equipment.

- Take regular breaks – once every two hours is recommended. Don't wait until you feel drowsy. Most people need a rest break of at least 15 minutes to restore alertness.
- Be aware that if you have several caffeine drinks over a long period, each dose of caffeine will have less effect.
- On long journeys plan a series of rest breaks, but recognise that each successive break will give less recovery than the one before.
- Physical exercise helps you recover from fatigue – a brisk 10-minute walk can energise you.

If you know you're tired, allow yourself a greater safety margin – slow down and be aware that you need more time to react.

Riders over 45 are more at risk of, and recover less quickly from, tiredness than younger riders. If you regularly start your shift feeling tired, or suffer from disturbed sleep, think about how to manage these problems as they will affect your riding.

Other physiological factors

Other things that may affect your concentration and reaction times are:

- minor illness (colds and other viral infections, hay fever, post-viral states)
- medications (especially those causing drowsiness)
- residual blood alcohol
- low blood sugar arising from hunger

- cyclical mood swings caused by hormone changes (this applies to men as well as women)
- life stress such as a bereavement.

Be aware that any of these are likely to affect your concentration and alertness. Take account of them, slow down and allow yourself a greater safety margin.

ECO As your ability to anticipate hazards increases, your riding will become smoother and your fuel consumption will decrease.

See Appendix 3, Fuel-efficient riding, page 298.

Anticipating hazards

Think about the last time you misjudged a hazard. Did this happen because you failed to observe a hazard? Or did you see the potential hazard but fail to anticipate what would happen next?

Did any human factors affect your ability to observe and anticipate? For example, tiredness, time pressure or lapse of concentration?

What can you learn from the situation to improve your anticipation of hazards in future?

Check your understanding

You should now be able to apply learning from this chapter in your rider training so that you can:

- [ ] explain how your brain processes information and how you can improve your ability to process complex information when riding
- [ ] explain the three main types of hazard you will meet on the road
- [ ] show how to use the information you gather from observation to plan your riding actions
- [ ] demonstrate good observation and anticipation skills
- [ ] identify human and physiological factors that can affect observation and anticipation, and show how you manage these.

Chapter 5

Anticipating hazards in the riding environment

Learning outcomes

The learning in this chapter, along with rider training, should enable you to:

- demonstrate awareness of hazards that you may meet at night, in poor weather conditions and on the road surface
- take appropriate steps to reduce or avoid potential dangers from these hazards
- show that you make full use of road signs and markings, your own local road knowledge and observation links to anticipate hazards.

Night riding

It's harder to see in anything less than full daylight and so observation yields less information. For example, pedestrians are harder to see unless there's significant backlighting. This section gives advice on what you can do to make the best of what you can see at night.

You

As the light fades, there's less contrast, colours fade and edges become indistinct. Your body naturally wants to slow down as night draws on and you're more likely to grow tired.

Night riding puts extra strain on your eyes. Even a slight eyesight irregularity can cause stress and tiredness. If you find you're unexpectedly tired from riding, especially at night, get your eyes tested as soon as possible.

Night fatigue

Night riding is tiring both because it strains your eyes and because your body naturally wants to slow down as night draws on. When tiredness starts to affect your judgement or performance, take action to deal with it. If you're having difficulty keeping your eyes open, you're a danger to yourself and other road users. Find somewhere safe to stop, and rest until you're alert enough to continue safely. Plan more stops on a long journey at night to allow for the additional tiredness.

See Chapter 4, page 85, Practical steps to combat tiredness.

Your machine and equipment

Make sure that your visor, glasses, mirrors and the lenses of lights and indicators are clean so that you can see clearly and be seen by other road users. The slightest film of moisture, grease or dirt on visors, mirrors or glasses will break up light and increase glare, making it harder to see what's going on. Scratches on a visor cause starring when struck by lights from other vehicles, which reduces visibility. If droplets form on your visor, try tilting your head so the airstream removes them. At night, don't wear tinted glasses or visors. If your helmet has a visor insert, refer to the manufacturer's guidelines.

Check your lights are correctly aligned and adjusted for the machine load. The bulbs should all work and the switching equipment should function properly.

See Appendix 2, Is your machine fit to ride?, page 293.

Your lights

On unlit roads put your headlight on main beam and only dip it for other road users.

Use a dipped headlight:

- in built-up areas with street lights
- in situations when a dipped headlight is more effective than the main beam – for example, when going round a left-hand bend or at a hump bridge
- in heavy rain, snow and fog, when these reflect glare from a headlight on full beam.

Dip your headlight to avoid dazzling oncoming drivers, the driver in front or other road users. When you overtake another vehicle, return to full beam when you're parallel with it.

> Always ride so that you can stop safely within the distance you can see to be clear on your own side of the road. At night, this is the area lit by your headlight unless there's other lighting. Even in the best conditions your ability to assess the speed and position of oncoming vehicles is reduced at night, so allow an extra safety margin.

If you use a satnav at night, experiment with different modes and find a way of using it that causes you least distraction in darkness.

Following other vehicles at night

When you follow another vehicle, dip your headlight and leave a long enough gap so that your light doesn't dazzle the driver in front. When you overtake, move out early with your headlight still dipped. Return to full beam when you're alongside the other vehicle. If you're being overtaken, dip your headlight when the overtaking vehicle draws alongside you and keep it dipped until you can raise it without dazzling the other driver.

Information from other vehicles' lights

You can get a great deal of useful information from the front and rear lights of other vehicles. For example, the sweep of the headlights of vehicles ahead approaching a bend may indicate the sharpness of the bend, and the brake lights of vehicles in front may give you an early warning to reduce speed. Use this information as a guide, but don't rely on it. Use other information as well.

Intelligent use of information given by lights can help your riding.

Dazzle

Headlights shining directly into your eyes may dazzle you. This can happen on sharp right-hand bends and steep inclines, and when the lights of oncoming vehicles are undipped or badly adjusted. The intensity of the light bleaches the retinas of your eyes so that you can see almost nothing for some moments.

To avoid dazzle, look towards the nearside edge of the road. This enables you to keep your road position but doesn't tell you what's happening in the road ahead, so reduce your speed. If you're dazzled, slow down or stop if necessary until you can see properly again.

Reflective studs and markings

Reflective studs and markings are a good source of information about road layout at night. To get the most out of them you need to be familiar with the *Highway Code*. Roadside marker posts reflect your headlight and show you the direction of a curve before you can see where the actual road goes.

Reflective studs or 'cat's eyes' indicate the type of white line along the centre of the road. Generally, the more white paint there is in the line, the greater the number of cat's eyes. They're particularly helpful when it's raining at night and the glare of headlights makes it difficult to see.

Centre lines: one cat's eye every other gap.

Hazard lines: one cat's eye every gap.

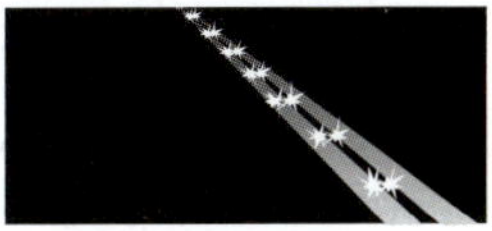

Double white lines: twice as many cat's eyes as hazard lines.

Other ways to improve observation at night

- Keep your speed down when you leave brightly lit areas to allow time for your eyes to adjust to the lower level of lighting.
- Some tinted or light-reactive visors and glasses may not be suitable for night riding. Check the manufacturer's advice.

When you ride at night, think about how to adapt your riding to take account of these factors:

- Your physiological and mental responses to night-time conditions. For each journey ask yourself whether you're fully physically and mentally alert for night-time riding.
- The condition of your machine. Is it properly equipped and prepared for night riding?
- Information in the environment. How do you adapt your observation and anticipation when you make a journey in darkness?

Weather conditions

You must take responsibility for how you deal with weather conditions. Bad weather is blamed for causing collisions when the cause may well be rider error, leading to riding inappropriately for the conditions. Careful observation, good anticipation, the correct speed and adequate braking distances are crucial for safe riding in difficult weather conditions.

Look for evidence of weather conditions before you start your journey. Anticipate changes that could happen during the journey, and, if necessary, check the weather again when you're under way.

In dense fog, you may need to ride so slowly that many journeys aren't worthwhile.

In extreme weather conditions, ask yourself: 'Is this journey really necessary?'

The weather affects your physical and mental condition, how far you can see, and your machine's road-holding. Remember: other road users also see less in poor visibility and will find it harder to see you.

Assessing the weather and its effects are central to your observation, anticipation and riding plan. When weather conditions reduce visibility, reduce your speed and regularly check your actual speed on the speedometer. You should always be able to stop within the distance you can see to be clear on your own side of the road. If it's foggy, follow the *Highway Code* advice on riding in fog.

Examples of weather conditions that reduce visibility are:

- fog and mist
- heavy rain
- snow and sleet
- bright sunshine, especially when it's low in the sky.

For more on dealing with these weather conditions, see Chapter 12, page 260, Bad weather conditions on fast-moving roads.

Riding in bad weather

Fog, rain or snow can cause misting or droplets to form on visors.

- Use anti-misting sprays on both surfaces and spray the mirrors as well.
- If misting occurs due to breath, raise your visor slightly to increase the airflow over the inner surface.
- Keep your visor clean, even if you have to stop to do so.
- Be aware that these problems can be worse on motorways because you're more exposed to the weather, and to the speed and spray of other vehicles.

Regularly check your speedometer for your actual speed. You can't rely on your eyes to judge speed accurately in these conditions because low visibility distorts your perception of speed.

Using lights in bad weather

Choose your lights according to the circumstances. Remember: your lights also help others to see you.

- Most modern bikes have a hard-wired headlight. Make sure it's adjusted correctly so it doesn't dazzle other road users.
- Do not rely on auto lighting systems. Consider manually switching on your dipped-beam headlight.
- Check that any additional lights are working.
- On a machine without a hard-wired headlight:
  - switch on your dipped headlight when visibility is poor in daylight or fading light
  - use a dipped headlight in rain, snow, mist or fog
  - use a dipped headlight when going from brighter into lower light (for example, when entering an avenue of trees).
- Don't use your main headlight beam when you're behind another vehicle in fog – it may dazzle the driver and will cast a shadow of the vehicle on the fog ahead, disrupting the driver's view as well as your own.

Observing when visibility is low

Always ride so you can stop in the distance you can see to be clear on your own side of the road. Use the edge of the carriageway, hazard lines and cat's eyes as a guide, especially when approaching a road junction or corner. Staring into featureless mist tires the eyes very quickly. Focus instead on what you can see: the vehicle in front, the edge of the road or the road ahead. But avoid fixing your focus on the tail lights of the vehicle in front because they'll tend to draw you towards it and you could collide if the vehicle stops suddenly. Be ready to use your horn to tell other road users you're there.

Always be prepared for a sudden stop in the traffic ahead. Don't follow closely, and only overtake other traffic when you can see that it's absolutely safe to do so. This is seldom possible in fog on a two-way road. At junctions when visibility is low, open your visor and listen for other vehicles, and consider using your horn.

Anticipating the effects of windy weather

Strong winds, especially crosswinds, are hazardous because they can blow you off course. Sudden gusts of crosswind are probably the most dangerous. These are likely to occur:

- when leaving the shelter of buildings and hedges at gateways, junctions and at the end of building/hedge lines
- when passing or being passed by a large vehicle
- in exposed places such as bridges, viaducts and hill crests.

When strong winds are likely, keep your speed low and plan your course to give additional space to your downwind side. At any speed, you may be blown about. Larger machines with full fairings and closed-in bodies are particularly at risk.

The road surface in winter

In winter, the ice or frost covering on road surfaces isn't always uniform. Isolated patches remain iced up when other parts have thawed out, and certain slopes are especially susceptible to this. Look out for patches of ice or frost, which you can detect by their appearance, by the behaviour of other vehicles and by the sudden absence of tyre noise: tyres travelling on ice make virtually no noise. Adjust your riding early to avoid skidding.

Micro climates

Look out for evidence of micro climates. These can cause frost, wet patches or fog to linger in some areas after they've disappeared elsewhere. Ice can linger in landscape features, such as valley bottoms, shaded hillsides and shaded slopes, or large areas of shadow cast by trees or buildings, and result in sudden loss of traction. Bridge surfaces are often colder than the surrounding roads because they're exposed on all sides, and can be icy when their approach roads are not. Patchy fog is particularly dangerous and is a common cause of multiple collisions.

Ice and wetness can linger in areas of shadow.

Road surface

Have you ever failed to spot a problem on the road surface that affected your tyre grip or machine handling?

The type and condition of the road surface affects tyre grip and machine-handling characteristics. Safe riding depends on scanning the road surface thoroughly and adapting to what you see. Riding control depends on tyre grip for steering, banking, acceleration and braking. Even the best tyres on a high-performance machine can lose traction on a poor road surface.

Always look well ahead to identify changes in the road surface. Avoid reacting late to an insignificant hazard as this could destabilise the machine. Looking well ahead will allow you to make a proportionate response to minor hazards on the road surface. Adjust the strength of your braking, acceleration and steering to retain adequate road holding.

These are common road surface hazards to look out for:

- country roads – tar-banding (the tar joint around repairs), mud or other deposits, wet leaves in autumn, spilt grain in summer
- urban roads – frequent drains and slippery metal covers; tar-banding and surface variation due to service excavations; oil, diesel and petrol spillages; road paint
- service stations and commercial vehicle depots – large amounts of fuels spilt on roads at bends and nearby roundabouts.

Always observe the camber of the road on a curve or bend. The slope of the camber increases stability if it falls in the direction of lean and it reduces stability if it rises in the direction of lean. If you cross over the centre of the road on a left-hand bend with **crown camber** you enter an area where the slope of the camber is destabilising.

See Chapter 8, page 159, Camber and superelevation.

Surfaces that slope downwards to the inside of the curve help cornering.

Surfaces that slope upwards to the inside of the curve make cornering more difficult.

The surfaces of most roads are good for road-holding when they're clean and dry. Snow, frost, ice, rain, oil, moist muddy patches, wet leaves, dry loose dust or gravel can cause tyres to lose grip, making skids and aquaplaning more likely. Rain may produce a slippery road surface, especially after a long dry spell. At hazards such as roundabouts or junctions, tyre deposits and diesel spillage may make the surface slippery at exactly the point where effective steering, braking and acceleration are needed to negotiate the hazard safely.

Road surface irregularities

Look out for irregularities, such as potholes, projecting manhole covers, sunken gullies and bits of debris, which can damage the tyres and suspension. If you can alter your road position in plenty of time to avoid them without endangering other traffic, do so. If you can't, carry out rear observation and slow down to reduce shock and maintain stability as you pass over them. Where possible, ride over them in an upright position.

Common surface irregularities to look out for

Road paint

Paint used in road markings can be very slippery when wet. Where possible avoid such markings, or choose a position that will minimise the danger. For example, where there's a 'SLOW' marking on the road, ride between the letters rather than over them.

Road joints

Take care where road repairs have left poor joints between the new and existing surface. Even slight differences in height can affect your bike's stability, deflecting it from your intended course. Avoid road joints running along the length of the road. Tar-banding provides less grip than the surrounding surfaces, especially when wet.

Traffic-calming measures

Avoid going straight over traffic-calming 'pillows' as this may destabilise the machine, especially at speed. Some pillows are rubberised to reduce noise for residents, and the surface may be very slippery when wet. Try and ride through the gap either to the nearside or offside, depending on the oncoming traffic.

Be aware that if you do ride over a pillow, the flash from your raised headlight may blind the driver or rider coming the other way, or may be misunderstood by the other person as a signal to proceed.

Metal hazards and physical defects

Rails at level crossings, cattle grids, metal covers and temporary metal sheeting provide poor grip, especially when dusty or wet. Tram lines can be especially dangerous, as they can trap motorcycle wheels between a track and the tarmac. When approaching a bridge, look out for expansion joints, which can be slippery, especially when wet or worn. Defects, such as potholes and general debris, also pose a serious danger. Scan effectively to see them early, so that you can ride around them in a gentle curve. Harsh steering because of a late decision to avoid the hazard can be problematic as you may destabilise the machine.

If these hazards appear on your preferred line and you can't avoid them, slow down on the approach if possible and pass over them carefully. Relax your grip and expect a momentary loss of traction.

See Chapter 8, Cornering, balance and avoiding skids.

Surfacing materials	Grip characteristics	Problems
Tarmac or asphalt 	Tarmac or asphalt surfaces give a good grip when they're dressed with stones or chips.	In time, they become polished and lose some of their skid-resistant properties.
Anti-skid surface 	High-grip anti-skid surfaces are designed to give extra grip on the approach to fixed hazards such as roundabouts, traffic lights and zebra crossings.	When newly laid, loose gravel on the surface can reduce grip; patches can become polished over time.
Concrete 	Concrete road surfaces often have roughened ribs, which give a good skid-resistant surface.	Some hold water, which freezes in cold weather and creates a slippery surface that isn't easily seen.
Cobbles **Brick paving** or **pavers** on roads in home zones **Road paint** 	Low grip when wet.	Rain increases the likelihood of skidding.
Metal hazards on the road surface such as tram lines, temporary metal sheeting, inspection covers, bridge expansion joints 	Poor grip when dusty, wet or worn. Tram lines can trap wheels.	Rain increases the likelihood of skidding. Spaces between tram lines and tarmac can widen over time.

Observation, anticipation and planning

Chapter 4 describes the key competences of observation, anticipation and planning. Use these competences to reduce your risks of losing stability.

Observe – weather and road conditions

Watch out for:

- weather conditions: rain, ice, snow; unexpected cold spots in shaded areas; a shower of rain after a long dry spell (accumulated rubber dust and oil mixed with water can create a very slippery surface)
- road surfaces: dry, loose dust or gravel; worn road surfaces polished smooth; setts or cobbles, which can be slippery when wet; potholes; the road surface on bridges, which may be icier or more slippery than the surrounding roads; concrete, which may hold surface water and become slippery when frozen
- slippery material on top of the road surface: wet mud or damp leaves; oil and fuel spillages, especially at junctions, roundabouts and service stations. The smell of diesel is distinctive and a strong warning sign, especially common in bus lanes and near junctions
- road surface features: metal grills and covers; cat's eyes, tar banding and road paint, including painted bus lanes, especially when wet; traffic-calming features.

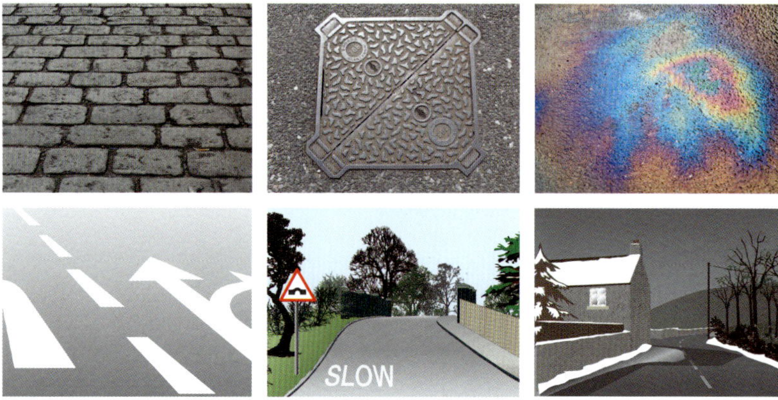

Keep a constant look out for weather and road conditions that create slippery hazards: cobbles, metal surfaces when wet, oily deposits, road paint, wet or icy surfaces on bridges, cold spots in shady areas.

These hazards pose a greater risk at corners and junctions, where you're more likely to combine braking or accelerating, and turning.

Anticipate and plan – consider the road conditions

Where bad weather or road conditions exist, you should firstly ask yourself if the journey is necessary, if it can be delayed until conditions have improved, or if a safer form of transport is available.

If you decide to proceed with your motorcycle journey, you should:

- Leave plenty of room for manoeuvres, reduce your speed and increase the distance you allow for stopping to match the road conditions – on a slippery surface, a bike can take many times the normal distance to stop.
- Use engine braking and a lower gear to reduce speed on a slippery road. It's essential that any gear change is accompanied by a smooth matching of engine speed to road speed.
- When moving off or travelling at low speeds in slippery conditions, use a higher gear to avoid wheel spin.
- On a slippery surface aim to brake, change gear and corner as smoothly as possible, so that the grip of the tyres isn't broken.

Riding through water

Avoid riding through water whenever possible.

Riding at speed through water can sharply deflect the front wheel and cause you to lose control.

See Chapter 8, page 185, Aquaplaning.

Take extra care at night, when it's difficult to distinguish between a wet road surface and flood water. Flood water can gather quickly where the road dips and at the sides of the road in poorly drained low-lying areas. Dips often occur under bridges.

Slow down as you approach a flooded area as water may conceal a hazard such as an object or deep hole. When you have to ride through water, slow to a walking pace and ride through the shallowest part but look out for hidden obstacles or subsidence.

If the road is entirely submerged, stop the machine in a safe place and cautiously find out how deep the water is. The depth of water that you can safely ride through depends on how high your machine stands off the ground and where the electrical components are positioned.

If you decide to ride on, follow the steps below:

- Engage first gear and keep the engine running fast by slipping the clutch. This prevents water entering the exhaust pipe. Use the rear brake to control the road speed, especially when riding downhill into a ford.
- Ride through the water at a slow even speed – a slow walking pace. Keep the bike upright.
- When you leave the water, continue riding slowly and apply the brakes lightly until they grip. Repeat this again after a short while until you're confident that both brakes are working normally. This also applies if you've pushed your machine through the water.

Road signs and markings

Road signs and markings warn of approaching hazards and give instructions and information about road use. Use your observation skills to read the road and link the signs to the hazards ahead, especially at night.

On road signs, the furthest hazard is shown at the bottom and the nearest at the top.

Use your own observations to link the signs to the road layout ahead. Observe all hazards from the distance to the foreground, and prioritise their importance.

Look for changes in the white lines in the centre of the road. A change from centre lines to hazard lines may help you to anticipate an unseen hazard.

Road markings	Explanation
	The centre line on a single carriageway road.
	The line that separates traffic travelling in the same direction on a single or dual carriageway road.
	This is a hazard warning line. It may be accompanied by an upright sign that specifies the type of hazard, such as a bend in the road. The marking is also used on the approach to a junction.
	This is seen at the edge of the carriageway, other than at junctions, exits from private drives and lay-bys. Used on the left-hand side of the road and alongside the central reservation of dual carriageway roads.
	This is seen at the edge of the main carriageway at a junction (particularly where a slip road leaves or joins), at an exit from a private drive or at a lay-by. Also used to divide the main carriageway from a traffic lane that leaves the main carriageway at a junction ahead (lane drop).
	Diagonal white lines (hatched markings) bounded by broken lines may be used in the centre of the road to separate opposing flows of traffic. They're often provided at junctions to protect traffic turning right. They may also be used on the approach to a central traffic island or the start of a dual carriageway. Hatched markings with a single, broken boundary line may be used at the edge of the road or next to the central reservation of a dual carriageway: the diagonal lines always slope towards the direction of travel. You should not enter any hatched area bounded by a broken line unless it's safe to do so.

The text for the table has been adapted from the sixth edition of *Know Your Traffic Signs*. It is reproduced here under the terms of the Open Government Licence.

Make the best possible use of road signs and markings:

- **Observe** – actively search for road signs and markings in your observation scans, and incorporate the information they give you into your riding plan as soon as possible. Many riders fail to see and make use of them, and so lose valuable information.
- **Understand** – be able to recognise them immediately. You should be familiar with the current editions of the *Highway Code* and *Know Your Traffic Signs*.
- **React** – react to a sign or marking by looking ahead to what it refers to and building the information into your riding plan. Where the sign or marking refers to an unseen hazard, anticipate the hazard and adapt your plan accordingly.

Unofficial road signs such as 'Mud on Road', 'Car Boot Sale' and 'Concealed Entrance' can also help you anticipate the road conditions ahead.

When was the last time you looked at road signs in the **most recent** edition of the *Highway Code*?

On your next few journeys, check whether you know the meaning of each sign or road marking you meet and match them to the road layout ahead.

Local road knowledge

Increasing your knowledge of the local roads can help your riding, but never take familiar roads for granted. Collisions are disproportionately frequent on familiar roads (the 'close to home' effect). Loss of attention is a major cause of collisions and riders are least attentive, and more likely to be distracted by secondary tasks, on roads they know well. Don't let your attention wander, even on roads you know well. You're also at risk from the wandering attention of other road users.

Town riding puts heavy demands on your observation, reactions and riding skills, and you need to be alert at all times. At complicated junctions, where it's important to get into the correct lane, local knowledge is useful. But even when you know the layout of main road junctions, one-way streets, roundabouts and other local features, always plan on the basis of what you can actually see – not what usually happens.

Making observation links

Observation links are clues to physical features and the likely behaviour of other road users. Aim to build up your own stock of observation links, which will help you to anticipate road and traffic conditions as you scan the environment.

Below are some examples of observation links.

When you see a cluster of lamp posts, look out for a probable roundabout ahead.

When you see a single lamp post on its own, look out for the exit point of a junction.

When you see no gap in a bank of trees ahead, look out for the road to curve to the left or right.

Some more observation links

When you see ...	Look out for ...
A railway line beside the road	The road will invariably go over or under it, often with sharp turns.
A row of parked vehicles	Doors opening, vehicles moving off. Pedestrians stepping out from behind vehicles. Small children hidden from view.
A bus at a stop	Pedestrians crossing the road to and from the bus. The bus moving off, possibly at an angle.
Cyclists	An inexperienced cyclist doing something erratic. A cyclist looking over their shoulder with the intention of turning right. Strong winds causing wobble. A young cyclist doing something dangerous.
A gap in a line of traffic	Cars emerging between queuing vehicles.
A recently laid road surface	Loose chippings causing loss of traction.
Flashing brake lights	A hazard a driver ahead has responded to by braking hard.

Practise using observation links, even on familiar roads. What would you look out for if you observed:

- a pedestrian calling a cab?
- a motorway slip road?
- a farm or quarry entrance?
- a petrol station or service station?
- horse droppings?
- signs warning of roadworks?
- a bus at a bus stop?
- new hedge clippings or grass cuttings on a narrow country road?
- bins out on the pavement?

Can you think of a recent occasion where you failed to spot the significance of something you observed?

Could you use this experience to improve your anticipation skills?

Check your understanding

You should now be able to apply learning from this chapter in your rider training so that you can:

- ☐ demonstrate awareness of hazards that you may meet at night, in poor weather conditions and on the road surface
- ☐ take appropriate steps to reduce or avoid potential dangers from these hazards
- ☐ show that you make full use of road signs and markings, your own local road knowledge and observation links to anticipate hazards.

Chapter 6

Acceleration, using gears and braking

Learning outcomes

The learning in this chapter, along with rider training, should enable you to:

- explain how acceleration, braking and cornering affect tyre grip and machine stability
- show that you can control your machine accurately in a range of situations
- show good acceleration sense, using the throttle accurately and smoothly
- show how to use gears accurately, selecting the correct gear in a range of circumstances and for different purposes
- explain the safe stopping distance
- show how to use the brakes and engine braking to slow the bike appropriately and safely in different circumstances
- explain the main factors that reduce fuel consumption.

Developing competence at controlling your bike

Riding smoothly reduces both fuel consumption and wear and tear on your machine.

See Appendix 3, Fuel-efficient riding, page 298.

The aim of this chapter is to give you complete control over moving, stopping and changing the direction of your machine at all times. To achieve this level of competence, you need to:

- accurately assess your current riding behaviour and the scope for improving your machine control skills
- understand in detail how the throttle, gears, brakes and steering controls work and how to make best use of them.

A moving machine is most stable when its weight is evenly distributed, its engine is just pulling without increasing road speed, and it's travelling in a straight line.

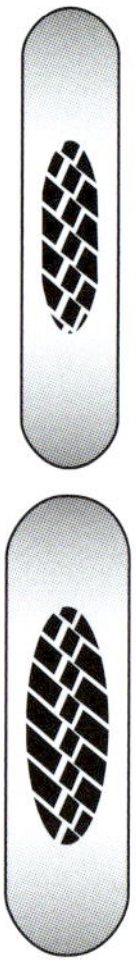

Control of your machine and your own and others' safety depends entirely on the grip between your tyres and the road. Check the condition of your tyres regularly. The wrong tyre pressure, worn treads, cracking, cuts, bulges, lumps or foreign objects can all reduce tyre grip and safety.

The patch of tyre in contact with the road on an average machine is about the size of a hand.

ECO All new tyres have a label that tells you about the tyre's wet grip, fuel efficiency and noise performance. Check tyre pressures regularly because under-inflated tyres can affect stability. Low tyre pressure also increases rolling resistance and fuel consumption.

See Appendix 3, Fuel-efficient riding, page 298.

The tyre grip trade-off

There's a limited amount of tyre grip available. The patch of tyre in contact with the road varies with the size of the bike and the width of the tyres. On an average machine the contact patch is about the same size as a hand. This is shared between accelerating, braking and cornering forces. If more tyre grip is used for braking or accelerating, there's less available for cornering, and vice versa.

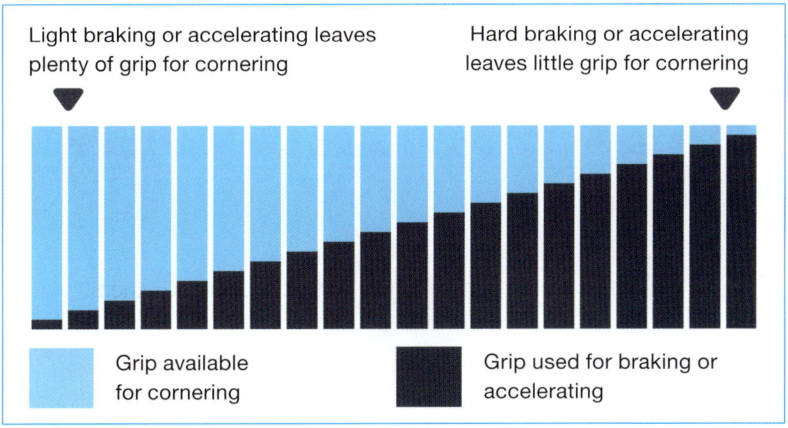

6

Develop your awareness of tyre grip

Analyse what's happening to your tyre grip as you alter course round a corner or bend.

Be aware of the trade-off between accelerating or braking on the one hand and cornering on the other.

Do you finish braking before you go into a bend?

Do you avoid accelerating harshly while riding through bends?

Balance and tyre grip

Tyre grip isn't necessarily the same on each wheel. It varies with the load on the wheel and this affects the machine's balance and how it handles. Braking, changing direction and accelerating each alter the distribution of the load.

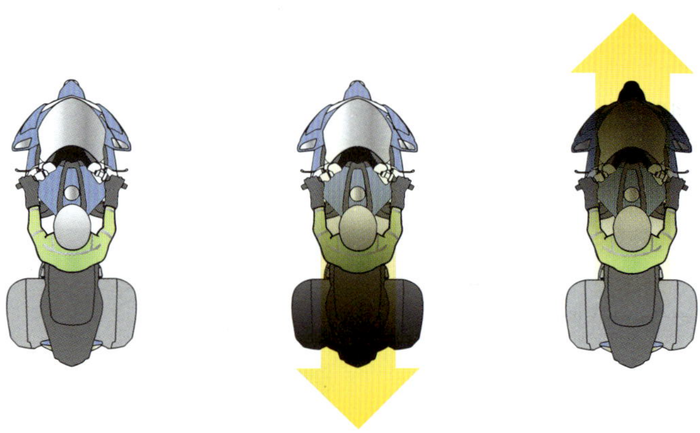

Steady speed
weight is evenly distributed

Accelerating
weight shifts to the back

Braking
weight shifts to the front

Braking, cornering and accelerating alter the machine's balance and tyre grip.

Excessive braking or accelerating as you ride round a corner or bend leaves less tyre grip for cornering. This reduces your control over the positioning of your machine. Eventually, if there isn't enough tyre grip for cornering, the bike will lose traction. The more slippery the road surface, the earlier this happens.

Braking is particularly hazardous on a banked (leaning) machine. Moderate use of the brakes is possible on a sound surface and with experience.

See Chapter 8, page 153, for specific advice on safe cornering.

Technology to help keep control of the machine

Many machines are now fitted with electronic safety features to help the rider keep control of the machine when harsh braking or acceleration might result in a loss of traction. These include cornering anti-lock braking systems, traction control and linked braking systems. The specific technology and how it works varies from one manufacturer to another. This technology is also developing fast, with increasing sophistication.

See Chapter 2, Advanced rider-assistance systems.

In Chapter 8, we look at some of the systems that can help riders to maintain stability.

Don't switch off safety features; they are there to help you. But whenever you do activate them, ask yourself why. Could you, for example, have anticipated the hazard that caused you to brake sharply?

See Chapter 8, page 183, Machine design developments.

Using the throttle

Open the throttle:

- to *increase* road speed
- to *maintain* road speed, for example, when cornering or going uphill (referred to as 'positive throttle').

Close the throttle:

- to reduce engine speed and slow the bike down.

If you're in the correct gear for your speed, opening the throttle will give you a responsive increase in engine speed. If you're in too high a gear, the engine may not respond because the load from the wheels is too great. Changing to a lower gear reduces the load and allows the engine to speed up and move the machine faster.

If you close the throttle, you get the opposite effect – deceleration. The engine speed slows down and cylinder compression slows the machine down. The lower the gear, the greater the slowing effect of the engine, or engine braking.

See page 129, Releasing the throttle – engine braking.

Acceleration and machine balance

Acceleration alters the distribution of weight between the wheels of the bike. When a machine accelerates the weight lifts from the front and pushes down on the back wheel, increasing the load on the rear tyre. During deceleration the opposite happens, increasing the load on the front wheel.

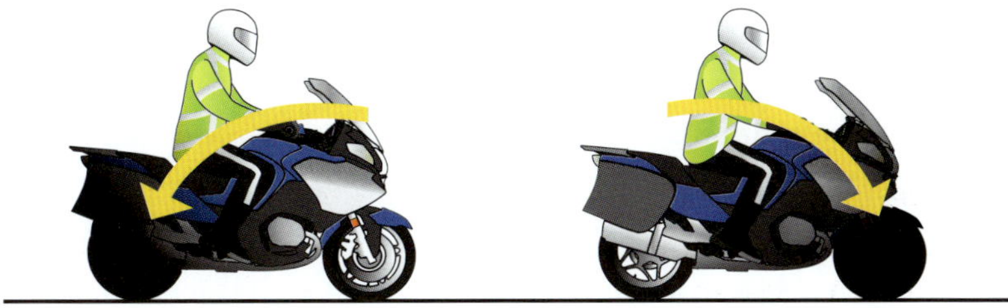

During acceleration

load on the rear wheel increases

load on the front wheel reduces

During deceleration

load on the rear wheel reduces

load on the front wheel increases

Develop your competence at using the throttle

How you use the throttle affects your own and others' safety. Motorcycles are very responsive to use of the throttle during acceleration and deceleration. Sudden sharp use of the throttle reduces tyre grip and jeopardises stability and control, especially when cornering. It could lift the front wheel of the bike or cause the rear wheel to spin.

Jerky use of the throttle is uncomfortable, puts unnecessary strains on the machine, reduces tyre grip and increases fuel consumption. Develop smooth control of the throttle: use gentle, progressive and accurate movements to open or close it.

Acceleration capability varies widely between machines and depends on the fuel or power source, the engine output, its efficiency, the power-to-weight ratio and its load. Take time to get to know the acceleration capability of any machine you ride. The safety of many manoeuvres, particularly overtaking, depends on judging it well. Remember: the faster you go, the further you'll travel before you can react to a hazard. It will take you longer to stop and, if you collide, the results of the impact will be worse.

Acceleration sense

Acceleration sense is the ability to vary machine speed in response to changing road and traffic conditions by accurate use of the throttle, so that you use the brakes less or not at all.

This uses less fuel, causes less wear on the tyres and reduces emissions.

See Appendix 3, Fuel-efficient riding, page 298.

You need acceleration sense in every riding situation: moving off, overtaking, complying with speed limits, following other traffic and negotiating hazards. Acceleration sense requires observation, anticipation, judgement of speed and distance, riding experience and knowledge of the machine's capabilities.

As your ability to anticipate hazards increases, your riding will become smoother and your fuel consumption will decrease.

See Appendix 3, Fuel-efficient riding, page 298.

When you come up behind another vehicle, how often do you need to brake to match the speed of the driver in front? If your answer is 'always' or 'nearly always', work at developing your acceleration sense.

Ride along a regular route using acceleration sense rather than braking. Notice how it improves your anticipation and increases the smoothness of the ride.

Acceleration sense helps you avoid unnecessary braking. Common mistakes are:

- accelerating hard away from a junction and then having to brake sharply to slow to the speed of the vehicles in front
- accelerating to move up behind a slower-moving vehicle and then having to brake before overtaking

- accelerating to overtake and then having to brake sharply to move back into a space
- accelerating into a closing gap.

Using the throttle on bends

To get the best stability while cornering, you need to keep your speed constant. Do this by gently opening the throttle enough to compensate for the speed lost due to cornering forces. Your aim is to maintain constant speed, not to increase it. Practice will help you judge how much to open the throttle for a steady speed.

Maintain a positive throttle (use the throttle to maintain a constant speed) through a bend. A constant speed keeps your weight evenly distributed front and rear, and ensures maximum tyre grip.

If you accelerate to *increase* road speed and alter direction at the same time, there may not be enough tyre grip available and you may lose cornering control.

If you need to change course and increase speed together, use the throttle sensitively and smoothly. Take extra care when accelerating in slippery conditions. If you misjudge it, you may experience loss of traction and control.

See Chapter 8, page 155, Cornering forces.

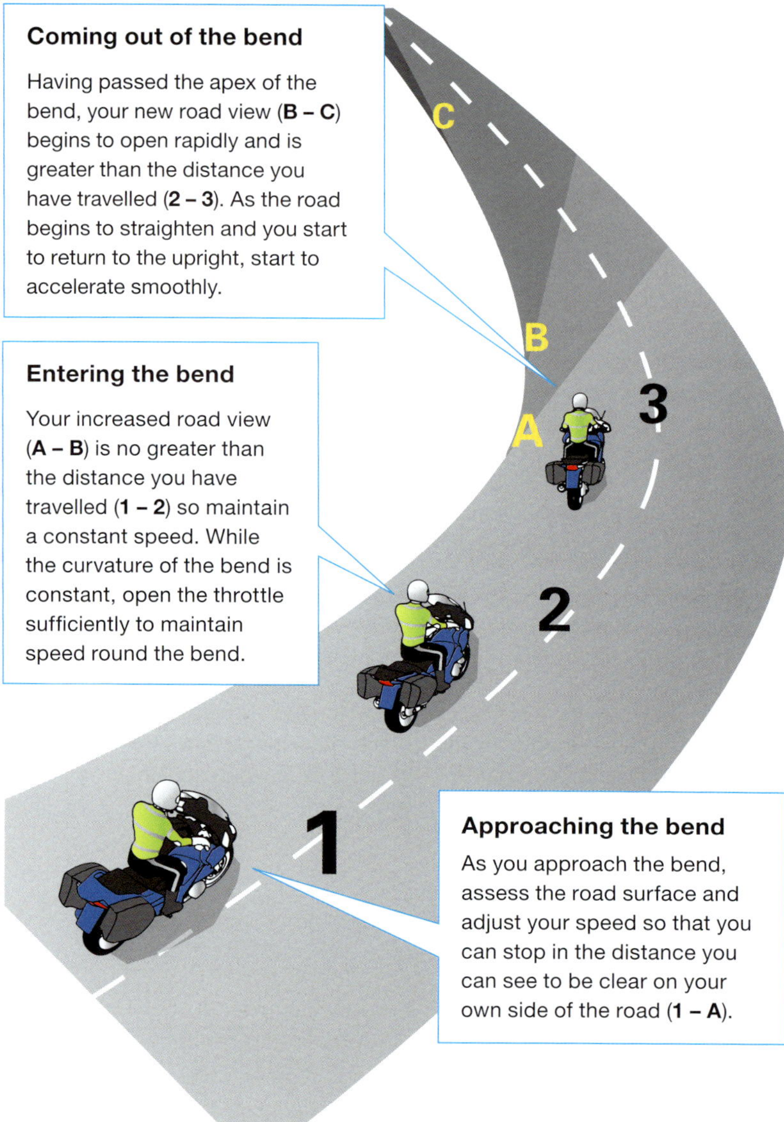

Coming out of the bend

Having passed the apex of the bend, your new road view (**B – C**) begins to open rapidly and is greater than the distance you have travelled (**2 – 3**). As the road begins to straighten and you start to return to the upright, start to accelerate smoothly.

Entering the bend

Your increased road view (**A – B**) is no greater than the distance you have travelled (**1 – 2**) so maintain a constant speed. While the curvature of the bend is constant, open the throttle sufficiently to maintain speed round the bend.

Approaching the bend

As you approach the bend, assess the road surface and adjust your speed so that you can stop in the distance you can see to be clear on your own side of the road (**1 – A**).

Follow the guiding safety principle – you must always be able to stop safely within the distance you can see to be clear on your own side of the road. If that distance shortens, you must slow to match it.

Key points

- **The harder you accelerate, the less your cornering ability.**
- **Use the throttle smoothly – jerkiness may cause loss of traction and is not fuel efficient.**
- **Use acceleration sense to vary your road speed without unnecessary braking.**
- **For cornering control and stability, use a positive throttle to maintain a steady speed through a bend.**

Factors that affect acceleration and engine braking

Engine configuration affects acceleration and engine braking. For example, a twin-cylinder four-stroke engine will give more low-down torque (pulling power) but will provide less free revving than a four-cylinder engine. The twin will also provide more engine braking when you close the throttle.

In addition, it is expected that as electric motorcycle technology develops, throttle and brake control is also likely to change. These technologies are expanding faster than at any time in recent years; always refer to the manufacturer's advice.

Using the gears

The way you use your gears can make or mar your riding. Correct use of the gears depends on accurately matching the engine speed through the chosen gear to the road speed, and using the clutch and throttle precisely. This will give you smooth gear changes and greater stability. Avoid selecting a lower gear instead of the brakes to slow the machine down.

See Braking and changing gear on page 126.

Moving off from stationary

From a standing start, accelerate smoothly and gather speed by steadily working up through the gears. You should only use maximum acceleration through the gears if there's a pressing need, and if the road surface and other conditions are safe. Over-accelerating in low gears or remaining in a gear beyond the limits of its best performance uses more fuel and may damage the engine. For this reason, some machines are fitted with rev-limiters.

Accurate use of the gears

Your machine can only increase speed if the engine can deliver the power, and it can only do this effectively if you're in the correct gear. Aim to:

- be in the correct gear for every road speed and traffic situation
- make all gear changes smoothly
- know the approximate maximum road speed for each gear
- know the most efficient point at which to change up.

The main effect of the gears is to transform engine revs into usable power:

- In a low gear, the engine is able to rev more freely, which allows the machine to accelerate rapidly and to climb steep slopes.
- In a higher gear, lower revs deliver more speed but less ability to accelerate or to climb slopes.
- Intermediate gears allow progress from one extreme to the other.
- A lower gear also restrains the machine's speed when descending a steep slope.

To climb a steep hill, select a low gear. This gives the back wheel plenty of turning power but less speed. To cruise on a level stretch of motorway, choose a high gear. This gives you speed but relatively little turning power.

The greater turning power of low gears also affects tyre grip. The greater the turning power, the more likely that the tyres will lose grip.

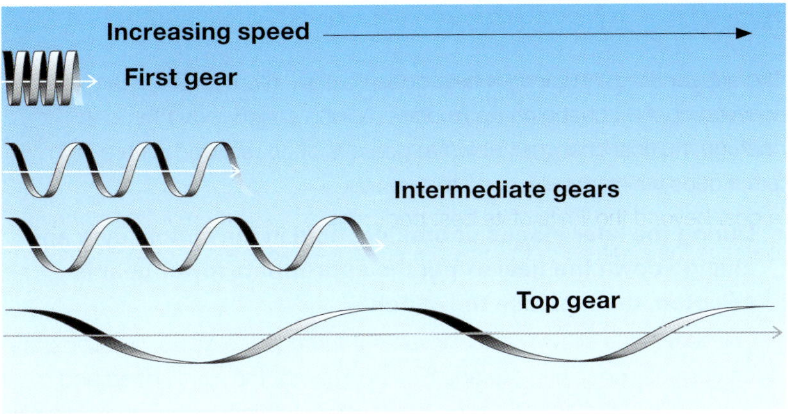

First gear

produces plenty of road wheel turning power but not much speed

Intermediate gears

produce varying combinations of wheel turning power and speed

Top gear

produces plenty of speed but not much wheel turning power

Changing to a lower gear helps when:

- travelling at low speeds
- going uphill
- going downhill, because engine compression slows the descent
- approaching a hazard
- on slippery roads, where you should ease off the throttle to lose speed gently, so as to avoid skidding.

High gears are good for:

- cruising at speed
- certain slippery conditions where lower gears may cause wheel spin.

Braking and changing gear

The sequential gearbox on a bike doesn't allow intermediate gears to be missed when changing up or down. When speed is lost through braking, multiple changing down of gears is often required. There are two techniques which can be used to do this:

- **During the later stages of braking, hold in the clutch lever and change down the gears until the appropriate lower gear is selected, then release the clutch.**

  This technique allows rapid movement through the gears, but depends on correctly choosing the appropriate gear for the road speed and accurately counting the gears. If you select too low a gear, there's a risk of locking the rear wheel and causing a skid.

- **During the later stages of braking, work down through each gear, releasing the clutch very briefly in the lower gear.**

  At each gear change, accurately match the engine speed to the road speed, to maintain smoothness and avoid locking the rear wheel.

  This technique is more suitable on machines where a multiple gear change in one clutch movement is inappropriate.

  Where conditions are so slippery that you need to reduce speed using the gears rather than using the brakes, make gear changes very carefully as you enter the optimum speed range for each gear.

You should be able to use both techniques, but whichever you use it must be properly incorporated into your planning.

The purpose of your journey may influence how you use your gears. For example, on routine journeys your goal is economic progress but, for emergency response, you need to make progress safely.

For economic progress – change up a little earlier. This reduces fuel consumption and carbon emissions. Many new machines are now fitted with a gear shift indicator (GSI) on the dashboard, to show you the most fuel-efficient point at which to change gear. Combine this with observation of the road ahead to avoid making unnecessarily frequent gear changes. For example, the GSI may suggest changing up just before you start to climb a steep hill, which would require you to change immediately to a lower gear.

For rapid progress – accelerate up to the engine's peak performance point and then change to a higher gear. Bear in mind the manufacturer's peak engine performance recommendations for your machine. This may differ from the maximum revs obtainable from the engine. Don't over-rev the engine.

Key points

- **Recognise when to change gear by the sound of the engine.**
- **Choose the correct gear for the road speed.**
- **Develop good coordination of hand and foot movements.**
- **Changing up a little early reduces fuel consumption. Take note of the gear shift indicator if fitted.**
- **Brake in good time to slow to the right road speed as you approach a hazard and, passing through the intermediate gears, select the appropriate gear.**
- **Match the revs to the road speed for the new gear to be engaged – you may need to blip the throttle when changing down.**
- **Use the brakes rather than engine compression to slow the machine (except during hill descents).**

Are you always in the correct gear?

When you fail to select the appropriate gear, ask yourself why. Are you focusing on other things and not your riding?

Do you ever find yourself changing gear halfway round a corner? Again, ask yourself why this happens, and how you can improve your use of gears.

Automatic transmission

Automatic transmissions operate and behave differently from manual gears and from each other, so always consult the machine handbook.

Some motorcycles have automatic or direct shift gearbox (DSG) options. These systems offer the ability to override the automatic function, as in a car, and manually select a gear using switches on the handlebars. When using the switches, they perform almost as a manual and allow a gear to be held or prioritised. If you're riding one of these machines, consult your handbook and follow the guidance on how to use the gearbox to best effect.

These machines may behave differently from a manual one and may not display as much engine braking as you expect from a manual-gearbox motorcycle.

Electric motorcycles

Electric motorcycles usually have no clutch or gear shifting, similar to a 'twist and go' scooter. They tend to accelerate more quickly because of the instant torque they provide and so throttle control is more critical, especially at low speeds or in turns. Because electrically propelled motorcycles are so quiet, they may also give a different impression of speed to the rider.

Some machines (including hybrids) recharge the battery while slowing down. This can affect how the throttle is used, and you may need to adjust the way that you use it to take account of this. The effect can be very noticeable, slowing the machine more and reducing the need to use the brakes. The slowing may be sufficiently pronounced that the rear brake light comes on to warn following drivers that the machine is slowing, much as if the brakes were actually being applied.

Familiarise yourself with your machine's characteristics. Making good use of this feature can prolong its range, make more efficient use of energy, and provide a smooth journey.

Slowing down and stopping

You need to be able to slow down or stop smoothly and with your machine fully under control. Anticipate the need to slow down or stop in good time and brake gently and progressively. Being able to accurately estimate the required braking distance at different speeds and in different conditions is a core skill for safe riding. There are two ways of slowing down (decelerating) or stopping:

- releasing or easing off the throttle
- using the brakes.

Releasing the throttle – engine braking

Engine braking depends on factors such as the type of machine, the power source (internal combustion or electric), the engine size, the cylinder configuration and the gear you've chosen to use.

When you release the throttle on an internal combustion engine, the engine slows and engine compression exerts a slowing force on the wheels. The loss of road speed is greater when you ease off the throttle in a low gear. On an electric motorcycle, releasing the throttle removes the drive allowing the bike to slow.

Releasing the throttle in this manner allows you to lose speed in conditions where normal braking might lock the wheels. It's also useful on long descents in hilly country.

With an internal combustion engine, engine braking operates only on the rear wheel, but it's an effective way of losing speed. Remember when you use engine braking that this gives no brake light signal to the traffic following you.

Using the brakes

See also Appendix 2, Testing the brakes, page 297.

Use the brakes when you need to slow more quickly than by using engine braking. Correct use of the brakes on a bike can slow you quickly and effectively. Incorrect use can cause you to lose control of your machine.

See Chapter 8, Cornering, balance and avoiding skids.

Follow these guidelines for braking:

- brake firmly only when travelling in a straight line
- brake in plenty of time
- adjust brake pressure to the condition of the road surface
- avoid using the front brake:
  - when the machine is banked
  - when turning
  - on loose or slippery surfaces
- on hills, brake on the straight stretches and ease off on the bends.

Braking as you approach a hazard

When and how firmly you apply the brakes depends on your judgement of speed and distance. You should consider:

- your initial speed
- the road surface
- the degree of banking

- weather conditions
- the specific road and traffic conditions.

Sometimes braking may need to be firm but it should never be harsh. Harsh braking usually indicates poor observation, anticipation and planning. Aim to lose speed steadily from the first moment until you achieve the right speed to negotiate the hazard. Timing is crucial: avoid braking so early that you have to re-accelerate to reach the hazard, or so late that you have to brake forcefully.

Getting the best out of your brakes

Many new bikes have linked brakes that, through the use of various sensors, apply braking pressure to both wheels regardless of rider input. This section explains methods you can use for bikes where that is not the case.

The front wheel of a bike produces the largest braking effort. The rear wheel produces a smaller but significant amount. In normal conditions use both brakes to achieve optimum braking. Under braking, the weight of the machine shifts forward onto the front wheel, improving front tyre grip and reducing back tyre grip.

Apply braking effort to the two wheels with sensitivity and good judgement. The shift in weight off the rear wheel onto the front wheel means that it's fairly easy to exceed the amount of tyre grip available at the rear wheel. Too much pressure on the rear brake can cause the rear wheel to lock.

Some riders are reluctant to use the front brake because they're afraid of locking the front wheel. But if you don't use the front brake you lose most of your braking capability.

There are situations where it's wise to avoid using the front brake but this isn't rigid advice. As you gain experience and a feel for your machine, you'll develop the ability to use the front brake in adverse situations. Your awareness of the tolerances of tyre grip and your finesse in operating the controls will increase with practice.

Don't rely on the rear brake alone. Using it alone, especially under hard braking, could cause the rear wheel to lock and bounce or slide along the road. Using the rear brake alone greatly increases your braking distance.

When to apply the brakes and by how much depends on:

- your speed
- the space available
- the road surface
- your assessment of the appropriate speed for approaching the hazard.

In normal circumstances, brake steadily until most of the unwanted speed has been lost, then decrease pressure on the brakes for maximum smoothness.

ECO Smooth braking uses less fuel.

See Appendix 3, Fuel-efficient riding, page 298.

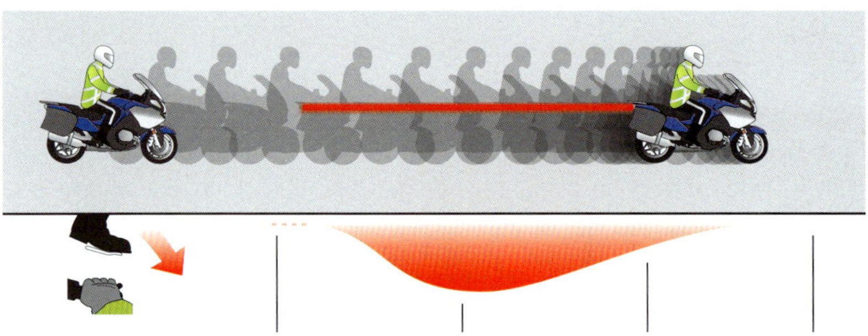

Do you know the braking capabilities of the machines you ride?

Find a suitable location with clear views and where you can test your brakes without affecting other road users.

Practise using:

- both brakes together
- the front brake on its own
- the rear brake on its own.

If you have ABS or linked brakes, follow the manufacturer's guidance on braking.

These trials should give you the confidence to use your brakes fully when necessary. Always be aware that cornering and slippery surfaces may increase the risk of locking the wheels.

Combining front and rear brakes

The best combination of front and rear braking varies with speed, direction of travel and road surface conditions.

During cornering

Generally, plan to brake in plenty of time on the approach to a corner or bend. Avoid braking firmly while cornering because this affects the stability of the machine.

If you have to brake, do it gently and steadily. Adjust the brake pressure for the condition of the road surface and avoid locking the wheels.

See The tyre grip trade-off, page 115.

On poor surfaces

Good observation and anticipation will help you respond sensitively to surface conditions. Loose gravel, damp, rain, road paint, leaves, dust and other hazards can create a poor road surface. Where the surface is poor and grip is reduced, brake on the part of the road that provides the best grip.

Adjust your brake pressure for the immediate surface conditions: increase pressure on a good surface, reduce pressure on a poor one. Where the surface is uncertain, ensure that any brake application is smooth and progressive. Gently use the back brake to bring the bike to a final halt.

Emergency braking on a good dry road

In an emergency, assess whether you can steer out of trouble or whether you have room to brake to a standstill on a straight course.

On machines fitted with ABS, fully apply the brakes; this is required for the system to work. You'll feel a 'pulsing' sensation through the levers. Don't view this as a fault, but as the system working as it should.

Where ABS is not fitted, the quickest and shortest way to stop on a good dry road is to brake as firmly as possible with the front brake while applying pressure to the rear brake, but avoid locking either wheel. As the machine slows, gradually relax the pressure on the front brake and increase the pressure on the rear brake to balance the weight of the bike. Continue to brake until the machine stops safely or until the danger has passed.

Remember:

- Your first application of the brakes must be smooth and progressive.
- Prepare for the stability of the bike to alter as the weight transfers to the front of the bike; this alters as the ratio of front and rear brake application is varied.
- Grip the bike with both knees to reduce the effect of being thrown forwards due to rapid deceleration.
- Prepare for the machine to 'sit up' if leaning.
- Focus on where you want to go, not on the hazard.

Emergency brake assist

Newer motorcycles may have emergency brake assist (BA or EBA) as well as ABS. EBA maximises braking pressure in an emergency situation. If you apply the brake with speed and force, EBA will activate and fully apply the brakes until the ABS takes over to prevent the wheels locking up. It's important to know what your motorcycle is likely to do in this situation, and what may activate the system.

Autonomous emergency braking

Many modern motorcycles are fitted with autonomous emergency braking (AEB) in some form. Make sure you understand which system your machine is equipped with and what will cause it to operate. You can then avoid making any decision that will trigger the system unexpectedly and understand what has happened should your motorcycle's AEB operate when you're not expecting it to.

See Chapter 8, page 183, Anti-lock braking systems.

Emergency braking on a slippery road

Avoid emergency braking on a slippery surface wherever possible. Use careful observation and anticipation, and adjust your speed in good time so you can avoid having to brake in these conditions.

If your bike has ABS, brake firmly and assess the levels of grip as you slow. Machines fitted with linked brakes and ABS can be braked heavily when upright on a slippery surface and remain stable.

On a bike without ABS, carefully apply braking force to both front and rear wheels, being careful not to allow a wheel to lock and lose traction. If a wheel starts to slide, carefully release some pressure from that braking system to allow the wheel to rotate again, then re-apply brake pressure.

Remember: if you activate the ABS, ask yourself why. Are you taking greater risks? Do you need to improve your technique?

The safe stopping distance rule

The safe stopping distance rule is one of the guiding principles of *Motorcycle Roadcraft.* By relating your speed to the distance within which you can stop, you can adopt a safe speed in any situation.

Always ride so that you can stop safely within the distance you can see to be clear on your own side of the road.

The importance of observing this rule for your own and other people's safety can't be overstated. It provides a guide to the speed at which you should corner and the distance you should keep from other vehicles in all other traffic conditions. Successfully applying this rule requires skill. You need to be aware of:

- the braking capabilities of your machine
- the type and condition of the road surface – in slippery or wet conditions braking distances increase greatly
- the effects of cornering, braking and machine balance on tyre grip.

In narrow and single-track lanes, allow twice the overall stopping distance that you can see to be clear to allow room for any oncoming vehicle to brake too.

Overall safe stopping distance

To work out the overall safe stopping distance, add thinking distance to braking distance.

Thinking distance + Braking distance = Stopping distance

Thinking distance is the distance travelled in the time between first observing the need for action and acting. This is why attitude, observation, anticipation and information-processing abilities are vital.

Actual thinking distance varies according to the speed of the machine, your physical and mental condition, your attentiveness and whether or not you're expecting something to happen.

Good anticipation gives you more stopping distance. Anticipation is much more important than fast reactions. It takes much longer to react to unexpected events than to expected ones – you need less thinking time if you're anticipating events and not just reacting to them.

Some common medicines (for example, some antihistamines for hay fever) can make you drowsy and slow your thinking. Be aware of their side effects.

Braking distance is the distance needed for braking. Actual braking distance depends on:

- the machine's capability, size and weight – larger, heavier machines take longer to stop
- the gradient of the road – rising or falling gradients affect deceleration and braking distances
- the condition of the road surface – slippery surfaces greatly increase braking distances
- the combined weight of bike, rider and kit
- the condition of the tyres
- how you use the brakes.

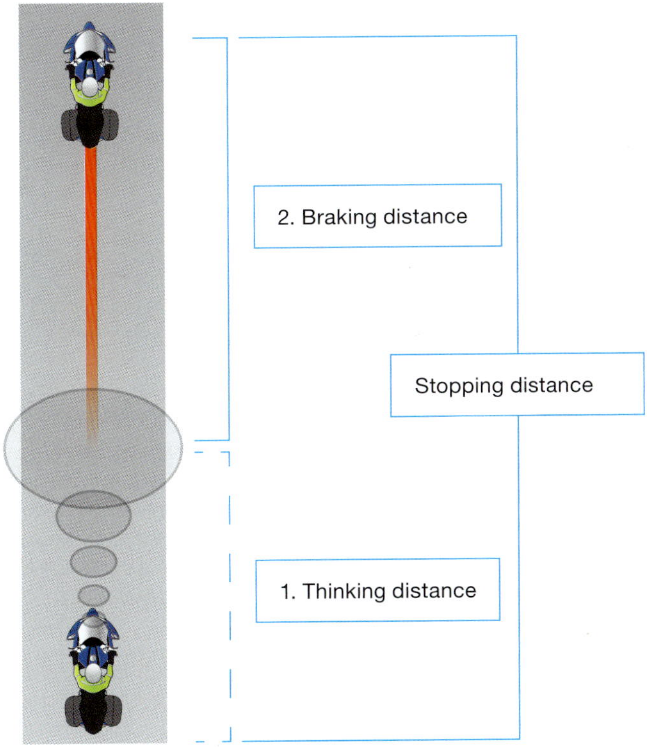

The two-second rule

To keep a safe distance between you and the vehicle in front, leave a gap of at least two seconds. But remember your overall stopping distance depends on your speed and the condition of the road surface. You need to allow at least double this distance in wet weather and even more in icy conditions.

An easy way to count two seconds is to say: 'Only a fool breaks the two-second rule'.

Note when the vehicle in front passes over a mark or shadow on the road.

If you pass over the mark or shadow on the road before you have counted two seconds, you are too close. Drop back and try the test again.

If the vehicle behind you is too close, drop back further from the vehicle in front. This will allow you to brake more gently in an emergency and may prevent you being rammed from behind.

Check your understanding

You should now be able to apply learning from this chapter in your rider training so that you can:

- ☐ explain how acceleration, braking and cornering affect tyre grip and machine stability
- ☐ show that you can control your machine accurately in a range of situations
- ☐ show good acceleration sense, using the throttle accurately and smoothly
- ☐ show how to use gears accurately, selecting the correct gear in a range of circumstances and for different purposes
- ☐ explain the safe stopping distance
- ☐ show how to use the brakes and engine braking to slow the bike appropriately and safely in different circumstances
- ☐ explain the main factors that reduce fuel consumption.

Chapter 7

Manual handling and manoeuvring at slow speeds

Learning outcomes

The learning in this chapter, along with rider training, should enable you to:

- explain and practise the competences needed to manually handle your machine safely
- explain the competences needed for slow-speed riding
- begin to practise slow-speed riding in a safe, controlled environment.

This chapter reviews some of the competences that experienced riders may have acquired when starting out and that new riders should aspire to master. A surprising number of minor collisions or injuries happen to riders when they are carrying out basic handling with the engine switched off, or manoeuvring a machine at slow speeds in confined spaces. Knowing how to do these manoeuvres safely is essential for all riders, especially those in the emergency services and other operational roles.

Manual handling

This section gives advice about how to handle your bike safely when the engine is switched off, especially when you're moving it in awkward conditions such as on a slippery surface or on an adverse camber.

See Chapter 8, page 159, Camber and superelevation.

Before you start

- Before you approach the bike, always check for a poor surface or adverse camber. Check for other trip hazards, including whether the side stand is out.
- Consider wearing your helmet even when moving the machine with the engine off. If you slip or drop the machine you could injure your face or head. Put the chin bar down and lock it before removing the machine from its stand.

Removing a bike from the centre stand

If your machine is fitted with a centre stand, some general advice is given here on how to remove the machine from the stand for manual manoeuvring. But you should follow the advice given by the manufacturer or your training instructor for specific machines and situations. The best method will vary depending on the size and weight of machine and the rider's build and strength.

Approach the machine from the nearside. Stand close enough so that your right leg is lightly resting against the machine, with the left leg slightly forward. Keep your leg clear of the foot peg and gear change. Ensure that the side stand is stowed in the upright position.

Firmly hold both handlebar grips and with a straight back look forward in the direction you want to go. Don't look down. Your grip on the handlebars should be firm but not tight. Cover the front brake and clutch with all four fingers so that you don't trap any fingers between the levers and handlebar. Bear in mind the machine may be in gear. Hold in the clutch lever to prevent a sudden stop and the bike toppling over.

In one continuous flowing motion, pull back on the bars to transfer the machine's weight to the rear then push forward. The ease with which you can transfer the weight depends upon whether the machine sits on the front wheel or rear wheel.

As the machine begins to drop from the stand, angle the handlebars slightly to the right to allow it to drop in towards you. Once both wheels are on the ground, apply the front brake to gain control.

Placing a bike onto the centre stand

Just like removing a bike from its centre stand, how easily you can place it will depend on the size and weight of the bike, and your own strength. The following is a guide as to how to best manage the task.

Identify a safe location, ideally on solid level ground, on which to leave the motorcycle. From the nearside of the machine, facing towards the machine and with the front brake applied, use your right foot to locate the footplate of the centre stand.

Make sure the footplate is in the middle of the sole of your foot to avoid slipping, especially if your boot is wet or muddy.

Apply pressure to the footplate while moving the machine gently from side to side to ensure that both feet of the stand are in contact with the ground. The machine will now be stable enough to release the front brake.

While still holding the left handlebar, take hold of the grab rail with the right hand. From this position and with the three points of contact, turn so that you're facing the nearside of the machine. This will help you keep your back straight during the lift. In one consecutive movement, straighten your right leg and transfer your body weight through the right foot. Pull up on the grab rail, while pulling back on the handlebar, until the stand fully extends.

Removing a bike from the side stand to get on it

Approach the machine from the nearside and stand perpendicular to it.

Firmly hold the left handlebar grip then apply the front brake. Push the left handlebar away from you so the bike tilts towards you and the angle of the machine lowers.

Swing your leg over the machine without putting undue weight on the stand. Then with a straight back and while looking up, raise the machine from the side stand into an upright position.

Use your left foot to sweep the side stand backwards and to make sure it's against the stop.

Applying the side stand to get off

Identify a safe location, ideally on solid level ground, on which to leave the motorcycle. Consider using the front brake to stop the motorcycle from moving. Use the left foot to push the stand forward and again make sure it connects with the stop, then reverse the steps for getting on the bike.

If you have to leave the machine pointing downhill, consider putting it into first gear before switching off. If the motorcycle is then to be placed on the centre stand, stow the side stand before following the instructions above.

Wheeling a bike in confined spaces

Once you've removed the machine from its stand, you can wheel it around. Check for a poor surface or adverse camber. Check for trip hazards.

Forwards

- From the nearside, firmly hold both handlebars and cover – but don't apply – the front brake.
- Look forward and always in the direction you want to go. Keep your back straight with your arms slightly bent.
- Keep close to the machine and aim to have it as upright as possible but with the weight still slightly towards you. This will lessen the effort required to push.
- Be aware of where the foot peg, centre and side stands and gear change are, and keep your right leg clear of them.

Backwards

- From the nearside, hold the left handlebar grip and either the seat, seat cowling or grab rail. This will enable you to turn and face in the direction you want to go while keeping control of the machine.
- Wheeling the bike backwards is far more difficult than going forwards, so whenever possible bring the machine to a stop in a position that avoids the need to do so.
- Consider leaving the bike in gear and using the clutch lever to control the speed of the machine if there is any camber or slope.

The risks of paddling

Be aware of the risks of paddling – sitting astride the machine to wheel it. If the ground is slippery or your boots are muddy, you could slip and injure yourself. The weight of the machine could cause or increase any injury.

Paddling backwards is more risky because it's difficult to see where you're going and you can't see any hazards directly behind the machine.

Problems that may need practice

Many riders find it difficult at first to manoeuvre a machine with the engine off. Common problems are:

- lack of confidence with the push-off or lift – this needs to be a firm positive movement
- poor technique or balance
- looking down instead of looking where you want to go
- the rider's physical attributes in relation to the weight of the machine – for example, short arms, short legs or low body weight may make a heavier machine harder to manoeuvre.

Practice will help you overcome these problems. Practise the technique for putting your machine on and taking it off its side or centre stand. Practise manoeuvring the machine forwards and backwards with the engine off and practise manual handling turns to see how the weight transfers when you move the handlebars away from you.

If you have the opportunity, practise these techniques on each of the machines that you ride.

Developing your competence at slow-speed riding

The slow-speed riding technique is a specific set of skills that takes a lot of practice, and is best developed under guidance from an experienced rider.

You need to be able to ride at slow speeds with confidence, especially in urban areas, in order to:

- travel slowly with prevailing traffic
- move slowly for operational tasks such as looking for suspects
- filter – move between lanes of stationary traffic

See also Chapter 11, page 238, Filtering.

- make tight turns in narrow streets
- make U-turns
- manoeuvre in confined spaces, such as garages and other parking areas.

Observation

Good observation is vital for safety. Take time to obtain information to give yourself an overall view of what you want to achieve, especially in tight or awkward situations:

- Check for adverse camber or slopes as these can make some parts of the manoeuvre easier or harder to control. Look for level areas, if possible, when you plan to make a manoeuvre at slow speed.
- Look out for poor road surfaces and irregularities on the surface that could cause you to lose grip or knock you off course.
- Before you choose a place to park up, check for and avoid if possible: adverse camber, gradients, uneven or broken-up road surfaces, and wet or slippery conditions.

See Chapter 5, page 99, Road surface.

Look where you want to go

- Always look where you want to go. At very low speeds, the importance of doing this is often underestimated. This is a simple, practical technique that makes a huge difference.

  See Chapter 4, page 71, Look where you want to go.

- For the same reason, don't look at the object you want to avoid. For example, look *through* a gap rather than at the edges of it. Look at where you want to be at the end of a tight turn, not at the pothole halfway through.

- When the machine needs to be turned in a very tight (full-lock) turn, look as far over your shoulder as you can in the direction you want to turn as this will help you make the turn. Consider moving your position on the seat to help you do this.

Balance

The ability to ride very slowly and calmly requires a high degree of balance. Think about how you load your panniers or top box as this will have an effect on balance. Don't overload the panniers; follow the manufacturer's guidelines on maximum load.

Machine control

Riding at very low speeds through tight curves requires specific machine control skills:

- using the brakes with a bias towards the rear brake (If your bike is fitted with linked brakes, linked rear to front, be aware that using the rear brake may also apply the front brake. If the machine has independent brakes, only apply the front brake as well as the rear with caution.)
- using the clutch at times – referred to as 'slipping' or 'feathering' the clutch
- in some circumstances, riding with the rear brake steadying the machine
- staying relaxed – tensing up reduces your ability to steer or lean.

Manoeuvres to practise

Proper practice is essential to become familiar with your machine. Always practise in a safe and controlled environment. A simple exercise is to ride repeatedly in a circle moving inward as your confidence builds. Try it travelling both to the left and right and notice the difference in turning circle depending on where you look.

Also try riding in a figure-of-eight manoeuvre, decreasing the radius of the turn progressively as your ability and confidence develop until you've achieved a 'full-lock' turn.

Use cones to practise. Set them up in a wide pattern to start with and decrease the distance and grouping according to your confidence and ability.

A short slalom course is a good way to practise slow control and will help you understand the benefits of good body position.

> Which aspects of manual handling or low-speed manoeuvring do you find more difficult?
>
> Assess yourself honestly and, in a safe environment, take opportunities to practise any manoeuvres at which you feel less confident.

Check your understanding

You should now be able to apply learning from this chapter in your rider training so that you can:

- ☐ explain and practise the competences needed to manually handle your machine safely
- ☐ explain the competences needed for slow-speed riding
- ☐ begin to practise slow-speed riding in a safe, controlled environment.

Chapter 8

Cornering, balance and avoiding skids

Learning outcomes

The learning in this chapter, along with rider training, should enable you to:

- explain the principles of safe cornering
- describe the forces involved in cornering and the factors which affect your balance and your machine's ability to corner
- show how to use the system of motorcycle control and the limit point for cornering
- show how to position your machine for the best view when cornering
- describe the principles of anti-lock braking systems, linked braking systems and traction control
- explain why active safety features can interfere with rider behaviour
- identify the causes of skidding and how to minimise the risk.

Developing your competence at cornering and balance

'Cornering' means riding a motorcycle round a corner, curve or bend. Cornering is one of the main riding activities, and it's important to get it right. When you corner, you place extra demands on the available tyre grip. The faster you go and the tighter the bend, the greater these demands are.

We start with some general principles and a simple explanation of the forces involved in cornering. We then look at the factors affecting your bike's ability to corner safely, and how to use the system in conjunction with limit point analysis to assess safe cornering speeds.

The system of motorcycle control and principles for safe cornering

See Chapter 3, The system of motorcycle control.

Cornering on a bike is very different from cornering in a car. If you get it wrong, the outcomes can be more serious for a rider. Use the system of motorcycle control to help you carry out the manoeuvre safely. Each phase of the system is relevant, but the information phase is especially important. Correctly assessing the severity of the bend is essential for safety.

Five key principles for safe cornering

You should:

- **be in the correct position on the approach**
- **be travelling at the right speed for the corner or bend**
- **have the right gear for that speed**
- **be able to stop in the distance you can see to be clear on your own side of the road**
- **open the throttle enough to maintain a constant speed round the bend – maintain positive throttle.**

Applying these principles to the variations in bends, traffic conditions, road surface conditions, visibility and other factors calls for judgement and planning. But before looking in more detail at using the system of motorcycle control for cornering, let's look at the other factors that affect a bike's ability to corner safely.

You – your riding position and balance for cornering

The way you sit on a bike affects its balance and handling.

When the bike is stationary you should be able either to place both feet on the ground or balance with one foot while the other works a control.

After moving off, place both feet on the foot pegs. Do this as soon as possible because it improves stability and control. When you're moving, sit in a comfortable position with your body slightly leaning forward. Sit so that you can reach the controls comfortably with a slight bend in your arms – avoid locking your arms straight.

Your forearms should be parallel to the ground, otherwise you have a tendency to lean down on them. This puts pressure on the handlebars, making steering more difficult, and giving you less control if you hit a bump or get a wobble.

Body position during banking.

The sharper the bend or the higher the speed, the more the machine needs to lean to maintain balance. As banking increases, there will be a point where the bike may 'ground' because the foot peg or exhaust pipe touches the road surface – potentially causing loss of control.

See Cornering forces, page 155.

On a left-hand bend, crown camber assists cornering because the road slopes down in the direction of turn.

On a right-hand bend, crown camber reduces the amount of lean available because the road slopes away from the direction of turn.

Your machine – roadworthiness

Motorcycles vary in their ability to corner, and they only corner to the best of their ability if they are well maintained. Steering, suspension, tyres, tyre pressures and the loading of the machine all affect its balance and road grip when cornering. Make sure that your bike and tyres are in good condition, and that your tyre pressures are kept at the recommended levels – good condition and correct pressures are vital for safe cornering. Take care to position loads so they don't upset the balance of the bike or restrict any moving parts.

Cornering forces

A moving motorcycle is at its most stable when travelling in a straight line on a level course and at constant speed. It will continue to travel on a straight course unless some other force is applied to alter its direction. When you steer, the turning force to alter direction comes from the action of the front tyre on the road.

Some riders mistakenly think that a moving motorcycle is unstable and that cornering is dangerous because a leaning bike is even more unstable. This isn't necessarily so. To understand motorcycle stability, it helps to understand some of the physical forces involved in cornering.

The design of the machine and tyres will reduce or accentuate these tendencies.

Factors that help stability

Because of the steering design on a motorcycle, it is stable when travelling in a straight line, and the front wheel has a self-straightening tendency when steered left or right. The forces involved will tend to pull the front wheel back in line if you release pressure on the handlebars.

The gyroscopic effect also tends to keep a motorcycle stable. Think of a spinning top. When you spin a top fast enough, it becomes stable around its spinning axis. The same applies to the wheels of a motorcycle once they're rotating fast enough.

These forces also help the front wheel to straighten if it's temporarily knocked off line, for example, by hitting a bump in the carriageway. This is why your position on the bike is important – with your body and arms in the correct position you get the most benefit from this self-correcting tendency.

See Chapter 7, page 147, Look where you want to go.

See page 153, You – your riding position and balance for cornering.

Steering

When you turn the handlebars, the tyre contact patch on the ground moves away from the machine's centre line. The centre of gravity is no longer above the centre line, so the machine will begin to lean. When this happens, cornering forces combine to help you to lean into the turn.

Counter-steering (positive steering)

At speeds above walking pace, steering input to the left will make the bike lean to the right. This is known as counter-steering or positive steering. Everyone counter-steers but the steering input required is minimal and often unnoticed. If you understand the principle, however, it increases your ability to manoeuvre accurately while cornering.

As the motorcycle leans, several forces are at work:

- Inertia is the tendency of an object to resist a change in its state of motion. Inertia tends to keep the motorcycle travelling in a straight line – this feels as though you're being pushed outwards.
- Other forces tend to move a bike travelling along a curved path towards the centre of the circle around which it's travelling.

When the forces tending to push the machine outwards equal the forces tending to pull it inwards, the bike will be balanced.

So, to start a turn and get the bike to lean, you must apply pressure on one side of the handlebars. To turn right, push on the right handlebar, and to turn left, push on the left handlebar. It's important to apply the pressure smoothly. When you reach the correct angle of lean for the bend, reduce pressure on the handlebars and the steering will self-align. Maintain a positive throttle to balance the effect of cornering forces.

See Chapter 6, page 118, Acceleration and machine balance.

Leaning, tyre grip and stability

Inexperienced riders are sometimes reluctant to lean a machine when cornering but leaning a machine at an *appropriate* angle is necessary to negotiate a bend and maintain stability.

There are various degrees of stability. A motorcycle becomes stable when ridden in a straight line at a constant speed. It also becomes stable when it's steered into a corner and takes a 'set' (becomes settled). This is when the cornering forces are balanced and a steady positive throttle is applied. The suspension and tyres will be compressed. The grip available at this point for cornering, braking and acceleration depends mainly on tyre compound and road compound (surface).

A safe and appropriate degree of lean varies with tyre profile and condition, speed, and the individual combination of rider and machine. Instruction and practice will develop your ability to judge this.

See Chapter 6, page 115, The tyre grip trade-off.

Stability when cornering therefore depends on the grip between the tyres and the road surface, and the rider's actions.

Using the limit point, look as far as you can along the course that you intend to travel, aiming to maintain stability of the bike.

See page 161, The limit point.

The rider's actions

The rider's actions on a path through the bend

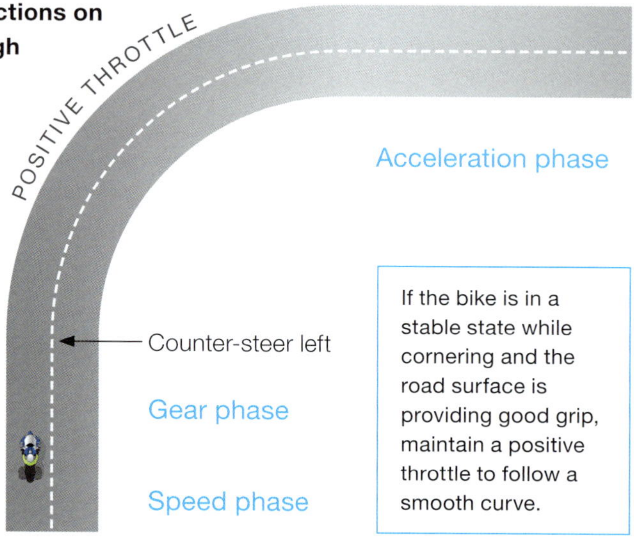

Weight transfer during cornering will alter the bike's stable state. Weight transfer forward during a turn will increase the self-aligning effect and straighten the steering. This will happen if you apply the front brake. If you don't anticipate and counter the effect of weight transfer, the bike will lift and straighten – 'sit up' – out of a turn. You can correct weight transfer by further counter-steering. But be aware that steering becomes far harder while braking.

Using the back brake while cornering causes oversteer and normally tightens the turn.

Using the throttle to increase speed has the opposite effect and tends to straighten the bike out of the turn.

Many bends tighten throughout the curve. **Counter-steering will allow a tighter turn**. The limiting factors will be the road surface grip and the angle of lean that the machine allows you before it grounds. If a foot peg, exhaust pipe or any other attachment touches the floor and can't bend or give this may cause the rear wheel to lift off the ground. When rear traction is lost, the motorcycle will slide towards the outside of the turn.

When approaching a bend, use your experience, good observation and the limit point to predict the correct entry speed. Remember that you must be able to stop in the distance you can see to be clear on your own side of the road. (Allow twice this distance in narrow and single-track lanes.) If you misjudge your entry speed, slowing or braking through the bend may produce the problems described.

Now that you have a basic understanding of the forces that affect stability and cornering, apply this when you ride. Practise so that you can use counter-steering accurately, and know how to apply the throttle or brakes appropriately and with great care when cornering.

> Always allow a margin for error when assessing the entry speed for a bend.

Camber and superelevation

Road surfaces usually slope to help drainage. The normal slope falls from the crown of the road to the edges and is called crown camber.

- **On a left-hand bend**, camber increases the effect of your steering because the road slopes down in the direction of the turn.
- **On a right-hand bend**, camber reduces the effect of steering because the road slopes away from the direction of the turn.

This applies if you keep to your own side of the road, but if you cross over the crown to the other side of the road, the camber will have the opposite effect on your steering.

In many places, especially at junctions, the slope across the road surface can be at an unexpected angle. Take this into account when deciding your position and speed for a bend.

Superelevation is where the whole width of the road is banked up towards the outside edge of the bend, making the slope favourable for cornering in both directions (similar to banking on a race track).

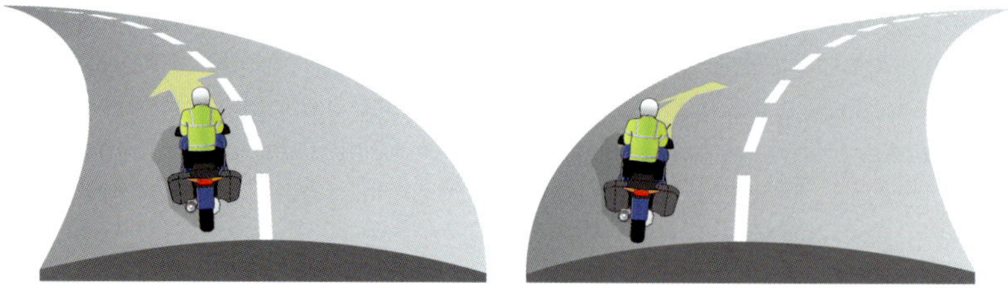

Crown camber

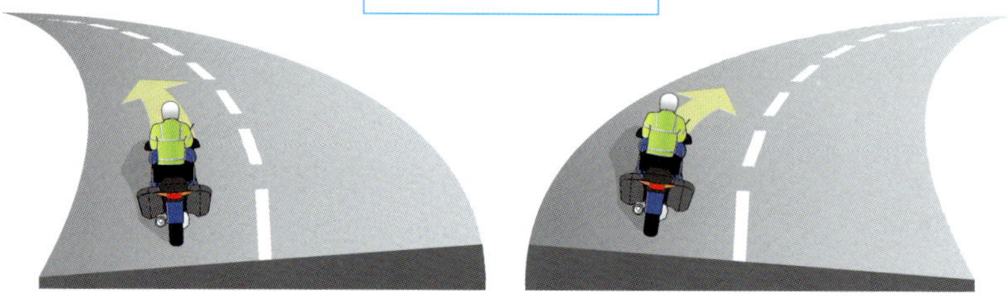

Superelevation

Pick out one or two sections of familiar road where cornering is tricky and work out whether unexpected camber is a factor.

Analyse how you took the corner and make an honest assessment of your riding. Did you make the correct decision about the best position and speed to adopt for the bend, for example?

Summary of factors affecting cornering

Your machine's ability to corner depends on your input. You need to accurately assess:

- your speed
- the amount of lean you apply
- the amount of acceleration or braking
- the slope across the road surface – camber and superelevation

- the road surface and how weather and other factors affect its grip
- the characteristics of the machine and its ground clearance
- the weight and distribution of any load you're carrying.

Once you understand the factors that affect your machine's ability to corner, you can use the system of motorcycle control and the limit point to corner safely.

Assessing the sharpness of a bend

As you approach a bend, seek as much information as possible about the severity of the bend using all the observational clues available to you (for example, weather, road surface, road signs, road markings, the line made by lamp posts and trees, the speed and position of oncoming traffic, the angle of headlights at night). The more information you gather about the bend, the more accurately you'll be able to judge the best position and speed to negotiate it.

See Chapter 4, page 64, Planning.

The limit point

To corner safely you must be able to stop within the distance you can see to be clear on your own side of the road. The limit point is the furthest point to which you have an uninterrupted view of the road surface. This is where the right-hand edge of the road appears to meet the left-hand edge in the distance. The more distant the limit point, the more quickly you can go because you have more space to stop in. The closer the limit point, the slower you must go because you have less space to stop in.

The limit point gives you a systematic way of judging the correct speed to use through the bend.

For a video explanation of limit points, see the Motorcycle Roadcraft e-learning course.

Watching the limit point enables you to match your speed to the speed at which this point appears to move. If the limit point is moving away from you, and you have a safe stopping distance between you and the limit point, you may accelerate. If the limit point is moving towards you, and your view of the road ahead reduces to below the safe stopping distance, you must decelerate or brake. Even when the bend isn't constant, you can still match your speed to the apparent movement of the limit point, because this will vary with the curvature of the bend. Acceleration sense is useful here.

Using the limit point together with the system helps you:

- adjust your speed so you can stop safely within the distance you can see to be clear on your own side of the road
- decide the correct speed to approach and negotiate the bend
- select the correct gear for the speed
- decide the point at which to start accelerating.

Left-hand bends

On a right-hand bend you have a view in front of you which includes the scenery (for example, hedges, trees, buildings) just beyond the side of the road, on the outside of the bend. On a left-hand bend these will seem to be further away because you're looking across the road. This may cause you to misjudge the amount of space available to you and approach the bend at a greater speed than is safe. On a left-hand bend, treat the centre of the road as the right verge.

On a left-hand bend, you should ride as though the limit point is where the edge of the road meets the central white line (or the centre of the road if there's no white line) so that you can stop safely on your own side of the road.

Using the limit point

Before you look at this diagram, make sure you have read pages 161–2. Read the diagram from the bottom of the page upwards.

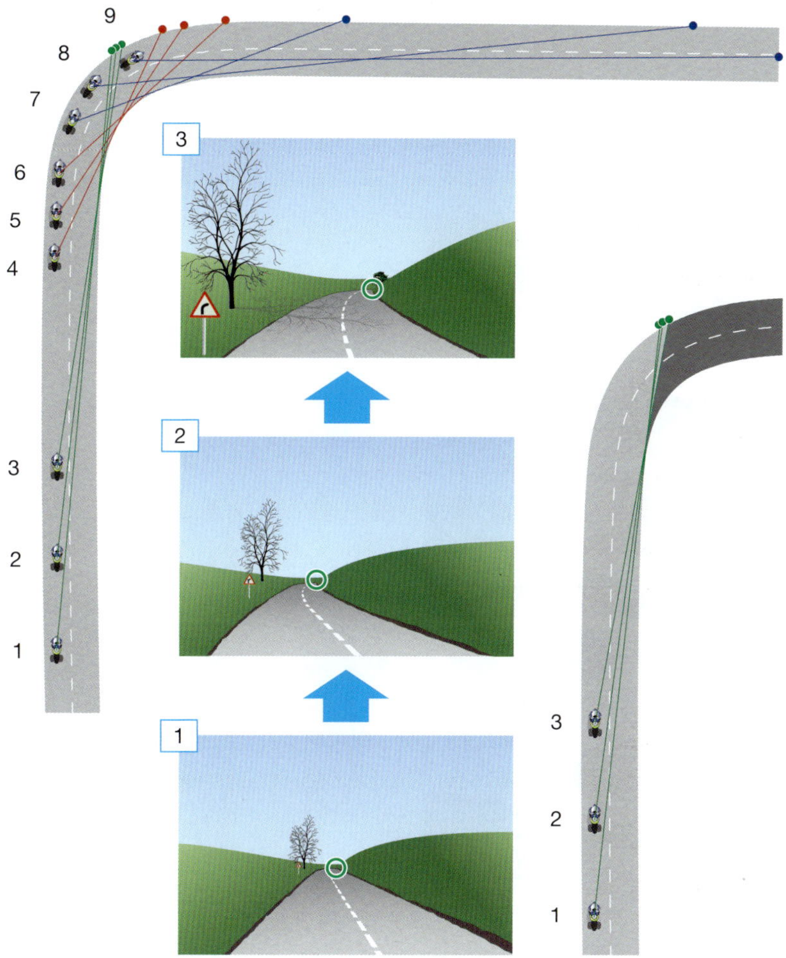

Approaching a right-hand bend

At first the limit point ○ ● appears to remain at the same point in the road.

Reduce your speed to be able to stop safely within the remaining distance.

As you approach the bend, take information about the sharpness of the bend and carefully assess the appropriate speed for cornering.

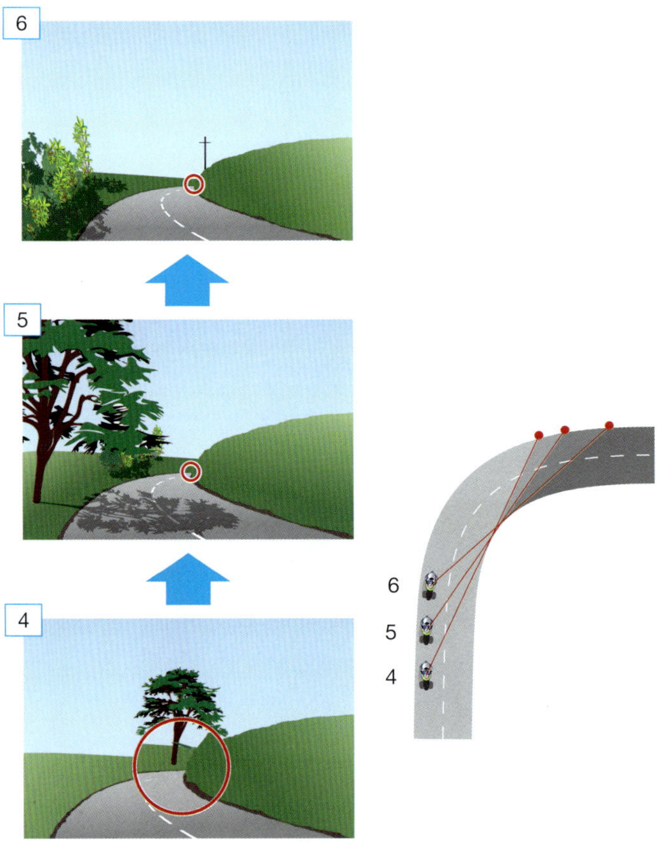

Just before you enter a right-hand bend

Just before you enter the bend, the limit point ○ ● begins to move round at a constant speed. Adjust your speed and gear, if necessary, to the speed of this movement.

You now have the correct speed and gear for the bend. Select the gear to match the speed before entering the bend.

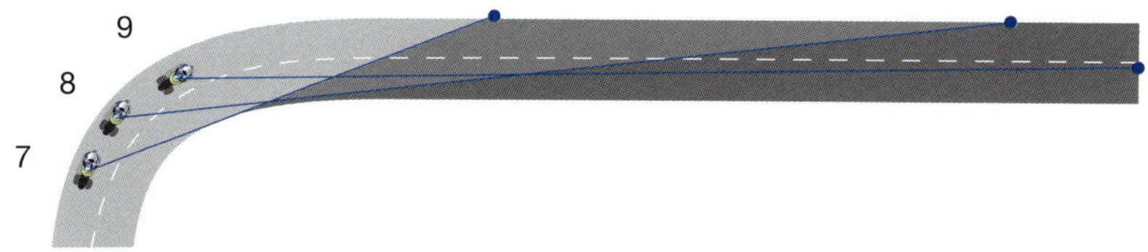

9

8

7

Going through a right-hand bend

As the bend starts to straighten, your view begins to extend and the limit point ○● starts to move away more quickly.

As your machine straightens and returns to an upright position, increase your acceleration towards the limit point.

As the bend comes to an end, continue to accelerate to catch the limit point until other considerations such as speed limits or new hazards restrict your acceleration.

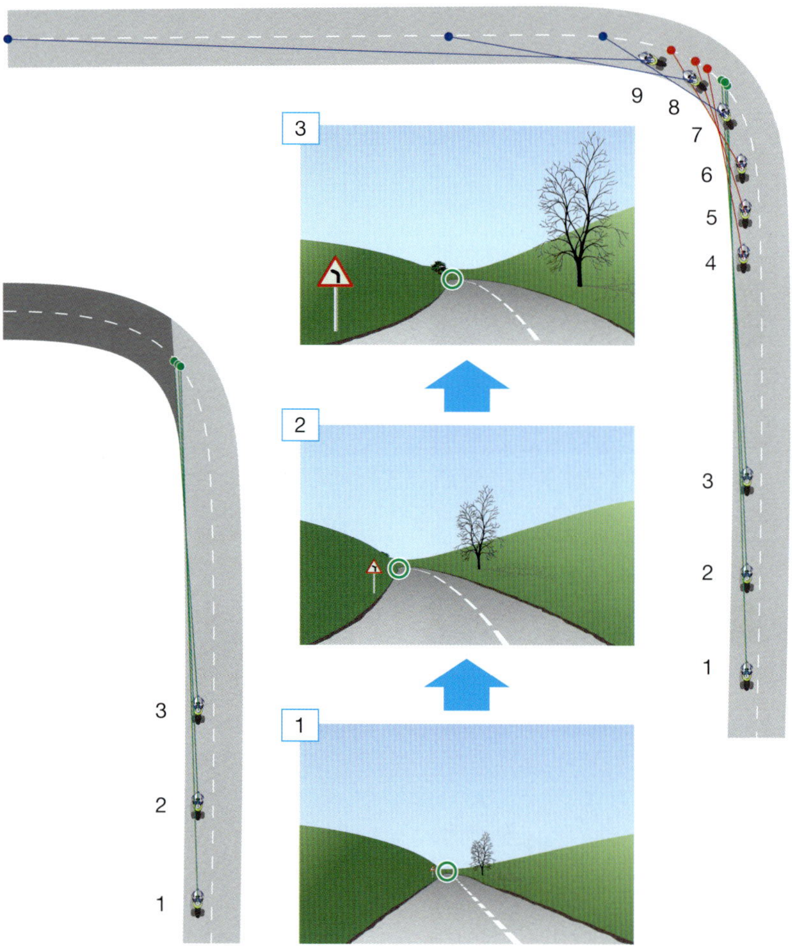

Approaching a left-hand bend

At first the limit point ○ ● appears to remain stationary.

Adjust your speed so you can stop safely within the remaining distance.

As you approach the bend, take information about the sharpness of the bend and carefully assess the appropriate speed for cornering.

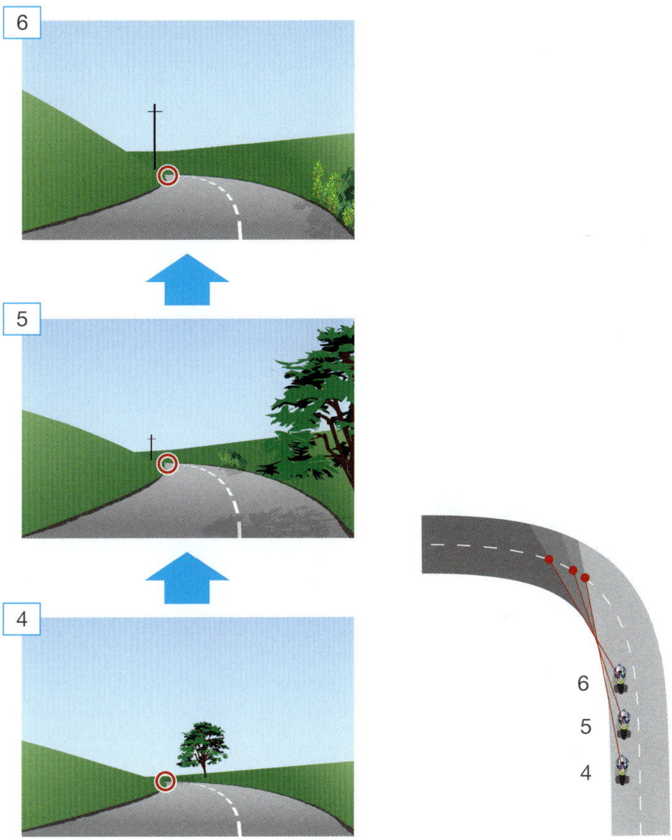

Just before you enter a left-hand bend

Just before you enter the bend, the limit point begins to move round at a constant speed. Adjust your speed to the speed of this movement.

You now have the correct speed to go round the bend. Select the gear to match this speed before entering the bend. Use the throttle to maintain a constant speed for maximum stability through the bend.

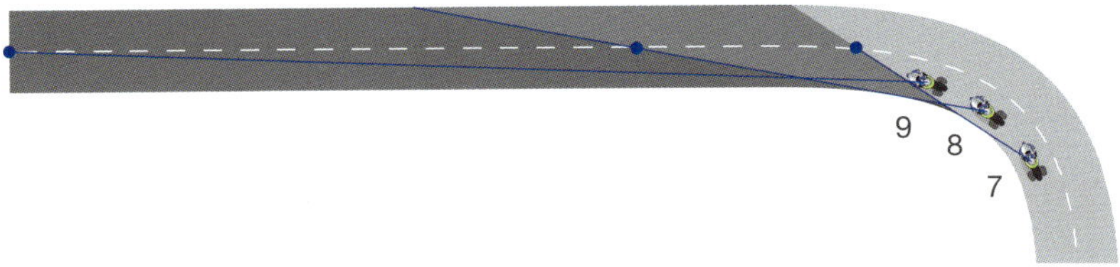

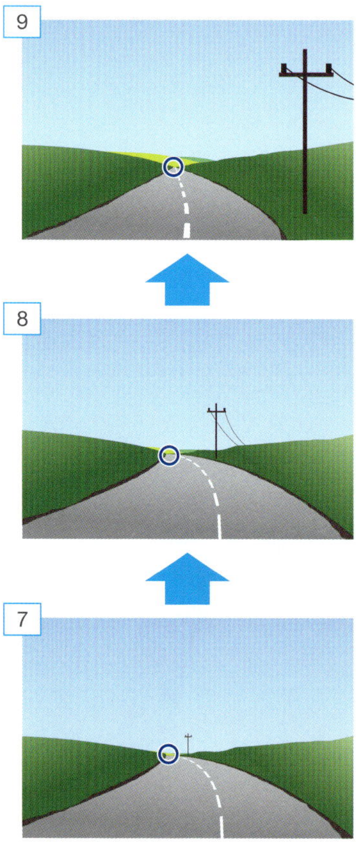

Going through a left-hand bend

As the bend starts to straighten, your view begins to extend and the limit point ○● starts to move away more quickly.

As your machine straightens and returns to an upright position, increase your acceleration towards the limit point.

As the bend comes to an end, continue to accelerate to catch the limit point until other considerations such as speed limits or new hazards restrict your acceleration.

The limit point technique is self-adjusting – as road visibility and conditions deteriorate you need more distance in which to stop, and so you must reduce your speed to compensate.

Use the limit point *as well* as other observation links – get into the habit of looking across or beyond the bend as you approach it. You may spot a hazard just *after* the bend, for example, a warning sign or a chevron marker indicating a further bend. In this case, it would be inappropriate to use the limit point alone to set your speed.

Where a road isn't wide enough for two vehicles to pass, consider doubling your stopping distance to give an oncoming vehicle enough space to stop as well. On a left-hand bend on a single-track road, the limit point is where the two kerb lines meet.

Practise matching your speed to the movement of the limit point

Try this on different types of bend – from very gradual to hairpin – and note how using the limit point enables you to adjust to the characteristics of each bend. Always adjust your speed so that you can stop safely within the distance you can see to be clear.

Make a special point of using the limit point to set your speed for bends and corners on roads you know well. It's on familiar routes that your attention is most likely to wander.

The double-apex bend

Some bends have been deliberately engineered with a tightening curve or 'double apex'. Misjudgement of the double-apex bend has proved a cause of serious collisions on left-hand bends, particularly for motorcyclists. In this type of bend, the curve that the rider initially sees on the approach to the bend continues to tighten so the final curve is much sharper. If you plan for the whole bend on the basis of the curve that you see initially, you run the risk of ending up in the path of oncoming traffic.

Careful observation and using the system of motorcycle control to match your speed to the limit point should help you to accurately negotiate deceptive bends like the one shown.

On an unfamiliar bend, be prepared if necessary to adjust your steering as you travel around the bend.

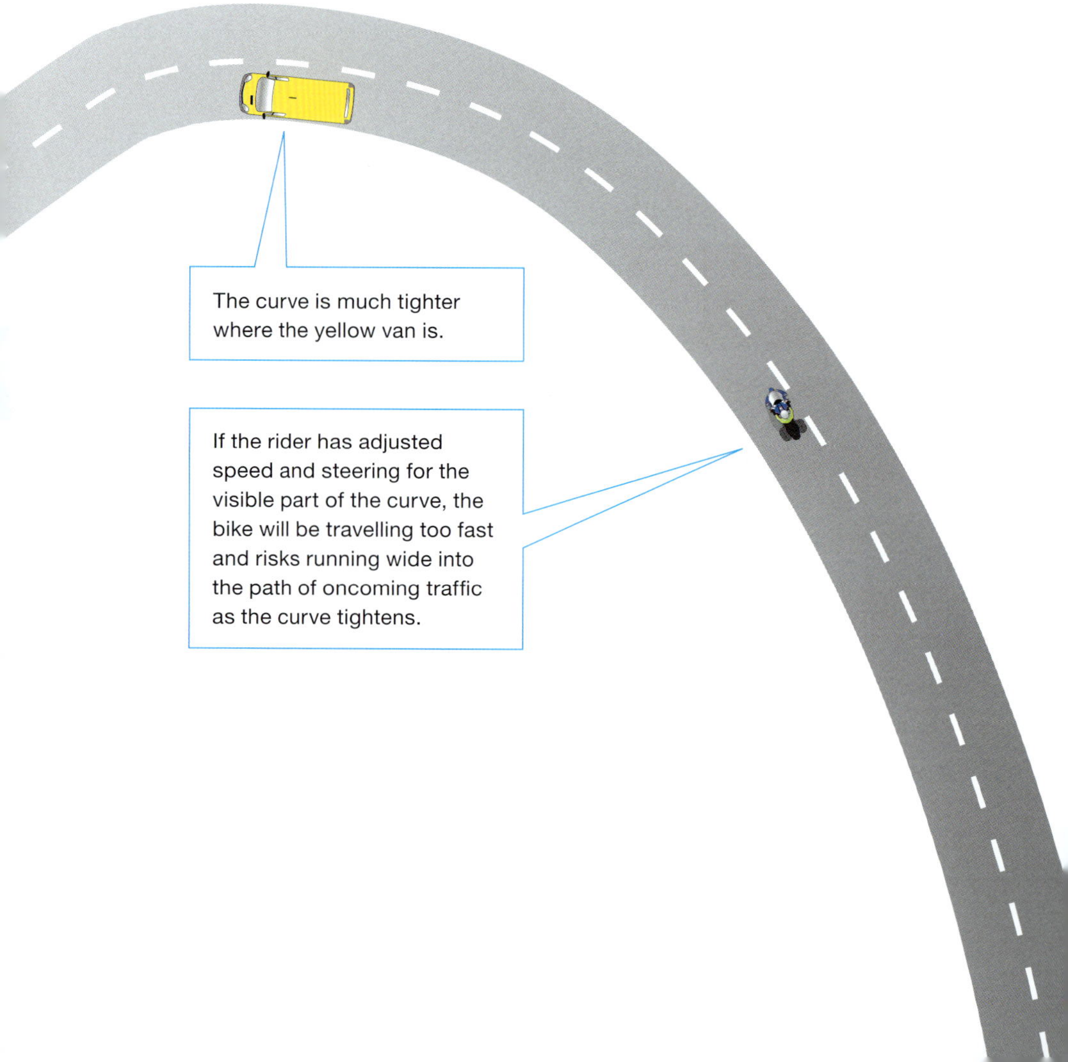

Using a cross view

You can plan a corner by using a cross view. As you approach the corner, first assess the direction of the corner, find the limit point, and then look across in the same direction as the corner for clues as to where the road goes. This can help you identify upcoming hazards, such as other road users, oncoming traffic, further bends, junctions and speed limit changes.

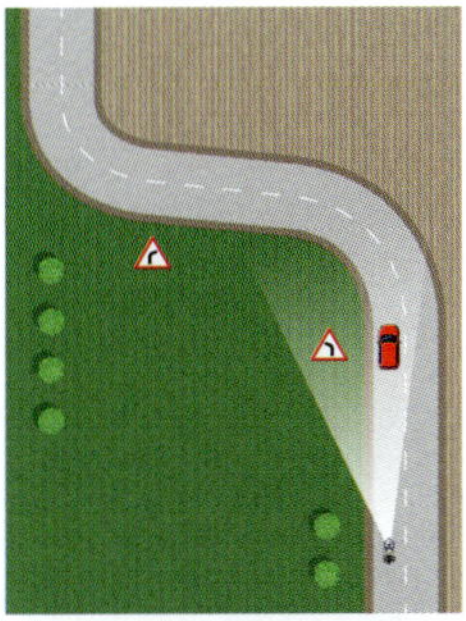

In this example, by scanning the road ahead, you can see a bend to the left and, by looking down the nearside of the red car, identify the limit point.

By using a cross view, you may be able to see where the road goes after the bend. In this example, you can see the red vehicle as it exits the bend. You can now also see that the road turns to the right following the left-hand bend.

You can now return your focus to using the limit point to negotiate the left-hand bend.

By using a cross view prior to the first left-hand bend, you can adopt an early position for the next right-hand bend. Assess the right-hand bend, then follow with a cross view, which, in this example, shows the red car having negotiated the right-hand bend and possibly braking for the 30 mph limit ahead.

Using a process of multiple cross views allows you to link bends and create a flow, rather than dealing with each bend in isolation.

How to use the system for cornering

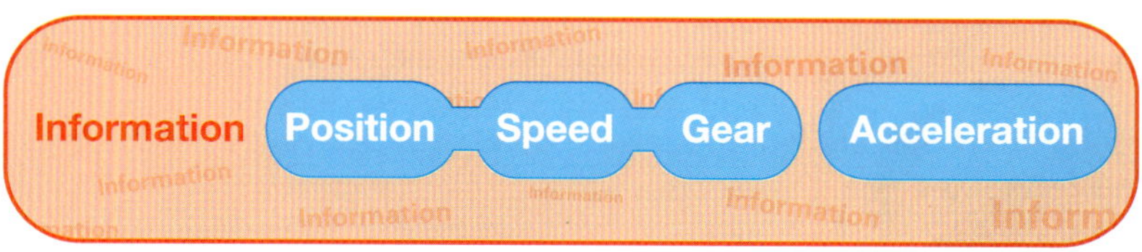

Information

On the approach to a corner or bend, you should be constantly scanning the road for information, especially about:

- the traffic in front and behind
- the road surface
- the effect of weather conditions on the road surface
- the severity of the bend and the limit point
- hazards – what you can see, what you can't see and what you can reasonably expect to happen.

Always keep your vision up. Remember: look where you want to go – don't focus only on the bend. Make effective use of lateral information. Whenever you can, look across the bend through gaps in hedges or between buildings for more information. Use the curved line of hedgerows and lamp posts to give you information about the severity of the bend. Look for early warning of other hazards as well. If you intend to alter your position to get a better view, remember to take rear observation first.

Position

You have great flexibility in positioning a motorcycle. Use this flexibility to compensate for your increased vulnerability as a rider. Consider four things when positioning your machine for cornering:

- safety
- stability
- getting the best view
- reducing the tightness of the bend.

Safety

Safety is the overriding consideration. Position yourself so as to minimise your risk of coming into conflict with other road users. Look out for hazards to your nearside and oncoming traffic to your offside. Be mindful of the width of your machine.

Always be prepared to sacrifice your road position for safety.

See Chapter 5, page 99, Road surface.

Stability

Select a course that will provide the best tyre grip.

Getting the best view

Your position will determine how much you can see when you enter a bend. Put the bike in the best position for you to see, with due regard to safety. The position that gives you the clearest view is different for a left-hand bend and a right-hand bend.

- **Right-hand bends** – position yourself towards the left of your road space. Watch out for:
  - blind junctions or exits
  - adverse camber
  - poor surface conditions towards the edge of the road.

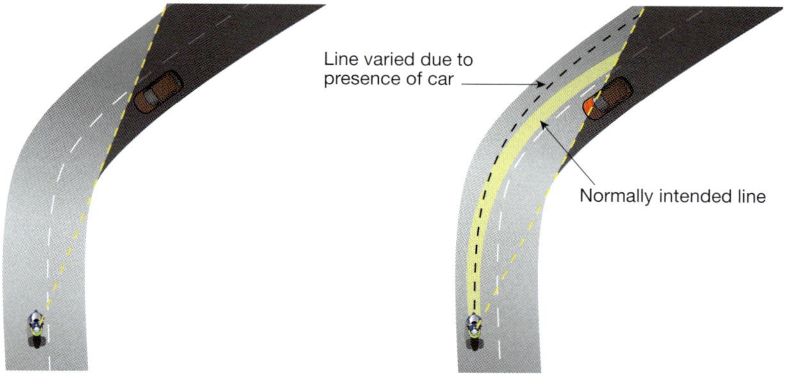

For right-hand bends, the nearside gives an earlier view into the bend.

- **Left-hand bends** – position yourself towards the centre line so that you get an early view round the bend. Before you take this position consider:
  - approaching traffic or other offside dangers which need a greater margin of safety
  - whether your position might mislead other traffic as to your intentions
  - whether you'll gain any advantage at low speed or on an open bend.

Don't position yourself in a way that causes concern to other road users. Be prepared to modify your road position in the interests of safety.

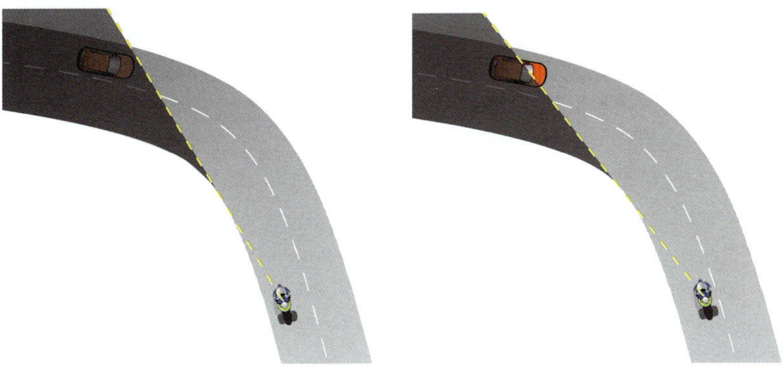

For left-hand bends, a position towards the centre of the road gives an earlier view.

Reducing the tightness of the bend

Where it's safe to do so, reducing the tightness of the curve through which you ride can help to improve stability. By moving your bike from one side of your road space to the other you can follow a shallower curve. The path you take is different for a right- or a left-hand bend, but always consider safety first. Don't take a straighter course unless you can see clearly across the bend. Often you won't be able to do this until the road begins to straighten out.

Riding through a series of bends

Try to plan your course through a series of bends so that the exit point from the first bend puts you in a good position to enter the second bend. Only link the bends in this way if you can see clearly across them and know that there are no additional hazards. Be careful of approaching the centre line if there's a possibility of oncoming traffic.

In planning your course through a series of bends ask yourself, 'Where do I want to be to approach the next bend?' Remember: always be prepared to sacrifice your road position for safety.

When you're cornering, practise using the available road space to improve your ability to observe and to reduce the curve of the bend. Make sure there's no possibility of coming into conflict with other road users and that your chosen course has a sound surface.

Practise this consistently. Notice how it improves your ability to see, and the smoothness and stability of the ride.

Speed

When you're in an appropriate position, choose the appropriate speed to enter and negotiate the bend.

Use the limit point to judge the safe speed to ride round the bend. Where the bend is a constant curve, the limit point remains at a constant distance from you. Keep your speed constant. If the curve changes, re-assess your speed and re-apply the system.

To assess the correct speed for a bend, you need to consider:

- your view into and round the bend
- the road and road surface conditions
- the traffic conditions
- your bike's characteristics
- the weather conditions
- your own ability.

> Remember: you should always be able to stop in the distance you can see to be clear on your own side of the road. This rule will give you a safe speed for the bend.

Gear

When you have the correct entry speed and before you enter the bend, select the appropriate gear for that speed. Select the gear that gives you the greatest flexibility to leave the bend safely.

See Chapter 6, page 123, Using the gears.

Acceleration

Open the throttle enough to maintain a constant speed round the bend. This will contribute to stability. If there are no additional hazards, start to accelerate when the limit point begins to move away and you begin to bring the machine upright. As you continue to straighten the bike, increase your acceleration to 'catch' the limit point. Accelerate until you reach the speed limit or the appropriate speed for the circumstances.

Match your speed to the speed at which the limit point moves away from you, provided you can stop safely within the distance that you can see to be clear on your own side of the road.

Safe cornering

Think about your riding behaviour on more open roads. As you plan your approach to corners, what's your priority?

- Does the purpose of your journey make a difference to your decision-making – for example, if you're under time pressure?
- What other human factors might affect your riding decisions?
- How do you think about the correct speed for the bend? Is your aim to maximise speed or to achieve a safe stopping distance?
- Do you make the best possible use of observation links to help plan your approach to a corner?
- Do you position yourself to get the best possible view when cornering, with due regard to safety?

Next time you meet a significant corner on an open road, ask yourself: 'What if there's a vehicle parked in the road just beyond my limit point?' Does this alter your riding?

Avoiding skids

Riding safely within the limits of the road conditions so that you're able to avoid a skid is much better than having to correct one. However skilful you are, skidding is dangerous and the chances of regaining control are limited. But if you're faced with a developing skid, you need to know exactly what to do to try to regain control, and how to avoid making the skid worse.

This section explains the principles and techniques for correcting a skid, but bear in mind that each skid is unique and each machine responds differently to skids. How you apply the principles and techniques will depend entirely on the circumstances and on the machine you're riding.

The best way to gain confidence in dealing with a skid is through formal loose-surface riding instruction. Because skidding should never be practised on a public road, there are no suggestions for practising techniques in this section.

What causes a skid?

Poor road or weather conditions increase the risk of skidding, and riders are certainly vulnerable to the effects of these conditions on a machine's stability. But a skid doesn't just happen – often it's not the road or weather conditions that are the cause but the rider's response to them. Skidding is often caused by altering course or speed too harshly for the road conditions.

Aim to ride and control your machine in such a way that it doesn't skid. This becomes more difficult when road or weather conditions deteriorate, but through good observation, anticipation and planning you can do a lot to minimise the risks of skidding.

First you need to understand how a skid happens, what warning signs to look out for and what actions to avoid.

How does a skid happen?

A machine skids when one or both tyres lose normal grip on the road surface. This happens when the grip of tyres on the road becomes less than the force or forces acting on the machine.

These forces act on a machine whenever you operate the controls – the brakes, the throttle, the clutch or the handlebars. If you brake or accelerate while cornering, two forces are combined. As Chapter 6 explains, there's only limited tyre grip available, and if these forces become too powerful they break the grip of the tyres on the road. Never ride to the limit of the tyre grip available – always leave a safety margin to allow for the unforeseen.

Skidding is usually the result of riding too fast for the conditions. This creates the circumstances from which a skid can develop. If a rider suddenly or forcibly accelerates, brakes, changes direction or releases the clutch without matching engine speed to road speed, this may cause loss of tyre grip. On a slippery road surface it takes much less force to break the grip of the tyres.

If you've ever experienced a skid, you'll probably remember that you were changing either the speed or direction of the machine – or both – just before the skid developed.

Causes of skidding

The commonest causes of skidding are the rider's input or external hazards.

When a skid develops, your first action should be to remove the cause. Later in this chapter we discuss the causes of skidding and how to remove them in more detail.

> If you start to skid – remove the cause.

Minimising the risks of skidding

You

Understanding the causes of skidding should help you to plan to avoid skidding in the first place. Skidding is more likely in bad weather conditions and on slippery road surfaces, so the first question to ask yourself in bad weather conditions is:

'Is my journey really necessary?'

Your machine

Most skids are the result of how a machine is ridden, but keeping your machine and tyres in good condition helps to minimise the risk of skidding:

- tyres should be correctly inflated and have adequate tread depth – check tyre treads and tyre pressure daily
- defective brakes and faulty suspension are especially dangerous on slippery surfaces and may help to cause or aggravate a skid – don't increase the risk by neglecting these problems.

Recognising and removing the cause of a skid

If your machine develops a full skid you're unlikely to have the time and space to correct it. You need full concentration and observation both to avoid skids and to be able to take immediate corrective action if one starts to develop.

When a skid develops, the first action is to recognise what type it is and remove the cause.

Rear-wheel skid

This occurs when the rear wheel loses its grip because of:

- excessive speed for the circumstances – ease off the throttle to reduce speed
- harsh acceleration, causing wheel spin – ease off the throttle to reduce speed
- excessive rear braking, locking the back wheel – ease the pressure on the rear brake to allow the wheel to rotate
- not matching engine speed to road speed when releasing the clutch – pull the clutch in.

A rear-wheel skid can cause the rear wheel to slide to either side. Remove the cause by easing off the throttle or reducing braking effort and bring the machine upright. When stability is restored, apply the throttle or brake but with greater sensitivity than before.

Of the two types of skid, a rear-wheel skid is the more controllable.

Front-wheel skid

This occurs when the front wheel loses its grip because of:

- excessive speed for the circumstances
- harsh or excessive braking
- poor contact with the road surface.

If you have the time and space, remove the cause of a front-wheel skid. There's very little time to recognise, react to and correct a front-wheel skid, so make every effort to avoid one.

Machine design developments

Manufacturers are constantly seeking to improve machine safety. Anti-lock braking systems (ABS), linked braking and traction control systems are safety devices that can help stability. Machines fitted with these features behave differently from other machines and require different techniques to get the best use from them.

Anti-lock braking systems

Most modern machines are now fitted with ABS and some with cornering ABS – a system that allows the ABS to work while cornering. The purpose of ABS is to retain tyre grip during harsh or emergency braking. Always refer to the manufacturer's guidelines.

ABS helps the rider to brake strongly without the wheels locking up when travelling in a straight line. During cornering, except on machines fitted with cornering ABS, the cornering forces can disrupt the system, allowing wheel lock to occur. If you activate the ABS during emergency braking, you should maintain maximum pressure on the relevant brake or brakes throughout the braking.

ABS does no more than provide the rider with an additional safety device. It doesn't increase the grip of the tyres on the road, nor can it prevent all types of skid. Depending on the circumstances, a machine equipped with ABS may stop within a shorter distance than if the wheels were locked up.

For many riders, ABS is a real benefit, especially when combined with a linked (front-to-back) braking system. This is because most riders are reluctant to use the full braking potential of their machines for fear of locking their wheels. ABS reduces this worry, encouraging fuller use of the brakes. But if you activate the ABS on your machine, you should always ask yourself 'Why?'

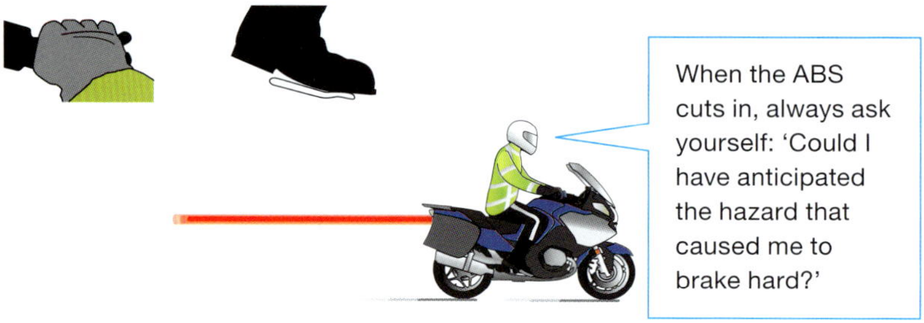

ABS is intended to help emergency braking but it doesn't allow you to ride faster in slippery conditions, and it doesn't make up for a lack of observation or anticipation.

Don't over-rely on the safety features fitted to your machine. Whenever you activate the ABS, work out why it cut in. Honestly assess your riding behaviour and whether you could have anticipated the hazard that caused you to brake hard.

Linked, coupled or combined braking systems

The front and rear brakes on most machines operate independently. Even experienced riders sometimes have difficulty achieving the best balance of braking between front and rear wheels. A linked or combined system links the brakes so that operation of one brake control activates both brakes in a predetermined optimum combination. On some machines both brake controls are linked to both brakes; on others only one brake control is linked to both brakes. The combination of linked brakes (front-to-rear) and ABS has been shown to provide a significant braking improvement on slippery surfaces for the average rider.

Traction control systems

Traction control systems improve control and stability by controlling excess wheel slip on the rear wheel when the engine speed increases. The systems monitor wheel slip (wheel spin) on the rear wheel and reduce the power supply to the wheel when slip exceeds a pre-set maximum. This allows the tyres to regain traction (grip) and stability. It allows the machine to make maximum use of tyre grip, especially on slippery surfaces.

Aquaplaning

Aquaplaning is dangerous. This is where a wedge of water builds up between the tyres and the road surface. It's caused by a combination of standing water, tyre tread and speed, which leads to increased braking distance at a minimum, and sometimes a loss of control. It can often be attributed to thin or worn tyre tread. When it happens, the safest solution is to maintain a firm hold on the handlebars and gradually close the throttle, allowing the machine to lose speed and the tyres to regain their grip.

Now that you have a fuller understanding of what causes a skid, think back over your own experience. For each skid you can remember, ask yourself:

- Was your journey really necessary?
- What were the causes of the skid? What type of skid was it?
- Could you have anticipated these conditions and avoided the skid altogether?
- Did you manage to quickly regain directional control? If not, how could you have improved your handling of the skid?
- How have you changed your riding as a result of the experience? Has this chapter made you aware of further changes that you need to make?

Check your understanding

You should now be able to apply learning from this chapter in your rider training so that you can:

- ☐ explain the principles of safe cornering
- ☐ describe the forces involved in cornering and the factors which affect your balance and your machine's ability to corner
- ☐ show how to use the system of motorcycle control and the limit point for cornering
- ☐ show how to position your machine for the best view when cornering
- ☐ describe the principles of anti-lock braking systems, linked braking systems and traction control
- ☐ explain why active safety features can interfere with rider behaviour
- ☐ identify the causes of skidding and how to minimise the risk.

Chapter 9

Rider's signals

Learning outcomes

The learning in this chapter, along with rider training, should enable you to:

- demonstrate appropriate use of the full range of signals available to you in different situations
- show appropriate responses to, and caution in, interpreting signals given by others
- show that you make active use of courtesy signals.

Developing your competence at using signals

Using signals may seem to be a basic skill, but many riders don't use the full range of available signals consistently or to best effect. This chapter will help you improve your competence at using signals.

Giving information to other road users is a key part of information processing in the system of motorcycle control.

See Chapter 3, page 41, The importance of information.

See also Chapter 13, Emergency response, for further information about the signals available to emergency services in response situations.

The purpose of signals

Signals inform other road users of your presence or intentions. Don't just consider those road users who can be seen – also consider those who can't be seen and those who you may reasonably expect to appear.

Think before you signal. Indiscriminate signalling isn't helpful to anyone.

> Give a signal whenever it could benefit other road users.

If you decide a signal is necessary, signal clearly and in good time. Always make sure the meaning of your signal is clear. Sometimes a signal is not in itself enough to make your intentions clear and other road users may use your position and speed to interpret what your signals mean. When negotiating a roundabout, for example, your signals may be misinterpreted if you haven't taken up the correct position for your intended exit. When appropriate, consider reinforcing the meaning of your signal with an arm signal.

Key points

- **Consider the need to give a signal on the approach to every hazard, and before you change direction or speed.**
- **Give a signal whenever it could benefit other road users.**
- **Remember that signalling doesn't give you any special right to carry out the actions you indicate.**
- **Follow the *Highway Code* – check your mirrors before you signal or manoeuvre.**

Interpreting signals given by others

You also need to be cautious about how you interpret the signals of other road users. For example, does a vehicle flashing the left-hand indicator mean that the driver intends to:

- park the vehicle, possibly immediately after a left-hand junction?
- turn into a left-hand junction?
- carry straight on, having forgotten to cancel the last signal?

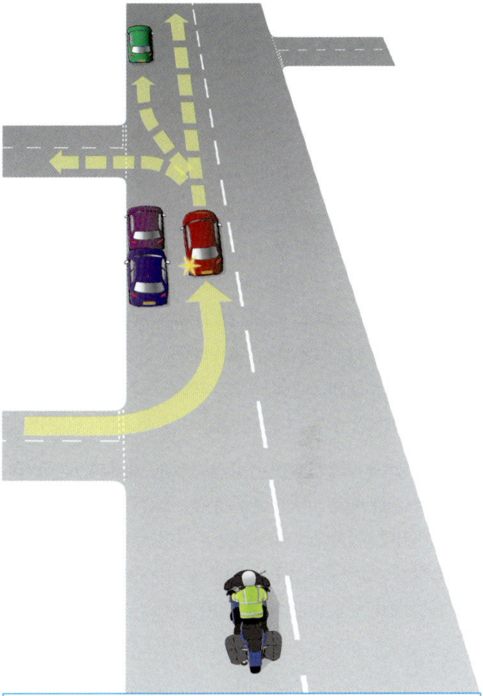

The indicator signal on the red car is ambiguous. Use the position and speed of the vehicle to help you interpret what the driver intends to do.

The range of signals

The signals available to you are:

- indicators
- hazard warning lights
- brake light
- headlight
- the position of your machine
- horn signals
- arm signals
- courtesy signals (for example, raising a hand to thank another driver).

Select the most effective signal for the job. You must give your signal in plenty of time if it's to benefit other road users. Be aware that when you change the speed or position of your machine you're also giving information to other road users.

Using the indicators

The indicators on some low-powered machines aren't very effective because the lamps are of relatively low wattage. This is especially true when direct sunlight shines on their lenses. Check that the indicator lamps on the machines you use are bright enough to attract the attention of other road users. If not, consider using arm signals instead.

The *Highway Code* advises you to give a signal when another road user could benefit. Use observation to anticipate when a signal may be needed. This encourages you to be aware of other road users at all times, especially those behind you. If in doubt, it's better to signal than not to signal, but always think before you do.

Do you avoid routine signalling? Ask yourself:

- Do I need to signal?
- What kind of signal should I give?
- To make my intentions as clear as possible, for how long should I signal and when should I stop signalling?
- Who could misunderstand my signal?

The purpose of signals is to warn other road users of your presence and/or your intention and to give you adequate time to achieve its purpose. Signals are informative and don't give right of way.

One signal should not cover two manoeuvres. Give a signal for each manoeuvre you intend to carry out.

Make sure that your signal can't be misinterpreted by other road users:

- Consider giving an arm signal to make your intentions clear, particularly in strong or low sunlight.
- Use your position to make your intentions clear to other road users. Move away from areas of increased danger.

Cancelling indicator signals

Leaving an indicator flashing after making a turn confuses other road users and can easily cause a collision. Never take an indicator signal as proof of another driver's intention when you're waiting to emerge from a side turning.

Look for supporting evidence such as an obvious slowing down, change of position or wheels turning in before you move out.

Most machines don't have indicator self-cancelling mechanisms. Always make sure you cancel a signal immediately after you've completed the manoeuvre. This is a key danger area and a common cause of collisions, particularly when a left indicator isn't cancelled.

Some machines are fitted with a self-cancelling mechanism that's activated either by the distance travelled or by the time that has elapsed, depending on the speed of the bike. If your machine has a self-cancelling system, make sure you know how it works.

These mechanisms sometimes cancel themselves when they're still needed, for example, when going round a large roundabout. Be alert to this possibility and be ready to switch your indicator back on.

Do you give clear signals to other road users?

- Do you always signal when another road user could benefit?
- Do you signal your intentions clearly and in good time?
- Where possible, do you choose a position that helps to make your intentions clear to other road users?
- Do you use arm signals where necessary to clarify your intentions?

Using hazard warning lights

Consider using hazard lights to alert other drivers to your presence when you've stopped. Don't use hazard lights when moving except on unrestricted multi-lane carriageways and motorways. Here you can use hazard lights briefly to warn the vehicles behind you that there's a hold-up ahead.

Don't use your hazard warning lights when filtering – it's illegal and causes confusion.

See Chapter 11, page 238, Filtering.

Using your brake light

Use your brake light to indicate either slowing down or your intention to stop. Always check your mirrors before using your brakes unless you're doing an emergency stop:

- Start braking well in advance of an anticipated hazard to alert the driver behind that you mean to slow down or stop, especially if the vehicle behind is too close.
- Avoid 'dabbing' the brakes: if your brake light flashes on and off but you don't slow down, you'll confuse the drivers behind you.
- Avoid resting your foot on the rear brake. This will distract a following road user and may also mean that they fail to react when you do actually brake.

Flashing your headlight

Flash your headlight when the horn would not be heard, and in place of the horn at night. You should flash your headlight for one purpose only: to inform other road users that you're there – not as a signal to come on. **Never assume that another driver flashing their headlights is a signal to proceed.**

Use a headlight flash in daylight:

- when speed makes it likely that the horn would not be heard – for example, on a motorway
- to alert other road users to your presence when you're approaching from behind.

Use your judgement to decide the duration of the flash and how far in advance you should give it. This is critical and will depend on your speed. The purpose of flashing your headlight is solely to inform the other road user of your presence. It doesn't give you the right to overtake regardless of the circumstances.

During darkness, flash your headlight to inform other road users of your presence, for example:

- on the approach to a hill crest
- when travelling along narrow, winding roads.

Don't flash your headlight when it might be misunderstood by road users for whom it's not intended, for example, as a signal to proceed.

Don't use your main beam when filtering through traffic. This may blind road users in front of you and cause them to wander into your path. If you feel the need to use your main beam, consider whether you need to slow down.

See Chapter 11, page 238, Filtering.

Using the horn

The horns on some machines have low power and may not be clearly audible to drivers. Check that the horn on any machine you ride is effective in traffic conditions before you rely on it to signal.

Only use the horn when it's necessary to warn other road users of your presence. If you see that another road user isn't aware of your presence, first choose an appropriate position and speed so that you can stop safely if necessary.

If you do need to use the horn:

- do it in good time
- adjust the length of the horn note to the circumstances.

Consider using the horn on the approach to hazards where the view is very limited, such as a blind summit or bridge on a single-track road.

Never use the horn to challenge or rebuke other road users. Give a wave of acknowledgement following use of the horn, for example, beep and wave. This helps to foster good relations between different groups of road users.

Always listen carefully for other road users' horn warnings and react appropriately – remember that your helmet can make a horn note difficult to hear.

As a last resort, it could be beneficial to use the horn:

- to warn another road user who is not aware of you (pedestrians and cyclists – especially children – are most at risk)

- when you approach a hazard where the view is very limited – for example, a blind bend or a steep hump bridge on a single track road

- to warn the occupants of parked vehicles of your presence.

Using arm signals

Arm signals can be helpful to other road users in certain circumstances. If you need to use an arm signal, follow the *Highway Code* advice. Be aware that many road users may not understand arm signals as they are rarely used.

Using courtesy signals

Courtesy signals encourage cooperative use of the road space and help to promote road safety. Acknowledging the courtesy of other road users encourages good driving, helps foster positive attitudes and promotes good relations between different groups of road users. Using a courtesy signal to defuse a potential conflict can make a real difference to road safety. Use courtesy signals:

- to thank another driver for letting you go first
- to apologise when you've unintentionally caused inconvenience to another road user
- if you have to use the horn (a wave of acknowledgement helps prevent misunderstanding; it shows other road users your use of the horn isn't meant to be confrontational).

You can use either hand to give a courtesy signal, but don't compromise your control or the stability of the bike. Alternatively, you can signal without removing your hand from the handlebars by raising your palm or nodding your head. But make sure that your courtesy signal can't be mistaken for a 'waving on' signal.

Do you think you tend to give courtesy signals more or less often than other road users?

On your next few journeys, make a conscious effort to give and acknowledge courtesy signals:

- How does this affect your own state of mind?
- How does it influence the actions of other road users?

Responding to other people's signals

Treat with caution any signals other than those given by authorised officials. If someone beckons you to move forward – for example, an arm signal from a cyclist or driver – always check for yourself whether it's safe to do so. Make sure you know and can use the range of arm signals set out in the *Highway Code*.

If someone beckons you to move forward, always check for yourself whether it is safe to do so.

Check your understanding

You should now be able to apply learning from this chapter in your rider training so that you can:

- ☐ demonstrate appropriate use of the full range of signals available to you in different situations
- ☐ show appropriate responses to, and caution in, interpreting signals given by others
- ☐ show that you make active use of courtesy signals.

Chapter 10

Positioning

Learning outcomes

The learning in this chapter, along with rider training, should enable you to:

- explain how to position your bike safely on the approach to hazards
- show how to position your bike to get the best view into nearside junctions
- show how to position your bike appropriately for following other vehicles, turning and stopping.

Developing competence at positioning your bike

For advice on positioning on the motorway, see Chapter 12, Riding on motorways and multi-lane carriageways.

Positioning is a crucial element in the system of motorcycle control.

See Chapter 3, page 45, Position.

The ideal road position depends on many things: safety, observation, road and traffic conditions, road layout, cornering, manoeuvrability, assisting traffic flow and making your intentions clear.

Always consider safety before anything else. Be prepared to sacrifice any other advantage in the interests of safety.

Aim to take a position that puts safety first, ensures good tyre grip and stability and provides the best view consistent with these objectives.

Put the bike in the best position for you to see and be seen, with due regard to safety.

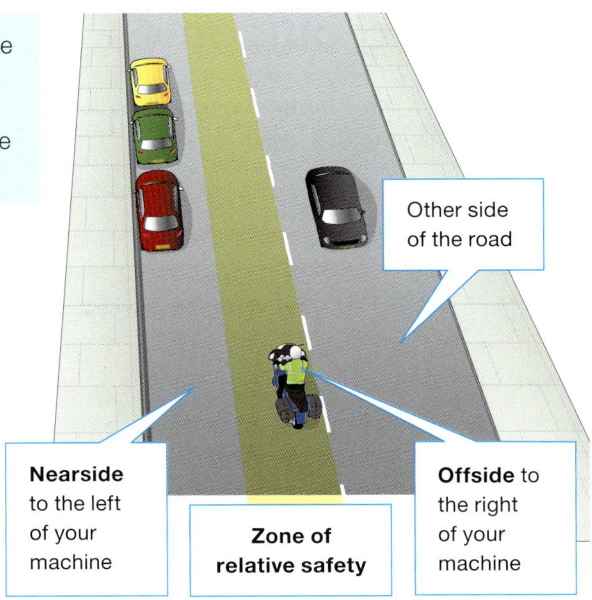

Positioning for advantage

The narrowness of rider and machine gives you great flexibility in the choice of position on your own side of the road. There are three positions to consider, as explained in the diagram.

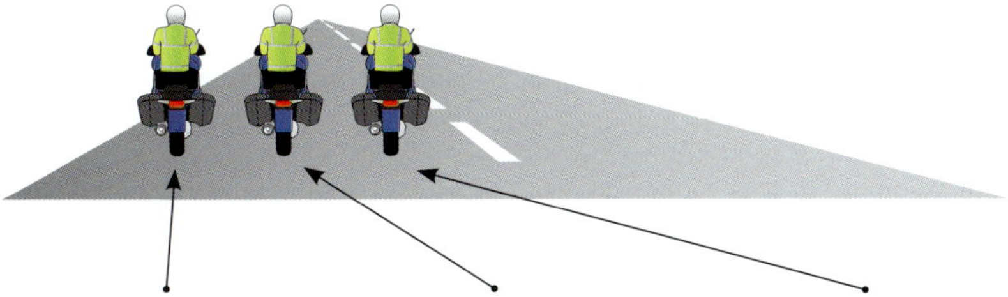

The nearside position

The benefits of this position are:

- it gives early views through right-hand bends
- it allows nearside views past lorries and other large vehicles
- it allows extra space for oncoming vehicles
- it's the best position for left-hand turns when there are no other hazards.

Make sure the nearside road surface is sound and free of drains, debris, dust and grit before using it.

The central position

This is midway between the better part of the nearside edge and the centre line.

The benefits of this position are:

- it gives you good margins of safety on both sides
- it allows you to change position to either side.

In wet weather, avoid the central position near junctions and on the final approach to bends, because oil and diesel tend to accumulate in it.

The offside position

The benefits of this position are:

- it gives early views on the approach to left-hand bends
- it provides increased safety margins away from nearside hazards
- it's generally the best position for right-hand turns.

Anticipate the possibility of large oncoming vehicles straddling the central line on bends and be prepared to move to the left.

Any of these positions should be sacrificed for safety.

When choosing a road position, always take into account the width of the road you're travelling on. Your choice of position will be different on, for example, a narrow or country road without white lines.

Always be prepared to sacrifice your road position for safety.

When you're riding through a series of bends in wet weather, follow the dry line of previous vehicles if this doesn't take you too far off course. Reduce your speed to compensate for deviating from your ideal line.

Safe positioning on the approach to hazards

The system of motorcycle control provides a safe and methodical approach to hazards.

By carefully choosing your position, you can reduce the risk of having a collision. Be aware of hazards on both sides of your motorcycle. In urban areas, to the nearside, there's a risk of colliding with cyclists and pedestrians, and parked vehicles and their occupants.

Be aware of other vehicles pulling out from junctions. Dangers can come from anywhere but be especially alert to moving hazards coming from the left. You'll generally have less time to react to these. To the offside, there's a risk of colliding with oncoming vehicles in the centre of the road.

Between the two extremes is a zone that is relatively free of hazards, but be aware of debris, oil and diesel, which tend to accumulate in this area.

Always adapt and adjust your position and speed to the circumstances. Where hazards are present on both sides, select a course that reduces your vulnerability and makes you more visible to other road users.

Roadside hazards

Common roadside hazards to look out for are:

- pedestrians, especially children, stepping off the footpath
- parked vehicles and their occupants
- cyclists, especially children
- horses
- runners – where there's no footpath
- concealed junctions
- surface water and spray from kerbside puddles.

Position your machine to avoid defects in the carriageway, road surface irregularities, debris and inspection covers, any of which may affect the stability of your machine.

If you identify hazards on the nearside, take a position closer to the centre of the road. This has two benefits:

- it gives you a better view
- it provides more space in which to take avoiding action if you need to.

If oncoming traffic makes it unsafe to take this position, or if the road is too narrow, reduce your speed. There's an important trade-off between your speed and the clearance around your machine. The narrower the gap, the slower your speed. Be prepared to stop if necessary.

Keep as far from rows of parked vehicles as circumstances allow. A good rule of thumb is to leave at least enough space for an opening door to the side of any parked vehicles. If you can't move out, slow down.

Child pedestrians may not look properly. Get into the habit of asking yourself: 'Could I stop in time if the child ran out?'

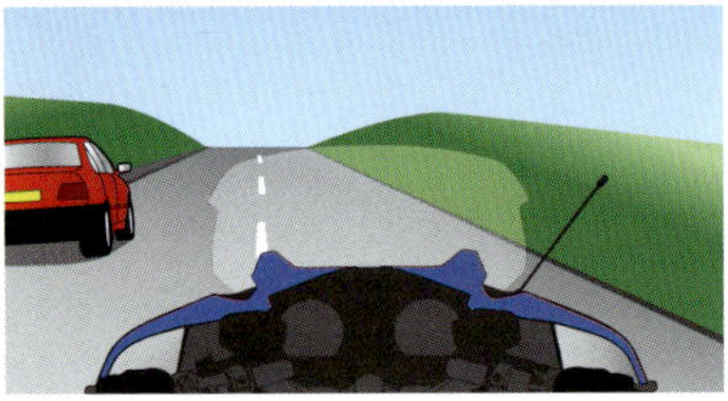

If traffic conditions are favourable, they allow a greater safety margin.

The less space you have, the slower you should go.

How well do you stand out against the background?

How visible are you at night?

Use rear observation to help you position yourself so that you're visible from the front and not lost against 'visual clutter' or larger vehicles.

Cyclists

When riding in heavy traffic, be alert to the behaviour of cyclists. Be aware that cyclists may attempt to pass on your nearside or filter through narrow gaps in the traffic that you may be planning to use.

Improving the view into nearside road junctions

Position yourself so that you can see as much of the road ahead as possible and so that other road users can see you. You can improve your view into nearside roads by positioning your bike towards the centre of the road. This also makes you more visible to vehicles pulling out from nearside junctions. Remember that you're a very small spot in the driver's field of vision and they may find it hard to judge how far away you are. Moving to a central position will make the driver more aware of your presence.

Check for eye contact and head movements but don't rely on these as evidence that the driver has seen you – they may be responding to a road user behind you.

In taking a central position you must take into account any vehicles on the other side of the road. Also consider the possibility that bikes or vehicles may move up on your inside if you do. Take a position that minimises the overall danger from both sides of the road. Carry out rear observation before you alter position either way.

Position to see and be seen.

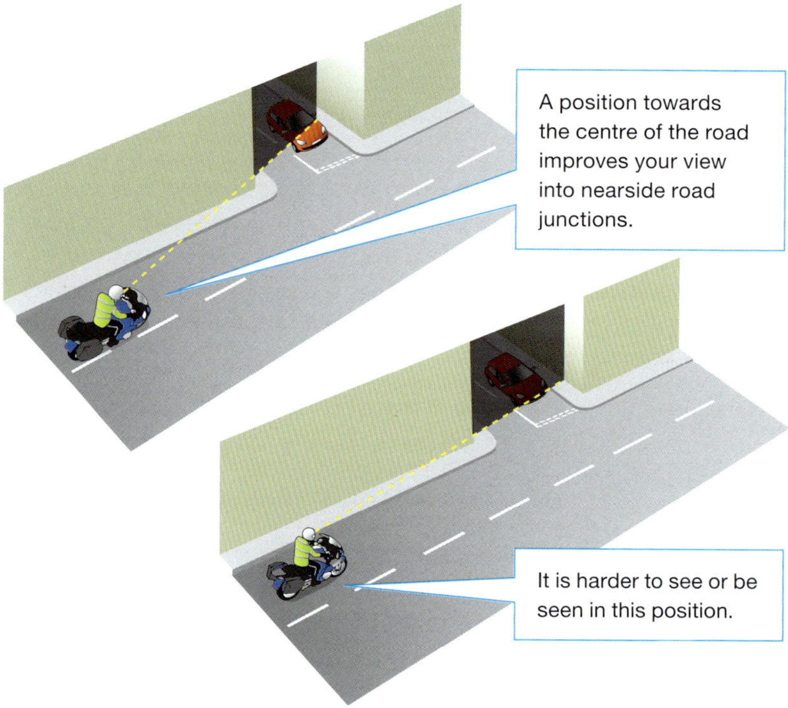

On your next journey, review your skill at positioning for safety. Do you pay enough attention to:

- nearside hazards?
- offside hazards?

Do you position your bike to obtain the best view in the circumstances, with due regard to safety?

How could you improve your positioning in order to increase safety?

Following position

In a stream of traffic, always keep a safe distance behind the vehicle in front. Follow the two-second rule: leave a gap of at least two seconds between you and the vehicle in front, depending on conditions.

See Chapter 6, page 138, The two-second rule.

Keeping your distance increases your safety because:

- you have a good view, and can increase it along both sides by slight changes of position – this enables you to be fully aware of what's happening on the road ahead
- you can stop your bike safely if the driver in front brakes firmly without warning
- you can extend your braking distance so that the driver behind has more time to react, especially if they're driving too close
- you can see when it's safe to move into the overtaking position
- in wet weather, you get less spray from the vehicle in front.

You should generally position your machine to the rear offside of the vehicle you're following. From this position you're:

- visible through the interior and offside door mirrors of the driver in front
- able to move into an overtaking position by reducing the following distance (that is, without needing to change position as well)
- able to escape to either side should an emergency arise.

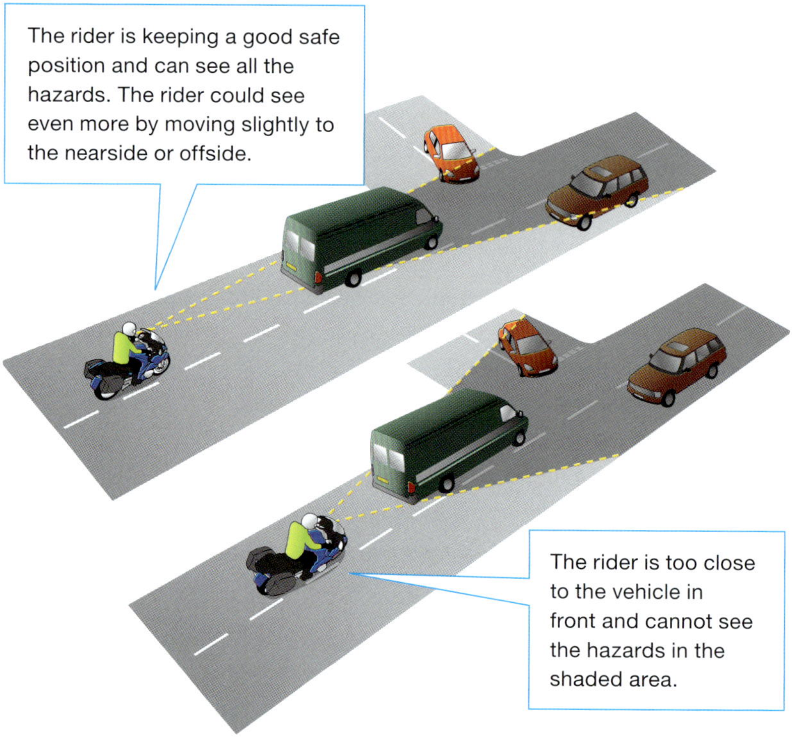

If you need to take a position further to the centre or nearside, increase your following distance to compensate for the loss of the offside escape route.

Position on bends

When approaching a bend, position yourself to get the best possible view of the road ahead. Take information on the approach to the bend to help you decide on the best position. This position will be different for right-hand and left-hand bends.

See Chapter 8, Cornering, balance and avoiding skids for further information.

Position for turning

Your position for turning depends on the other traffic, your safety, road surface conditions, the road width and layout, the position of any obstacles and the effect of these obstacles on traffic behaviour. Take information on the approach to help you decide on the best position. Generally, the best position on the approach to a junction is on the nearside for a left turn and towards the centre line for a right turn.

When positioning for turning, give careful consideration to:

carriageway markings

other traffic

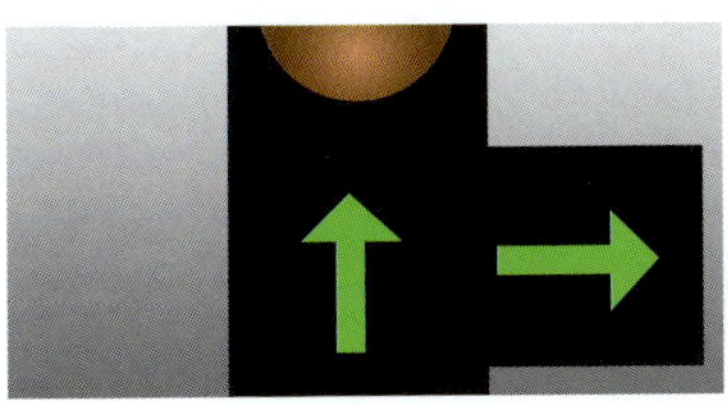

traffic light filter arrows

obstructions

If you intend to turn right and oncoming traffic is encroaching on your side of the road, move back in from the centre line.

If you intend to turn left and the corner has a sharp angle, is obscured, or pedestrians are present, approach the corner from further out than normal. Move further out in good time. Avoid 'swan necking' – approaching close to the nearside and then swinging out to the right just before turning the junction. This can mislead other road users about your intentions.

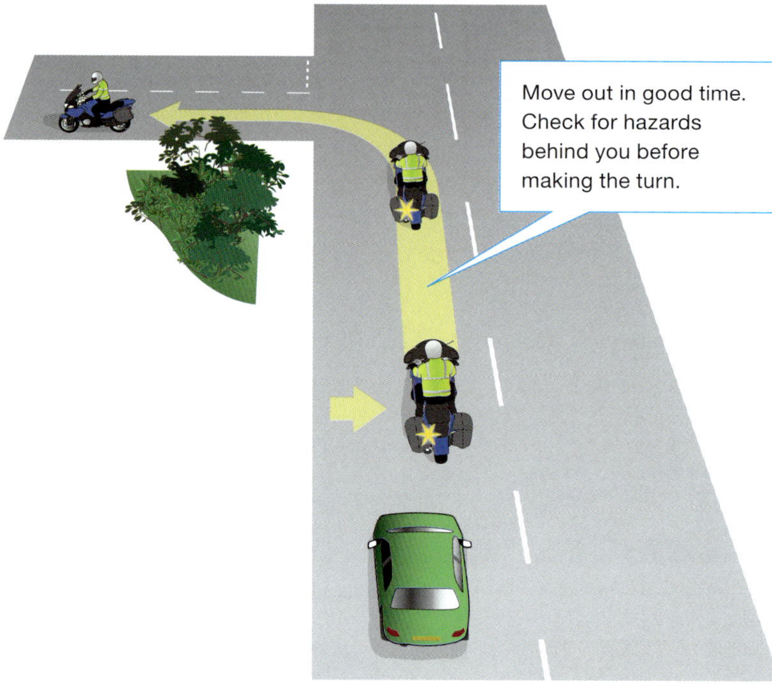

Position at crossroads

When you're turning right at crossroads and the oncoming vehicle is also turning right, there's a choice of two positions. Your choice will depend on the road layout and markings, and the position of the other vehicle:

- pass offside to offside – this gives you a better view
- pass nearside to nearside where traffic conditions, the junction layout or the position of the other vehicle makes offside to offside impractical.

Take extra care on a nearside to nearside pass, especially if your view of the road is blocked by a tall van or lorry. Look carefully for oncoming traffic. Riders are extremely vulnerable when carrying out this manoeuvre.

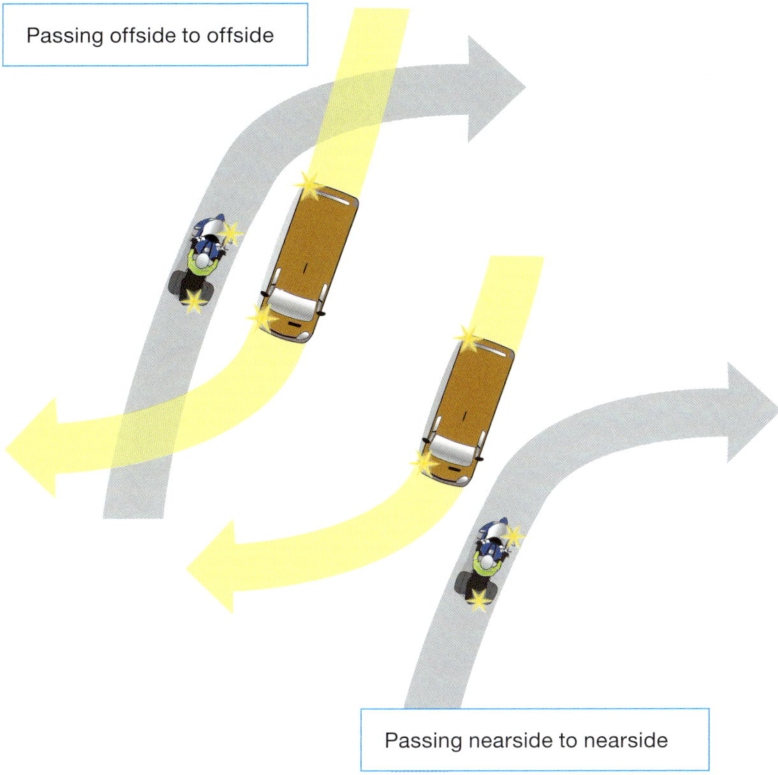

Take extra care on a nearside to nearside pass because your view of the road is obstructed by the other vehicle.

Position for stopping behind other vehicles

Before you come to a stop, think about your next move. Position your bike so that you can continue with minimum inconvenience to yourself and other road users. You should be able to see the rear tyres of the vehicle in front and some empty tarmac.

Remember: think 'rubber and road' or 'tyres and tarmac'.

Stopping well short of the vehicle in front gives you several advantages:

- a good view of the road
- room to move around the vehicle ahead if it stalls or hesitates
- the space in front of you is a safe haven for a cycle or another motorcycle
- if you become aware that a vehicle approaching behind has left braking too late, you can move forward to allow it extra space to stop in
- facing uphill, if the vehicle ahead starts to roll back towards you, you have time to warn the driver or take avoiding action.

Where the situation allows, consider stopping half a car's length short of pedestrian crossings or traffic lights to provide yourself with a safety margin should your motorcycle be shunted from behind.

An example of using your stopping position to increase safety is where there are traffic lights at roadworks close to a bend. Consider stopping before or on the approach to the bend so that drivers who come up behind can see you.

Leave yourself enough room to pull out and pass the vehicle in front if necessary. You should be able to see the rear tyres of the vehicle in front and some empty tarmac.

Position for approaching the brow of a hill

When approaching the brow of a hill, maintain a central position in your lane. This will minimise the risk of colliding with an as yet unseen vehicle approaching on your offside, but also avoid risk to any unseen pedestrian or cyclist on your nearside just over the brow.

Check your understanding

You should now be able to apply learning from this chapter in your rider training so that you can:

- [ ] explain how to position your bike safely on the approach to hazards
- [ ] show how to position your bike to get the best view into nearside junctions
- [ ] show how to position your bike appropriately for following other vehicles, turning and stopping.

Chapter 11
Overtaking

Learning outcomes

The learning in this chapter, along with rider training, should enable you to:

- explain the risks of overtaking
- show how to use the following and overtaking positions safely
- show how to assess and overtake different types of hazards safely in a wide range of circumstances
- explain how to help other road users to overtake you.

Developing your competence at overtaking safely

The height, manoeuvrability and rapid acceleration of motorcycles are great advantages when overtaking. These features, together with their need for less road space than vehicles on four wheels, should make motorcycles the safest of all vehicles on which to overtake. The fact that they're not is because riders fail to appreciate all the hazards involved.

Overtaking is hazardous because it requires you to negotiate dynamic hazards (for example, moving vehicles) as well as fixed ones (for example, road layout) and it may bring you into the path of other vehicles. It's a complex manoeuvre in which you need to consider the vehicle(s) you want to overtake as well as a number of other hazards as the vehicle to be overtaken moves among them.

There are three things about these elements to consider:

- the vehicle you're overtaking
- external factors
- the interaction between the vehicle you're overtaking and those external factors.

This section describes the general principles of using the system of motorcycle control to do this manoeuvre safely. Training will further develop your ability to apply the system to dynamic hazards in practice.

Overtaking is a high-risk manoeuvre because you're potentially putting your bike into the path of oncoming traffic. If you're travelling at high speed and collide with an oncoming vehicle, the speed of impact will be the combined speed of vehicle and bike.

- Many overtaking deaths are due to head-on collisions on rural roads.
- On rural roads, 1 in 8 collisions in which the rider is killed or seriously injured happens when the rider is overtaking a moving vehicle on the offside, compared with 1 in 10 on urban roads.
- Riders are more vulnerable than car occupants when overtaking.

Is your machine capable of overtaking?

- Are you familiar with the bike's capabilities and characteristics?
- Are you sure that the bike will give you enough acceleration?
- Can you legally achieve the necessary speed?
- Have you assessed your bike's capability in relation to the road user you're overtaking? For example, overtaking a long vehicle will require more capability than overtaking a cyclist.

Passing a stationary vehicle

Passing a stationary vehicle is the simplest possible overtaking situation.

The stationary vehicle is your hazard. Use the system to approach and assess the hazard and to pass it safely. Take account of the position and speed of oncoming traffic, the position and speed of following traffic and the presence of pedestrians or other roadside hazards, especially on the nearside. If the situation allows, leave at least a door's width when passing a stationary vehicle.

See Chapter 10, Positioning.

Other external factors may affect your decision to overtake. For example, an oncoming vehicle may mean you have to wait before overtaking.

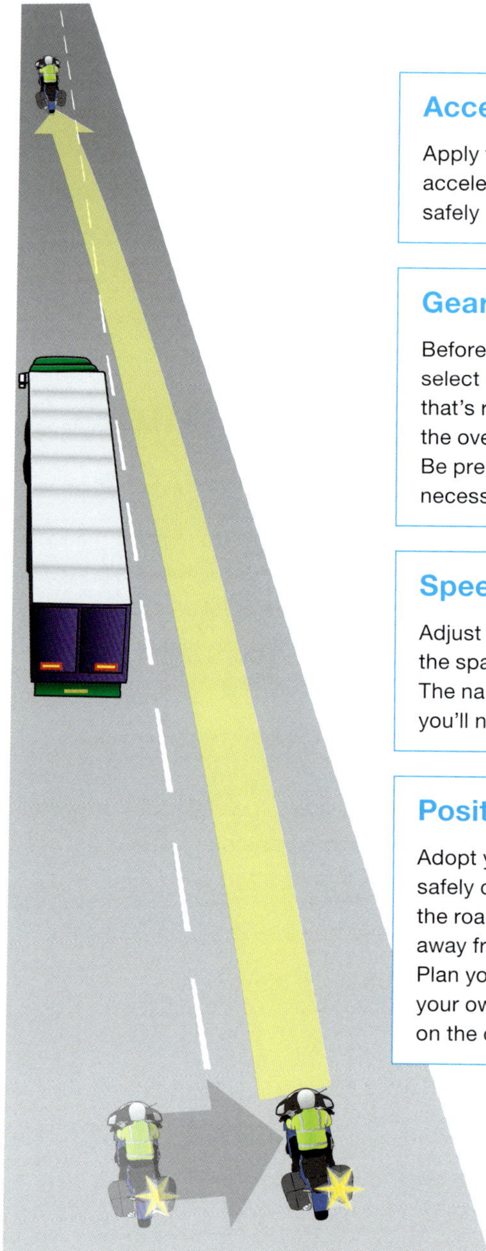

Acceleration

Apply the appropriate degree of acceleration to complete the pass safely and leave the hazard.

Gear

Before you start the overtake, select an appropriate gear that's responsive enough for the overtaking manoeuvre.
Be prepared to change gear if necessary.

Speed

Adjust your speed to the size of the space you're travelling through. The narrower the space, the slower you'll need to go.

Position

Adopt your position as early as you safely can, ideally to the offside of the road, at least a door's width away from the stationary vehicle. Plan your path when you return to your own side. Check for hazards on the offside.

Information

Observe and assess the road and traffic conditions ahead for an opportunity to pass safely. Ask yourself the questions below.

Does the road layout present a hazard?

Is there enough road width for me to pass?

Is the vehicle I'm passing likely to move off?

What's the speed and proximity of any oncoming vehicles?

Is there a possibility of as yet unseen vehicles approaching?

Is there a blind area I can't see into before starting the overtake?

What's happening behind? Are any of the following vehicles likely to overtake me?

What distance do I need to pass and safely regain a nearside position?

Have I noted any relevant road signs, markings and speed limits?

Overtaking moving vehicles

Overtaking a moving vehicle is more complicated because the situation is changing all the time. You need to consider the speed and acceleration capabilities of your machine, the physical features of the road and the relative speeds of other vehicles. You also need a good sense of where your bike and other vehicles are in relation to gaps in the traffic.

Whenever you consider overtaking, always ask yourself:

- Do I need to?
- Is it safe in the circumstances?
- Is my bike capable of overtaking?

The following pages describe two overtaking situations:

- **a single-stage overtake** where you're able to overtake immediately (approaching, overtaking and returning to your own side of the road) in one continuous manoeuvre
- **a three-stage overtake** where other hazards require you to take up a following position before you can safely overtake.

Overtaking usually involves multiple hazards. Any overtaking situation can change rapidly and become complicated by further hazards (for example, new oncoming vehicles, or slower vehicles further ahead on your side of the road). While you're learning to negotiate these complex hazards, you may have to consider and apply the system more than once in an overtaking manoeuvre. As you gain practice and confidence, you'll learn to view the number of hazards as one complex picture, and to use fewer applications.

The vehicle in front

Assess what sort of hazard the vehicle in front presents.

- Is the driver of the vehicle aware of you?
- Can you predict from earlier behaviour whether the driver's response is likely to be aggressive?
- Does the size or the load of the vehicle prevent the driver from seeing you or prevent you from seeing the road ahead clearly?
- Does the vehicle have left-hand drive?

Consider signalling your intention to overtake to the driver in front. Your road position will help you to do this but take care not to appear aggressive. This can be counter-productive and provoke an aggressive response in the other driver, who might speed up as you try to overtake. If the driver in front appears to be obstructive, consider whether it's worth overtaking at all. If you decide to go ahead, think about how much extra speed and space you need to allow to take into account any actions the driver may take.

If the driver in front isn't aware of you, consider altering position and using your headlight to signal that you're there.

Take extra care before overtaking a long vehicle or vehicles with wide or high loads. Assess the road ahead very carefully for any possible dangers. If you can, take views to both sides of the vehicle and make sure you have plenty of space to overtake and return safely to your own side. Be aware that if you can't see the wing mirrors of a heavy goods vehicle, the driver can't see you.

The vehicles behind

Assess whether the vehicles behind pose a risk. Note their speed, position and progress, and judge whether any of them may want to overtake you. Be aware that other following vehicles could overtake the vehicle following you. Use your mirrors and check to the side to monitor the situation behind you, especially before changing your speed or position. Decide whether you need to signal. At higher speeds, don't turn your head fully to look behind, because the situation ahead may alter while your head is turned.

Other hazards to consider before overtaking

Be aware of hazards that might cause the vehicles you're overtaking to alter their position. The illustrations on the next page show some common overtaking collisions.

The rider doesn't realise that the motorcyclist leaving the side road can only see the slow-moving van and may pull out onto the main road. This is a common cause of collisions when filtering.

The rider doesn't anticipate that the orange car may turn without warning into the side road.

The rider doesn't realise that the driver of the green car is looking only to their right and may pull out.

The rider thinks that the van is going to pass the parked car ahead, but the van is turning right, so will move and alter speed very differently.

The rider doesn't anticipate that the tractor may turn without warning into an entrance or gateway.

The rider doesn't realise that the red car is approaching. The lorry may slip safely into a return gap, leaving the rider facing the oncoming vehicle.

Make sure you have a full view of the road ahead of the vehicle you intend to overtake. Consider the possible actions of the driver of that vehicle and any others that may come into view.

A single-stage overtake

The basic principles of a single-stage overtake are the same as passing a stationary vehicle, but you'll now have additional questions to ask yourself:

What's the speed of the vehicle(s) to be overtaken?

Have I taken into account the speed and performance of my machine?

What's the likely response of the driver and occupants of the vehicle in front?

Information

Observe the road ahead for other actual and potential dangers – physical features, position and movement of other road users and weather/road conditions.

Identify:

- a safe stretch of road along which you have adequate vision to assess the whole overtake
- what's happening behind
- a gap into which you can safely return
- the relative speed of your machine and the vehicle(s) you intend to overtake
- a stretch of road long enough to accommodate the relative speeds of the vehicles – this will be much longer than the distance needed to pass a stationary vehicle.

Consider signalling if it will benefit other road users. Make sure that your signal is clear and can't be misinterpreted.

Think about the likely response of the driver and occupants of the vehicle in front. Consider the need to give information to any other road users.

The next diagram shows a typical single-stage overtake.

> Remember that much of the decision-making will happen *before* you get to the point shown in the diagram.

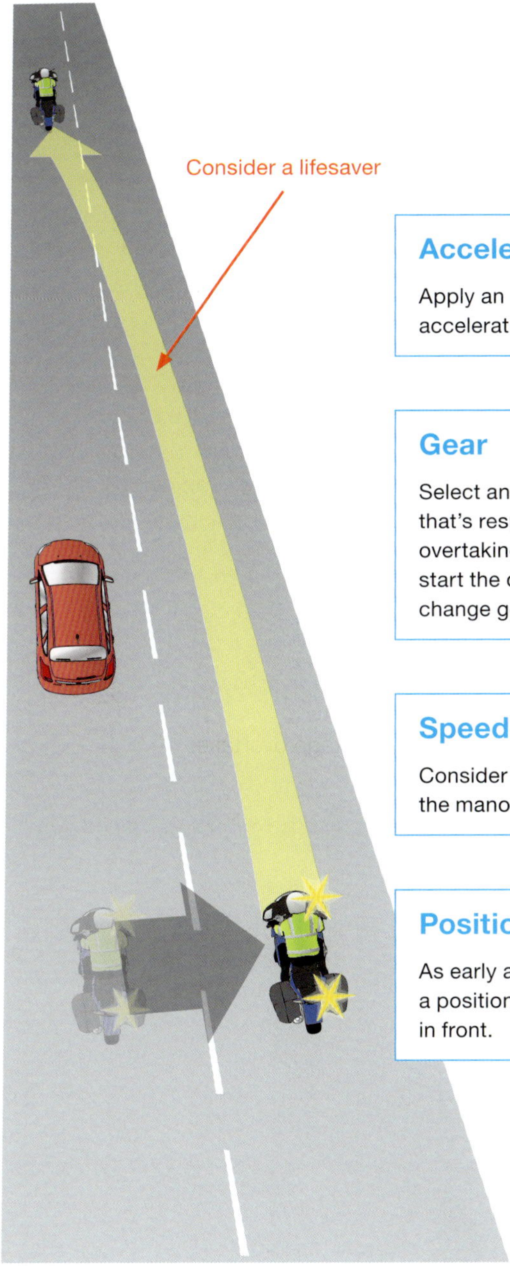

Acceleration

Apply an appropriate degree of acceleration to overtake safely.

Gear

Select an appropriate gear that's responsive enough for the overtaking manoeuvre before you start the overtake. Be prepared to change gear if necessary.

Speed

Consider your speed throughout the manoeuvre. Is it appropriate?

Position

As early as you safely can, take a position to overtake the vehicle in front.

A three-stage overtake

Stage one: following position

Where you're gaining on a vehicle in front but can see it isn't possible to overtake immediately, reduce your speed so that you can follow at a safe distance while you look for a safe opportunity to overtake on a suitable piece of road.

See Chapter 10, page 207, Following position.

In order to overtake in these circumstances, you'll need to observe and assess the road and traffic conditions ahead for an opportunity to overtake safely. When you anticipate one, move into an overtaking position. This is the most complex of the three overtaking stages, so you must ask yourself a number of questions:

Does the road layout present a hazard?

Is there enough road width for me to overtake?

What's the speed of the vehicle(s) to be overtaken?

What's the likely response of the driver and occupants of the vehicle in front?

Is/are the driver(s) ahead likely to overtake?

What's the speed and proximity of oncoming vehicles?

Is there a possibility of as yet unseen vehicles approaching at high speed?

What's happening behind? Are any of the following vehicles likely to overtake me?

What's an appropriate speed to complete the overtake, taking account of the hazards beyond the vehicle I'm overtaking?

What distance do I need to overtake and regain a nearside gap safely?

Have I taken into account the speed and performance of my machine?

Have I noted any relevant road signs, markings and speed limits?

Your priorities may change as you go through the manoeuvre. Continue to observe, plan and process information so that you can adjust your hazard priorities as the overtake develops. Observe what's happening in the far distance, the middle distance, the immediate foreground and behind. Do this repeatedly. Remember that good observation alone isn't enough. Your safety depends on correctly interpreting what you see.

See pages 222–3 for examples of situations where riders don't correctly interpret what they see.

In some cases, you might plan to take the following position but then find, as you close up on the vehicle in front, that you have a clear view of the road ahead and there are no additional hazards. In this case, you could go straight into the overtake.

Otherwise, once you think you've found a safe place to overtake, start to close some of the distance between you and the vehicle ahead.

Stage two: overtaking position

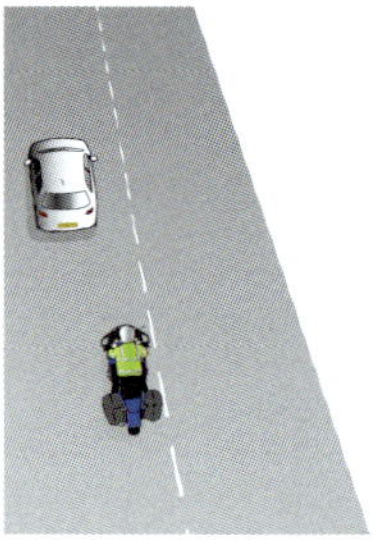

Position your bike to get the best possible view and opportunity by moving into the overtaking position. This is generally closer to the vehicle in front than the following position and you should only use it in readiness for overtaking. Always have due regard for safety. If a hazard (for example, an oncoming vehicle, a road junction) comes into view, move back to an appropriate following distance from the vehicle in front.

Remember the need for rear observation if you don't know what's in your blind spot. Consider the need to signal.

As you move closer to the vehicle in front, the driver is likely to realise that you want to overtake. Be careful not to intimidate the driver in front or to appear aggressive by following too closely, which is dangerous and counter-productive. Following too closely may cause the other driver to speed up, making it more difficult to overtake.

Before you move into the overtaking position, take views to the offside, nearside, under, over and through the windows of the vehicle in front. Generally, position your machine towards the offside rear corner of the vehicle in front. This position has two advantages:

- the driver in front can see you through their interior mirror and side mirror
- you have an escape route to the offside.

Avoid sitting in the blind spot of any vehicles you intend to overtake.

Select the most responsive gear for the speed at which you'll overtake, so you don't have to change gear during the overtaking manoeuvre. Good observation, judgement and acceleration sense should enable you to return to the nearside without braking.

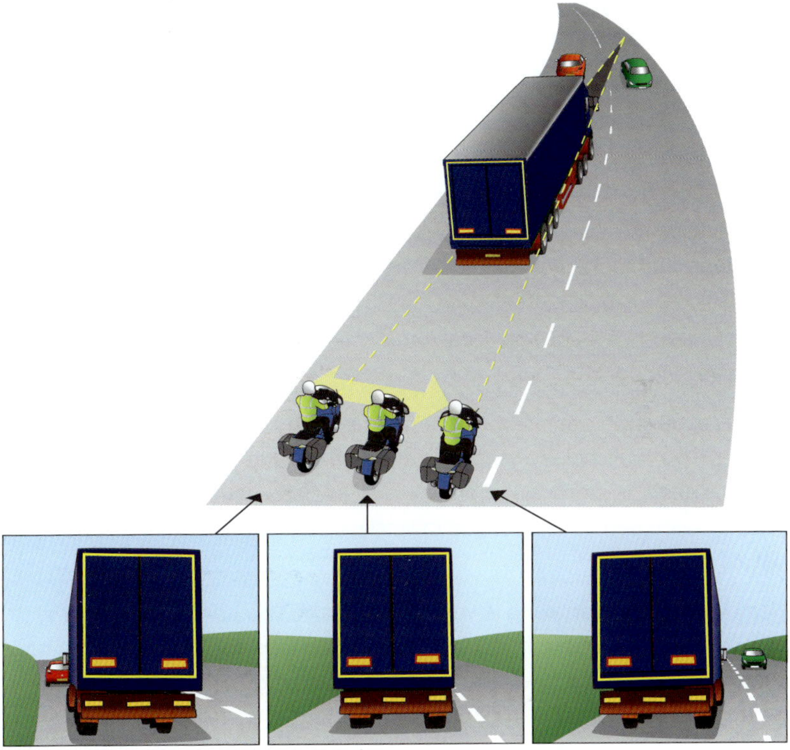

When you're following a large lorry, keep well back and take views to both sides of it.

Can you see both mirrors on a high-sided vehicle? If you can't, the driver may not be able to see you.

Look at the driver's face in the mirror. It gives you a lot of information. If the driver turns their head, it's more likely that they've seen you.

Stage three: overtaking

From the overtaking position, adjust your position so that you have a clear path beyond the vehicle you wish to pass, without accelerating. Consider rear observation.

From this position:

- make sure there's a safe gap ahead of the vehicle you overtake
- in assessing the safe gap, consider the effect on the road user you pull in front of
- if you see the manoeuvre wouldn't be safe, return to the following or overtaking position as appropriate
- if the manoeuvre can be completed safely, accelerate past.

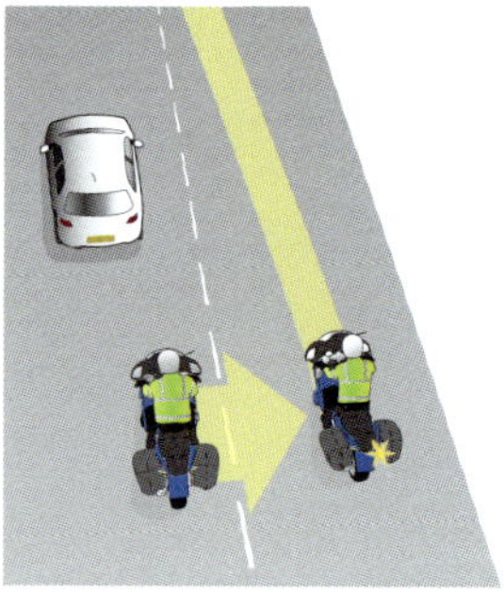

As you accelerate past, reconsider the hazards ahead of the overtaken vehicle. This may include other vehicles you want to overtake, physical features such as junctions or bends, or 'dead ground' – any part of the road that you can't see because of landscape features or the curve or nature of the road.

Remember that overtaking is your decision and you can reconsider it at any point. But be aware if you start to overtake and then in the light of new information you abort, the vehicle behind could move into your space, leaving you marooned. If in doubt, hold back.

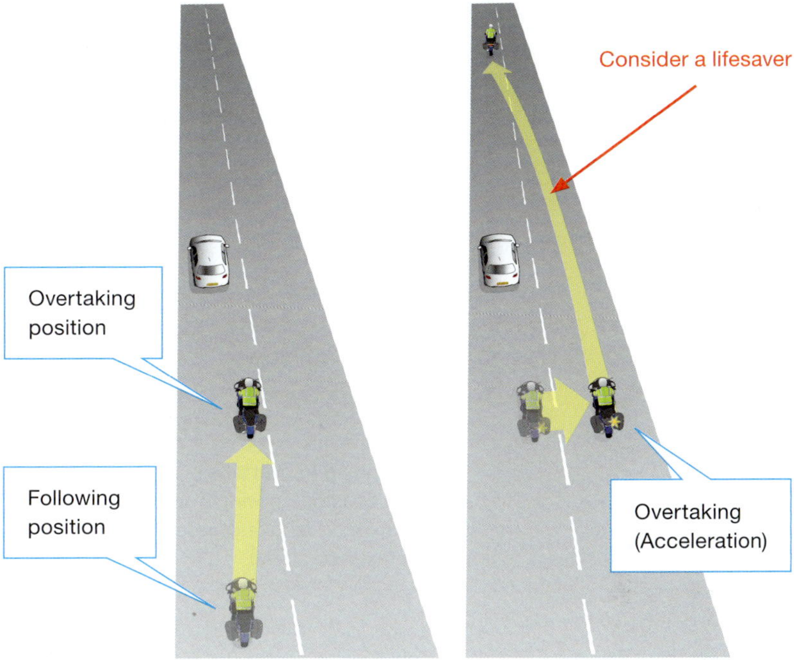

Overtaking vehicles in a line of traffic

Overtaking in a line of traffic is more difficult because it takes more time. You also have to take into account the possible actions of more drivers, both in front and behind. Drivers in front may not be aware that you're there or intend to overtake; drivers behind might try to overtake you. Always signal your intentions clearly to other road users.

Before you overtake, identify a clear gap between the vehicles in front that you can enter safely. This gap may get smaller before you arrive, so choose one that's large enough to allow for this. Don't overtake if you'll have to force your machine into a gap.

Consider moving out onto the other side of the road to give yourself a clearer view of the road ahead. Hold this position if you can see that the road ahead is clear, and if you can identify a clear return gap and have enough time to reach it. Allow for the possibility that the driver following you might move up into the gap that you have just left. When you reach the first return gap, you may not need to enter it. If it's safe, hold your position while you decide whether you can overtake more vehicles.

Apply the system. If there's more than one vehicle, you may wish to consider a series of overtakes as one manoeuvre. While you may be able to plan these as one manoeuvre, re-appraise each one separately as you approach the vehicle.

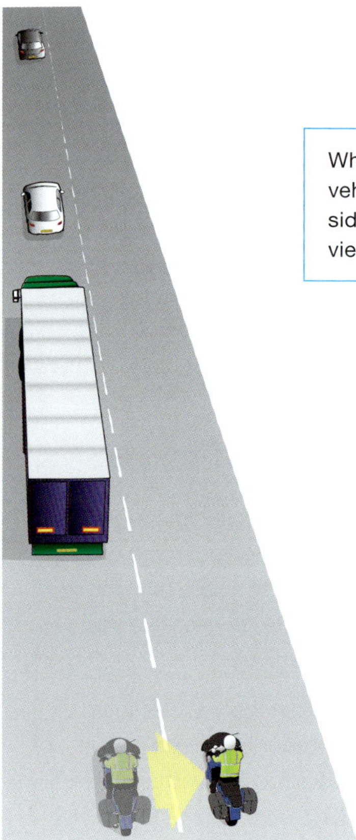

When planning to overtake in a stream of vehicles, consider moving out onto the other side of the road to give yourself a clearer view of the road ahead.

From the point of accelerating past the previous vehicle in the line, consider whether to continue or to return to a safe position in the line yourself. Each of these decisions is a separate application of the system.

Don't be tempted to increase your speed for each overtake in a line of traffic.

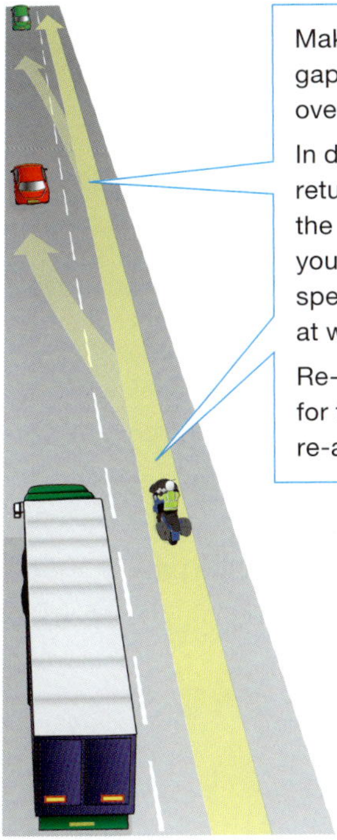

Make sure there's a safe gap ahead of the vehicle you overtake.

In deciding whether the return gap is safe, consider the effect on the road user you pull in front of and the speed you'll need to be riding at when you return.

Re-appraise the opportunities for further overtakes and re-apply the system.

Other overtaking situations

Overtaking on a single carriageway

This is perhaps the most hazardous form of overtaking because you potentially put your bike in the path of any oncoming vehicles – so plan this manoeuvre with great care. Remember that you can always reconsider your decision and hold back.

You need to be able to judge the speed and distance of oncoming vehicles accurately to assess whether you can reach the return gap before they do. This can be extremely difficult, especially on long, straight roads.

The size and type of the oncoming vehicle can give you clues about its possible speed.

As well as looking for vehicles, train yourself to look specifically for cyclists, pedestrians and horses before you overtake. Riders as well as drivers sometimes fail to spot an unexpected solo road user.

See Chapter 4, page 71, Drivers who look but fail to see you.

Next time you plan to overtake on a single carriageway road, review your decision-making. Ask yourself:

- Do I need to overtake?
- How will I assess the speed of any oncoming vehicles?
- Have I checked for pedestrians, cyclists or any other unexpected hazards?
- Will my overtaking manoeuvre put me in the path of oncoming vehicles?

Overtaking on bends

Overtaking on bends is potentially dangerous and you should always ensure that you have the available view to do this safely. In certain circumstances, it's possible to get a good clear view of the road through the bend before you enter it. If you're sure there are no other hazards, position yourself to overtake before the road straightens out. The diagrams that follow give some examples of how to consider making an overtake using this information.

Left-hand bends

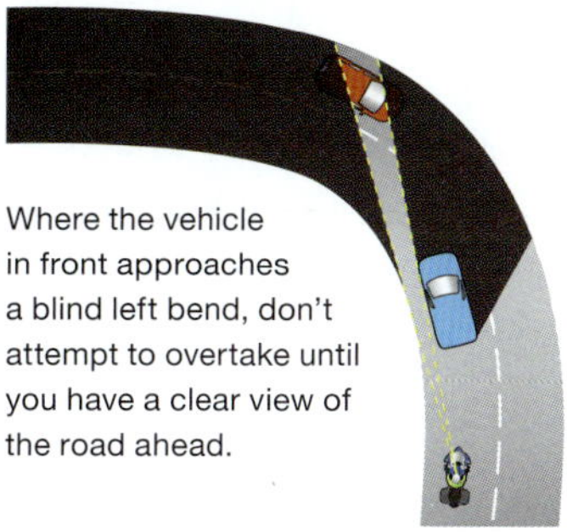

Where the vehicle in front approaches a blind left bend, don't attempt to overtake until you have a clear view of the road ahead.

Right-hand bends

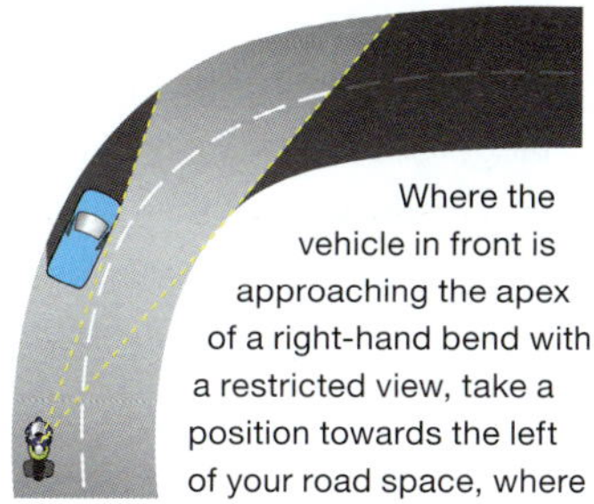

Where the vehicle in front is approaching the apex of a right-hand bend with a restricted view, take a position towards the left of your road space, where appropriate. But watch out for poor condition of the nearside road surface, adverse camber and blind junctions or exits.

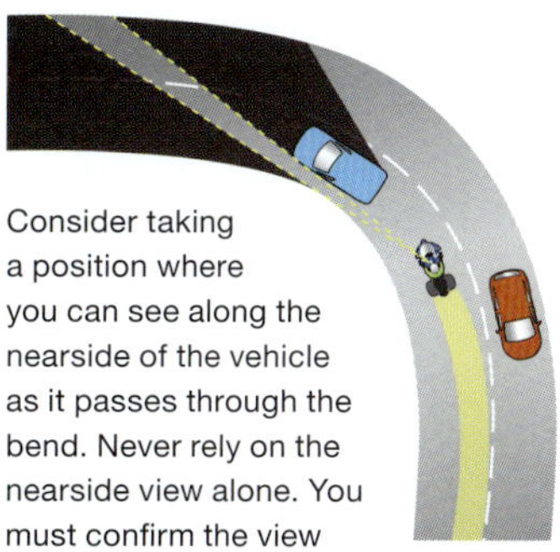

Consider taking a position where you can see along the nearside of the vehicle as it passes through the bend. Never rely on the nearside view alone. You must confirm the view along the offside before you start to overtake.

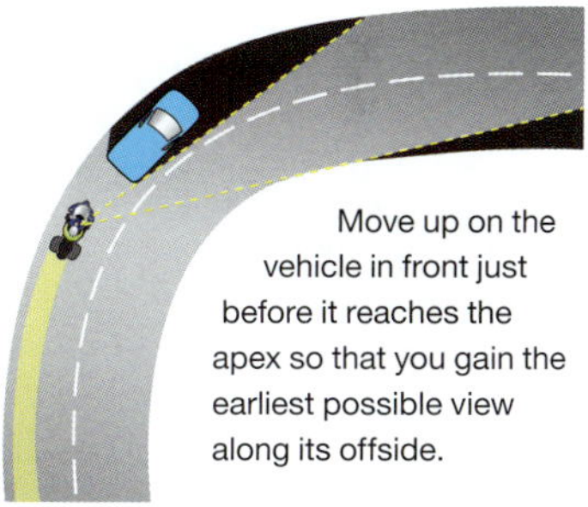

Move up on the vehicle in front just before it reaches the apex so that you gain the earliest possible view along its offside.

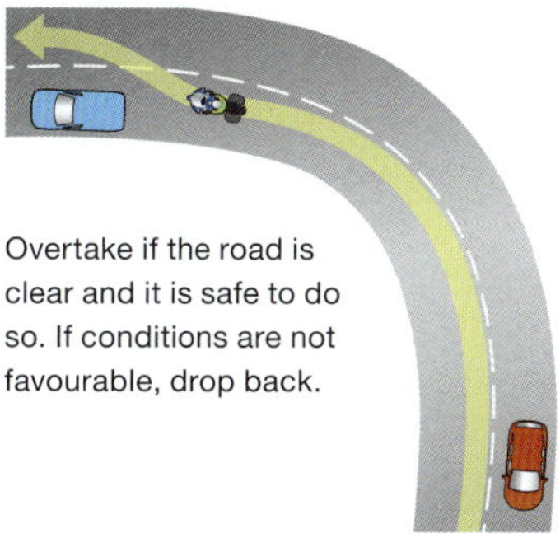

Overtake if the road is clear and it is safe to do so. If conditions are not favourable, drop back.

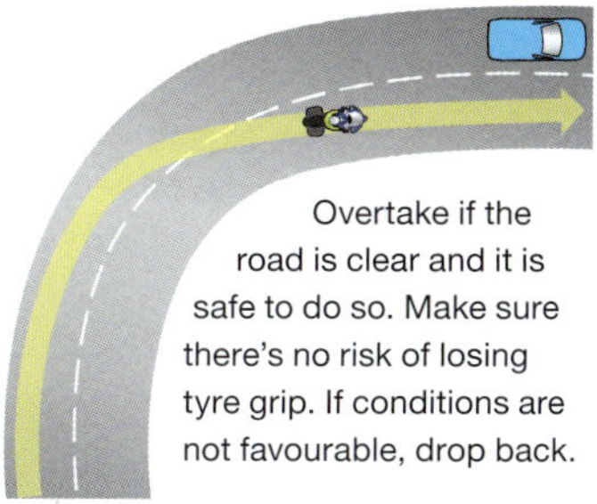

Overtake if the road is clear and it is safe to do so. Make sure there's no risk of losing tyre grip. If conditions are not favourable, drop back.

11

Overtaking on single carriageway roads marked with three lanes

Single carriageway roads marked with three lanes are potentially very dangerous as traffic in both directions shares the centre lane for overtaking. Never try to overtake if there's the possibility of an oncoming vehicle moving into the centre lane. Avoid overtaking when you would make a third line of moving vehicles, unless you're sure it's absolutely safe to do so.

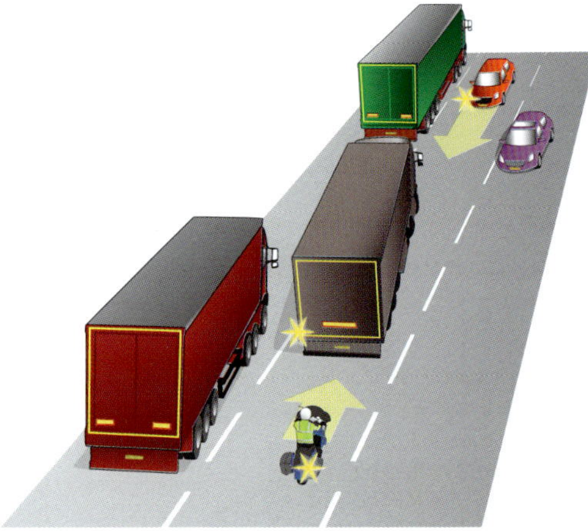

Don't be tempted to follow another vehicle through an apparently safe gap on a three-lane single carriageway. Always identify a safe return gap of your own. The vehicle in front may slip safely into a small return gap leaving you in the middle lane facing oncoming vehicles.

When you're planning to overtake, always look out for the 'lurker' who closes right up unseen behind other vehicles and then sweeps out to overtake.

Overtaking on multi-lane carriageways

On multi-lane carriageways, it can be more difficult to judge the speed of traffic approaching from behind.

Before overtaking, check the intentions of drivers in the nearside lanes. If a vehicle is closing up on the one in front, the driver may pull out without signalling or only signal after the vehicle starts to move out. Watch the distance between the wheels of the vehicle and the lane markings. If the gap narrows, the vehicle could be moving out. Follow these key principles:

- Leave yourself room for manoeuvre at all times; generally avoid overtaking three abreast. (This may be unavoidable if traffic is dense.)
- Overtake on the nearside only if traffic in all lanes is moving in queues.
- Take particular care when planning to overtake large vehicles at roundabout exits and on left-hand bends.
- On carriageways with three or more lanes, maintain your observation of the gaps between vehicles. A shortening gap may indicate a vehicle preparing to overtake into a lane closer to you.

See also Chapter 12, Riding on motorways and multi-lane carriageways.

Where a large vehicle such as a lorry or coach is blocking your view of lane 1, hold your position until you can see that lane 1 is clear ahead and the driver won't need to move out. Then continue with the overtaking manoeuvre.

Remember that when you overtake a large vehicle you may be buffeted by displaced air. In high winds you may suddenly encounter strong crosswinds as you move beyond the shelter of a large vehicle. In either situation, take a firmer hold on the handlebars as you pass, but keep your arms and body flexible and consider pushing weight through the foot pegs, so as to maintain balance and stability of the machine.

See Chapter 5, page 97, Anticipating the effects of windy weather.

Filtering

When traffic is stationary or moving in queues, motorcyclists can use their manoeuvrability and limited space requirements to make progress. The advantages of filtering along or between stopped or slow-moving traffic have to be weighed against the disadvantage of your increased vulnerability while filtering.

In some areas, motorcycles are permitted to use bus lanes. Here, the rider may not realise that the two cars in the main carriageway have slowed to allow the purple car to turn into the junction on the rider's left. The driver of the purple car cannot see clearly past the red and yellow cars and cannot see any buses approaching, so turns blind across the bus lane as the rider approaches.

Slow down where necessary when you travel in bus lanes to anticipate this common hazard.

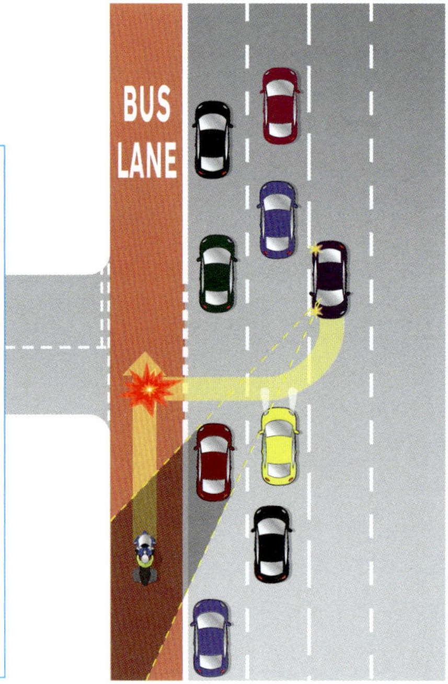

If you decide to filter:

- take extreme care
- watch out for debris, objects or loose gravel, especially on parts of the carriageway that aren't often used
- keep your speed low – you need to be able to stop suddenly if circumstances change
- always identify a place where you can rejoin the traffic flow before you move out
- make yourself visible – consider using a dipped headlight
- be ready to brake and/or use the horn
- use the opportunity to make progress but be courteous and avoid conflict with other road users.

Never use your hazard warning lights when filtering – this is illegal and causes confusion.

Don't use your main beam when filtering. If you feel you need to use your main beam, consider whether you should slow down.

Watch out for and anticipate:

- pedestrians crossing between vehicles
- vehicles emerging from junctions, which may be indicated by a gap in queuing traffic
- vehicles changing lanes or making U-turns without warning
- vehicle doors opening
- reflective paint and studs which could throw the bike off line
- traffic islands
- other bikes also filtering
- the tyres of a car turning in your direction.

When approaching two lanes of slow-moving traffic (for example, on a dual carriageway), anticipate:

- vehicles changing lanes
- vehicles jostling for position
- traffic joining the rear of the queue.

Be mindful of these possible hazards before joining the queue and filtering.

The range of hazards

Before overtaking, consider the full range of possible hazards that each situation presents. You've already considered the hazards presented by the vehicle in front and any vehicles behind, and the hazards associated with particular types of carriageway, but the road conditions and other road users present hazards too, for example:

- pedestrians
- cyclists and horses
- oncoming vehicles not yet in view
- the road layout and conditions
- the road surface.

You'll also need to note any relevant road signs, markings and speed limits before attempting to overtake.

Some of these hazards are discussed in more depth below.

Cyclists and horses

Although bicycles don't take up much road space, they have a tiny tyre contact area and may have limited tyre grip. They're inherently unstable – they get blown around both by weather and passing traffic and are susceptible to hazards on the road surface such as potholes. They also have limited braking capacity. Cyclists have little physical protection, usually have no mirrors, may be wearing earphones and may be untrained in riding safety.

When you overtake a pedal cycle:

- **Allow the cyclist space to manoeuvre** – at least 1.5 metres, but more if you're travelling at a high speed relative to the cycle.
- **Overtake only on the offside except in complex traffic systems** – and then only on the nearside, with care.
- **Don't overtake a cycle then turn in across its path** – the cycle has limited braking capability and this is inconsiderate in any case. Judge the cyclist's speed with care – it's easy to underestimate this.

At traffic lights with advanced stop lines for cycles, you may need to overtake shortly after starting off. The cyclist may be in the centre of the road and may weave as they pick up speed, so be prepared to give them additional space.

Allow horses plenty of room and avoid using warning equipment. Be prepared to stop if necessary. Speed or the sound of a horn can startle horses. The British Horse Society recommends that riders pass horses at no more than 10 mph and allow at least 2 metres of space when passing.

Road layout and conditions

When you plan to overtake, look for possible hazards in the layout of the road ahead. Watch out for nearside obstructions or junctions, including pathways, tracks, entrances and farm gates. Vehicles, pedestrians or animals could emerge from these, causing the vehicle(s) in front of you to veer towards the centre of the road. Look for right-hand junctions and entrances concealing vehicles or other hazards that could move out into your path.

Look for lay-bys on both sides of the road and watch out for vehicles pulling out of them. Drivers pulling out of a lay-by on the other side of the road may not see you because they're watching what's happening behind rather than in front of them. Try to position yourself so that drivers in nearside lay-bys can see you.

Assess the width of the road and look out for any features that could obscure your view, such as vegetation, bends, hidden dips, hill crests and hump bridges. There may be fast-moving vehicles approaching you on the sections of road you can't see.

Make sure you've observed the whole stretch of road necessary to complete the manoeuvre, and know that it doesn't include any other hazards. Look especially for hazards that might cause the vehicles you're overtaking to alter their position. Make full use of road signs and road markings, especially those giving instructions or warning you of hazards ahead.

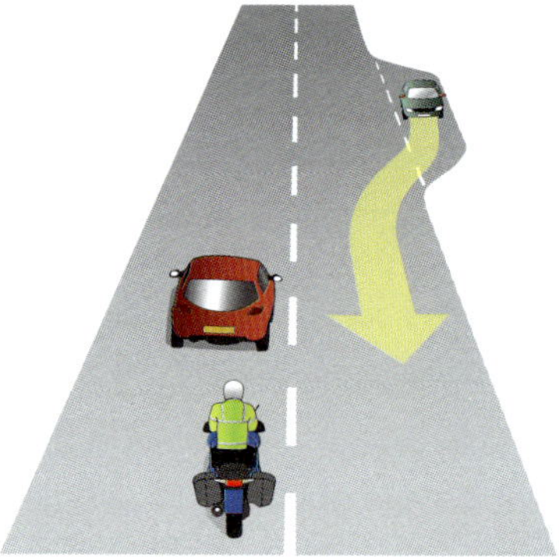

See Chapter 5, page 106, Road signs and markings.

The road surface

Before you overtake, position your motorcycle to avoid defects in the carriageway, road surface irregularities, debris and inspection covers, any of which may upset the handling of your machine. Watch out for surface water, which could cause a curtain of spray at a critical moment. Be aware that bad weather may affect your bike's road-holding and how well you can see the road.

See Chapter 5, Anticipating hazards in the riding environment, pages 94 and 99.

Human factors in overtaking

Overtaking is a particularly hazardous element of any riding task you may need to perform. Human factors affect not just you but also the other road users you encounter. The interaction between all those factors and the changing environment as you move along will influence your decision about whether to overtake.

Overtaking safely

What human factor risks should you consider? Ask yourself:

- What human factors might affect my ability to accurately perceive hazards before overtaking?
- How might human factors interfere with my ability to overtake safely (for example, 'red mist', noble cause risk-taking, thrill-seeking tendencies)?
- Does the specific purpose of the journey affect my decisions to overtake? Should it?

Helping other road users to overtake

Helping other road users to overtake eases tensions and contributes to a cooperative driving culture that increases safety. Use your mirrors and be alert to the intentions of road users behind you. If another rider or driver is overtaking you, try to make it easier by leaving enough distance between you and the vehicle in front to give them a safe return gap, but don't suddenly reduce speed to achieve this.

Be aware that other road users may try to overtake you when you keep to the legal speed limit. This is quite likely when you slow down to enter or as you're about to leave a lower speed limit area.

Overtaking: key safety points

- **Only overtake if you can see far enough ahead to be sure it's safe.**
- **Avoid causing other vehicles (overtaken, following or oncoming) to alter position or speed.**
- **Before you overtake, assess whether your machine is capable of the overtaking manoeuvre you're planning.**
- **Before starting to overtake, always ensure you can move back to the nearside in plenty of time.**
- **Always be ready to re-assess if a new hazard comes into view.**
- **Only overtake in situations where you won't come into conflict with other road users and it can be performed legally.**
- **When possible, avoid overtaking three abreast to leave yourself a margin of safety.**
- **Be aware of the potential dangers when filtering.**
- **On multi-lane carriageways, only overtake on the nearside if there are slow-moving queues of traffic and offside queues are moving more slowly.**
- **Never use the hard shoulder for overtaking.**
- **Consider signalling if it will benefit any other road user. Make sure that your signal is clear and can't be misinterpreted.**
- **Always be patient and leave a margin of safety to allow for errors.**

Check your understanding

You should now be able to apply learning from this chapter in your rider training so that you can:

- ☐ explain the risks of overtaking
- ☐ show how to use the following and overtaking positions safely
- ☐ show how to assess and overtake different types of hazards safely in a wide range of circumstances
- ☐ explain how to help other road users to overtake you.

Chapter 12

Riding on motorways and multi-lane carriageways

Learning outcomes

The learning in this chapter, along with rider training, should enable you to:

- show that you can join and leave a motorway or multi-lane carriageway correctly
- show that you can use the appropriate lane for traffic conditions
- show that you can safely adapt your position and speed for overtaking, motorway junctions and other hazards, including weather conditions
- demonstrate correct use of the hard shoulder
- explain the human factor risks in motorway riding and show how you manage these.

Riding on multi-lane carriageways

Safe riding on motorways and other fast-moving multi-lane carriageways depends on developing your awareness of the extra hazards that arise on these roads and rigorously applying to them the riding competences and methods explained in *Motorcycle Roadcraft*.

Despite the higher speeds and volume of motorway traffic, there are fewer collisions on motorways for each mile travelled than on other roads. But motorway collisions are more likely to be fatal because of the high speeds involved.

However, other fast-moving multi-lane roads such as dual carriageways combine traffic moving at equally high speed with additional hazards such as junctions to right and left, roundabouts, slow-moving vehicles and the absence of a hard shoulder.

See page 265, Additional hazards on fast-moving multi-lane carriageways.

Much of this chapter applies to all multi-lane carriageways, but motorways have specific features that you'll need to take into account:

- slip roads for entering and leaving the motorway (not always present on other multi-lane carriageways)
- dangers created by the presence of the hard shoulder
- dangers created by the absence of a hard shoulder on some motorways, which means that there could be stranded vehicles on the carriageway or vehicles pulling into or out of emergency refuge areas
- legal restrictions on which types of vehicle can use motorways, and the lane restrictions and speed limits for each type.

It takes time to develop accuracy in assessing speeds and stopping distances in a fast-moving riding environment. Always ride well within your own competence and aim to steadily develop your experience so that you're comfortable and confident within your existing speed range before moving on to higher speeds. Plan how you're going to address the fast-moving traffic conditions before you start your journey. Always take into account the size and limitations of your machine.

ECO Remember that higher speeds on fast-moving roads burn more fuel. Smooth acceleration and braking reduce fuel consumption.

See Appendix 3, Fuel-efficient riding, page 298.

Layout of the carriageway

Here we use the numbering system used by the police and other emergency services to refer to the lanes on motorways and other multilane carriageways.

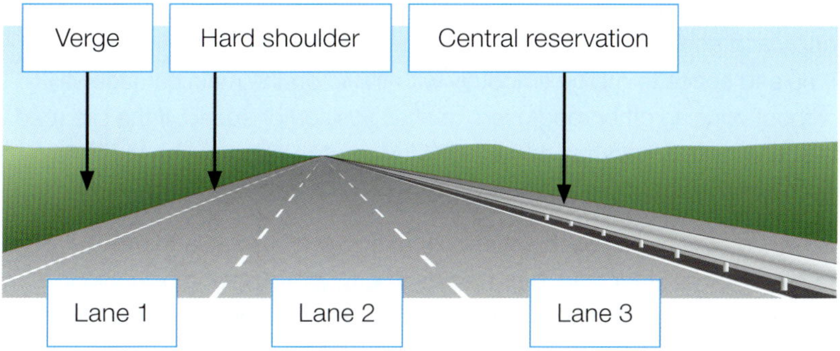

The nearside lane is lane 1, the next is lane 2 and so on. On a traditional three-lane motorway, lane 1 is the lane next to the hard shoulder and lane 3 is the lane next to the central reservation. The hard shoulder isn't counted as a carriageway lane.

See page 258, Using the hard shoulder.

New motorway layouts

An increasing proportion of the motorway network (smart motorways) uses technology to monitor and manage flow from regional centres. In addition to traditional motorways, there are two newer types of motorway:

- All lane running (ALR) – the full width of the road is available to drivers, with emergency refuge areas at intervals.
- Controlled motorways – with three or more lanes, a hard shoulder and variable speed limits.

Joining the motorway

Joining the motorway at a slip road or where motorways merge is potentially hazardous; you should use the system of motorcycle control to approach and join. Slip roads are designed to give drivers and riders the time and space to merge smoothly with traffic on the main carriageway without causing other road users to alter position or speed. If the slip road is raised, take advantage of the high viewpoint to observe the traffic flow and to plan your approach.

Drivers on the motorway have priority and may not be able to move over to allow you to enter lane 1, but looking early, planning and using your acceleration sense will assist you in merging safely. Only poor planning or exceptionally heavy traffic should cause you to stop in the slip road.

Slip roads have one or more lanes. If you're travelling in the outside lane of the slip road, consider how your speed and position will affect vehicles in the inside lane. If you overtake a vehicle on your nearside just before you join the motorway, you could block its path on to the motorway. You risk colliding with it if you can't move straight into lane 2 of the motorway.

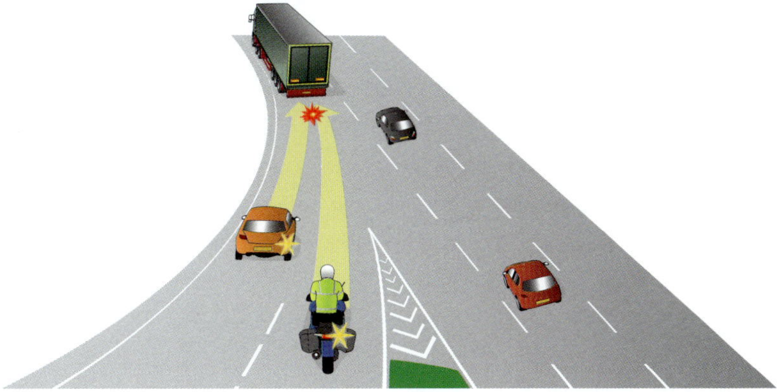

Do not overtake a vehicle that is on the inside lane of the slip road if you will block its path on to the motorway.

Use the system

As you enter the motorway, process information about the traffic on the slip road and motorway so that you're in the correct position, at the correct speed and in the correct gear to accelerate onto the motorway smoothly and safely.

Signalling

Well before you enter lane 1, decide whether you need to signal to let motorists on the motorway know that you intend to join the traffic flow.

Before you join the motorway, check over your shoulder to make sure there's nothing in your blind spot. Good use of your mirrors will allow you to keep the time spent doing this to a minimum.

Acceleration

Allow yourself time to adjust to the higher motorway speed and to gauge the speeds of other vehicles.

Riding on the motorway

Good observation is key to safe motorway riding. Due to the speeds involved, it's vital to extend your observation:

- look ahead and behind you all the way up to the road horizons
- scan ahead, to the sides and to the rear frequently and thoroughly
- use your mirrors regularly – you should always know what's happening behind you
- be aware of your own and other road users' blind spots and be prepared to move your body and alter machine position to observe what's happening in those areas
- monitor what's happening to your machine – regularly check that the instruments are giving normal readings and listen to the sound of your engine and to the noise of the tyres on the road surface
- check your speed regularly – it's very easy to increase speed without realising
- be especially alert around junctions – traffic patterns change rapidly in these areas.

On your next motorway journey, practise extending your observation.

Make a point of scanning as far as the road horizon, front and back. Use rear observation frequently. Regularly scan to the sides as well.

Aim to give yourself the longest possible time in which to react. Active scanning helps enhance your level of awareness, which in turn increases your overall safety.

Adapting to higher speeds

At 70 mph, you travel 31 metres (102 feet, about three coach lengths) per second. To give yourself as much time to react as possible:

- extend your observations in all directions and to the road horizons
- anticipate early and maintain a safe following distance – in good weather the two-second rule is a good guide but in bad weather you must allow a much greater distance
- use all controls smoothly, particularly steering, when travelling at high speed
- give other drivers enough time to see your signals before making a manoeuvre
- wind and engine noise can drown the sound of your horn at high speeds, so consider using your headlight as an alternative if it's necessary to alert other road users to your presence.

Remember that drivers travelling at high speed may fail to see you in the distance and so pull out in front of you.

Lane discipline

You need good lane discipline for safe motorway riding. There are no slow or fast lanes. Overtake only to the right, except when traffic is moving in queues and the queue on your right is moving more slowly than you are.

Don't overtake by using a lane to your left.

Overtaking

Before you overtake, watch out for:

- slower vehicles moving out in front of you
- faster vehicles coming up behind you.

Apply the system of motorcycle control to overtake safely on motorways and other multi-lane carriageways, paying special attention to taking, using and giving information.

Taking information

Scan regularly so that you're continually aware of what the surrounding traffic is doing. You should know which vehicles are closing up on other vehicles in front, and which vehicles are moving up behind. Constantly monitor opportunities to overtake and match your speed of approach to coincide with an opportunity. Make allowances for the additional hazards presented by lane closures and motorway junctions.

Look for early warnings that other vehicles intend to overtake:

- relative speeds
- head movements
- body movements
- vehicle movement from the centre of the lane towards the white lane markers.

You're likely to see all these before the driver signals: many drivers only signal as they start to change lanes.

Over a motorway journey of reasonable length (say 20 miles), practise spotting the warning signs described above to predict when other vehicles are about to change lanes.

Use this anticipation to help your planning.

Think carefully before overtaking on left-hand bends where there are mainly heavy goods or large vehicles in lanes 1 and 2. A car may be hidden between the heavy goods vehicles and be about to pull out into lane 3. Make sure you can stop safely within the distance you can see to be clear. Don't attempt to overtake unless you're sure you can see all the vehicles in lane 2.

The rider is about to move out to overtake. The rider checks the mirror but cannot see the fast-closing car in lane 3. The driver in lane 3 cannot see the rider about to pull out.

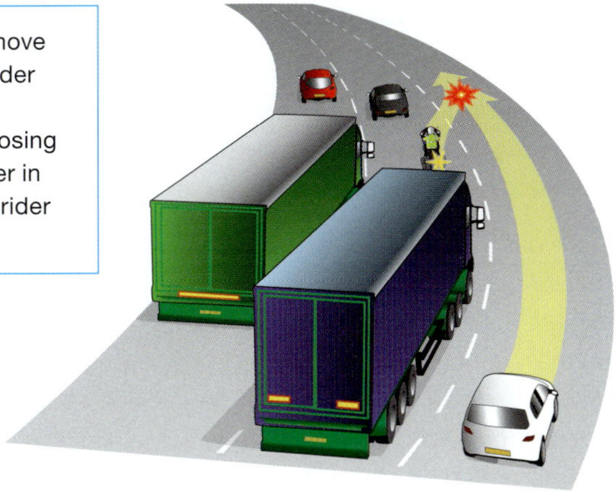

Just before you overtake, carefully check the position and speed of the vehicles behind. For example, before you move into lane 2 to overtake a vehicle in lane 1, check there are no fast-closing vehicles moving back into lane 2 from lane 3.

As you move from lane 1 to lane 2, beware of vehicles moving up behind you into lane 2 from lane 3.

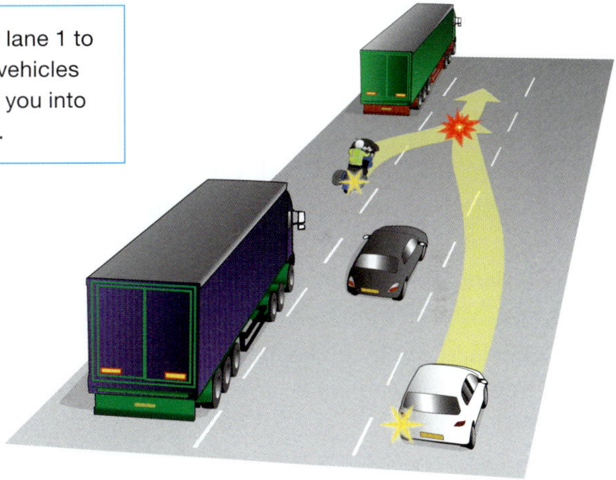

Move your head to increase your view either side of your blind spot. Re-check the position and speed of vehicles to the front and then consider the information that you need to give to the surrounding traffic. Be aware of being buffeted by air displaced by high-sided vehicles.

Giving information

Don't sit in the blind spot of a vehicle you're trying to overtake. Aim to move rapidly through a driver's blind spot or don't enter it if you can't see or move beyond it. If you find yourself in a driver's blind spot and are unable to overtake, drop back so that you're visible to the driver.

Consider alerting other road users to your presence, especially if you're travelling at speed. If you decide a headlight flash would be helpful, give it in plenty of time for the other person to react. Give a single flash: decide on the length of flash according to your speed and the response of other drivers. Take care not to appear aggressive to other road users, and avoid dazzling oncoming drivers. Be aware that flashing your headlight could be misinterpreted by others as an invitation to move out in front of you.

Indicator signals

Consider indicating before changing lanes. Let the indicator flash long enough for other vehicles to see and react to it.

When you've passed the vehicle or vehicles in front, return to the appropriate lane when you see an opportunity. But don't keep weaving in and out.

Leaving yourself room to manoeuvre

If you're travelling in lane 2 and traffic in your lane ahead has come to a standstill, slow down so you approach the queue less quickly. If traffic is flowing freely in lane 1, there's a particular danger from left-hand-drive lorries approaching from behind and pulling into lane 2 to overtake the lorry ahead.

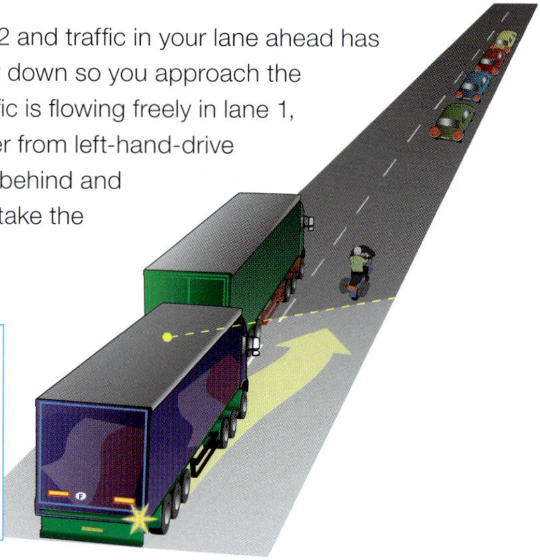

The sight line from the left-hand-drive lorry means the driver will not see your bike until almost totally out into your lane.

Being overtaken

Anticipate what the drivers behind you intend to do by their lane position and their speed of approach. This will help you to avoid potentially dangerous situations. As the other vehicle overtakes you, be aware that you're in the overtaking driver's blind spot.

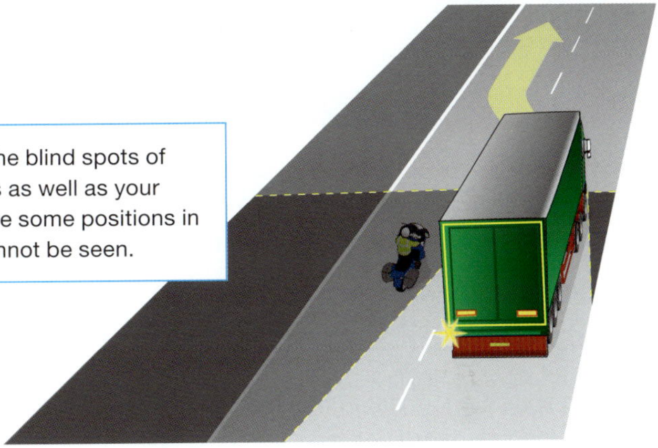

Be aware of the blind spots of other vehicles as well as your own. There are some positions in which you cannot be seen.

Motorway junctions

At junctions and service areas, you're likely to meet variations in traffic speed and more vehicles changing lanes. Watch for drivers who only change lanes for an exit at the last minute. When you see a motorway exit, anticipate a slip road ahead and the possibility of traffic joining the motorway.

If you're on the main carriageway, check your mirrors early and allow traffic to join the motorway by making slight adjustments to your speed or changing lane. Vehicles on the motorway have right of way, so don't do this if it would force other vehicles to change their speed or position.

Watch out for fuel spilled on the road surface at motorway junctions from large goods vehicles. Large goods vehicle drivers who fill their tanks at the services may then spill excess fuel as they accelerate firmly to join the motorway.

Using the hard shoulder

The hard shoulder forms part of a motorway; on a traditional motorway it's intended for emergency use only. It must only be used in accordance with the *Highway Code* and, for emergency services riders, the most recent professional guidelines. Stopping on the hard shoulder is dangerous both for the rider and for other motorway users because there's a high risk of collision. Never use the hard shoulder for overtaking.

On stretches of smart motorway, you may find that the hard shoulder is being used permanently as a running lane; that is, 'all lanes running' (ALR), or as an additional lane during periods of congestion. In these conditions, be extra vigilant and watch out for stationary vehicles in any of the live lanes. Also look out for vehicles pulling into or out of emergency refuge areas, spaced at regular intervals along the carriageway and marked by blue signs with an orange SOS telephone symbol.

Entering or leaving the hard shoulder

When you move onto the hard shoulder, or into an emergency refuge area, be aware that the road surface may contain loose gravel and other debris, which could reduce the available grip for stopping. Look out for debris such as screws, nails and other sharp objects that could damage your tyres when you enter or leave the hard shoulder.

When you leave the hard shoulder or an emergency refuge area, carefully observe the traffic approaching from behind. Depending on the volume of traffic, choose an appropriate moment to move off. If you're leaving the hard shoulder, build up your speed to match the speed of vehicles in lane 1 **before** you move on to lane 1 of the carriageway.

Leaving the motorway

Plan your exit. Make sure you know your exit junction well in advance. Assess the road and traffic conditions as you approach the junction and use the information provided by road signs and markings.

The diagram shows a typical sequence of information given at motorway exits. Note that some motorways have signs at different points, so always read distance marker signs carefully.

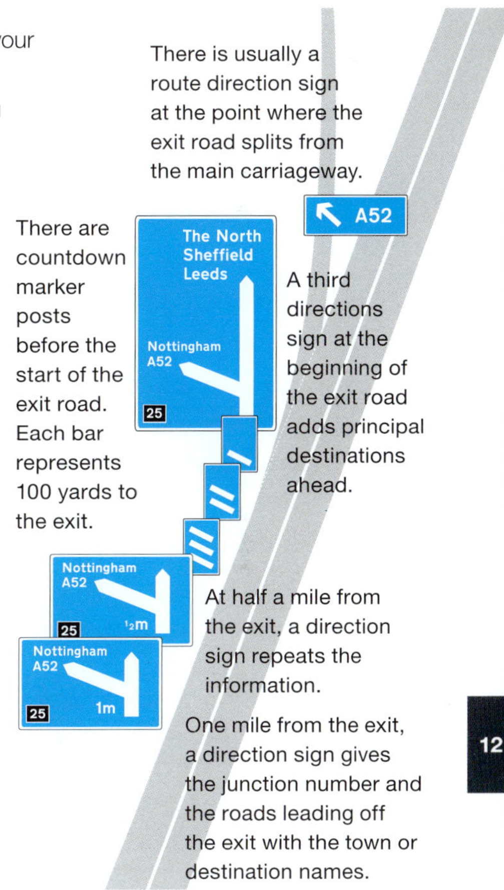

As you approach your exit junction, look for the advance direction signs and use the system of motorcycle control to plan and carry out your exit. If the motorway is busy, consider joining lane 1 earlier rather than later. If a signal is necessary, always allow plenty of time for other drivers to react. Indicate at the 300-yard countdown marker. If your machine has self-cancelling indicators, monitor them to make sure they don't switch off too soon.

Avoid braking on the main carriageway if possible. Plan to lose unwanted speed in the exit road – which acts as a deceleration lane – and well before you reach the junction at the end of the exit road. But be aware that other road users may not do this and may start to slow down before reaching the exit road. On busy motorways, watch out for vehicles leaving the motorway at the last minute from lanes 2 or 3 and cutting across your path.

Riding at high speed affects your perception of speed when you leave the motorway:

- check your speedometer regularly to help you adjust to the slower speeds of ordinary roads
- plan for the point at which you'll meet two-way traffic
- be ready for acute bends at the end of motorway exit roads
- watch out for oil or other deposits which can make these areas exceptionally slippery.

Bad weather conditions on fast-moving roads

Chapter 5 explains how weather conditions affect your ability to observe and anticipate. This section looks at planning for bad weather conditions at higher speeds.

See Chapter 5, page 94, Weather conditions.

Bad weather reduces visibility and tyre grip, so it's more dangerous at high speed because you need a much greater overall safe stopping distance.

You should always be able to stop safely in the distance you can see to be clear on your own side of the road.

Do not rely on auto lighting systems. Consider manually switching on your dipped-beam headlight. When you can't see clearly, reduce your speed and consider using your dipped headlight. You must use it if visibility drops below 100 metres (328 feet). The gap between motorway marker posts is about 100 metres so use these to assess how far you can see.

Fog

Fog reduces your perception of speed due to the lack of visual reference points. In poor visibility, some drivers may reduce their following distance in order to keep the vehicle lights ahead in view. Be aware also that not all vehicles will be displaying the appropriate lights.

Fog reduces your perception of speed and risk because you can't see. At the same time, it encourages you to ride close enough to keep in sight the vehicle lights ahead.

Adjust your speed to ensure that you can stop within the range of visibility. The denser the fog, the slower your speed. Riding in fog can be very tiring and stressful. If you start to feel tired, take a break at the next available rest area.

Rain

High speed increases the risk created by rain and standing water on the road surface. This is because your bike's tyres have to displace water more quickly. If they're unable to do this, a wedge of water will form between the tyres and the road, resulting in aquaplaning. During such conditions, remain vigilant to the possibility of unexpected sections of deep water and adjust your speed on the approach.

See Chapter 8, page 185, Aquaplaning, for further advice.

During and after rain, heavy spray from large vehicles travelling fast may restrict your visibility. Consider using a dipped headlight and, if it's safe to do so, overtake in the lane furthest away.

See Chapter 5, page 95, Riding in bad weather.

After a long, hot, dry spell, a deposit of tyre and other dust builds up on the road surface. These deposits create a slippery surface especially during and after rain. Avoid heavy braking, steering or accelerating or you could lose tyre grip.

Snow, sleet and ice

If there's snow, sleet or ice on the motorway, always ask yourself: 'Is a motorcycle journey really necessary?'

Snow and sleet reduce visibility and tyre grip. At speed, spray thrown up by the wheels of the vehicle in front reduces visibility further, and stability problems may arise when ruts develop in the snow. Often stability can be maintained only by travelling at walking pace with both feet ready to support the bike.

Reduce speed and increase following distances in icy conditions, especially if the road surface isn't gritted.

High winds

Sections of carriageway that are raised above the surrounding countryside are affected by high winds. Be prepared for particularly strong gusts of wind as you leave a cutting, enter or emerge from under a bridge, cross a valley or go into open country. Take particular care on viaducts and bridges.

In windy conditions, high-sided vehicles can suddenly veer; they also tend to act as wind breaks buffeting smaller vehicles and motorcycles as they draw past them. Keep a firm grip on the handlebars with both hands.

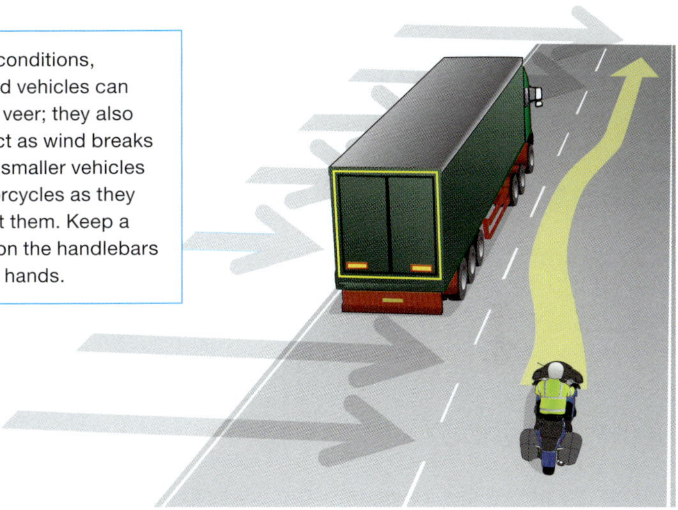

High-sided vehicles displace air, which tends to pull smaller vehicles and motorcycles towards them during overtaking. As the smaller vehicle moves in front, it breaks free of the suction and tends to veer out. Correct this with a firm grip on the handlebars and consider leaning the machine into the wind and pushing weight through the foot pegs to compensate for the sideways force.

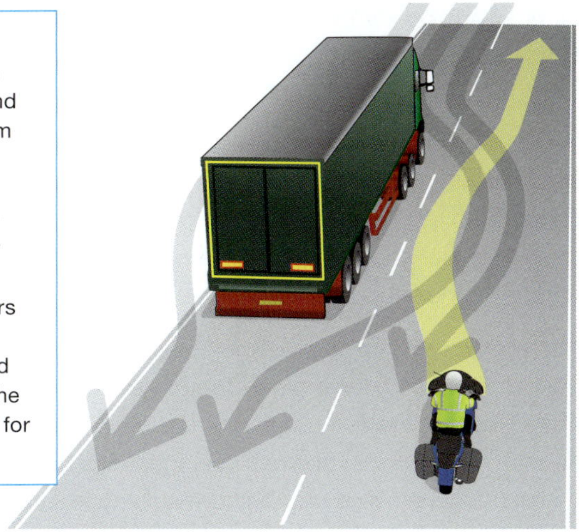

Bright sun

Bright sun low in the sky can cause serious dazzle, especially on east/west sections of road. If the sun is shining in your mirrors, adjust them to give you the best visibility with minimum glare. If you're dazzled by bright sun, other road users may be too, so allow for this when overtaking.

Other hazards

Debris

Regularly scan the road surface for debris that may have fallen from vehicles. This can damage tyres and cause other vehicles to suddenly alter position.

Lane closures

Roadworks are a regular feature of motorway journeys. Contraflow systems aren't dangerous in themselves but become dangerous when road users ignore advance warnings. All roadworks are signed on approach and you should know the sequence of signs. Keep to the mandatory speed limits through roadworks, even when conditions seem to be suitable for a higher speed.

Merging with other traffic requires judgement and courtesy. It's sensible for vehicles from each lane to merge alternately. But these situations often create conflict and result in collisions. Allow a reasonable following gap and never close up to prevent other vehicles merging.

Matrix signs and signals warn of lane closures or other changes in riding conditions ahead. On a smart motorway, look out for a red X or reduced speed limit on the overhead gantries. You may not immediately be able to see the need to slow down or change lanes but don't assume the sign is a mistake. The incident may be some distance further along the motorway.

Additional hazards on fast-moving multi-lane carriageways

On multi-lane carriageways, you need to watch out for a range of additional hazards that aren't present on motorways:

- slow-moving traffic
- traffic lights
- roundabouts
- right-hand junctions
- crossroads
- traffic moving into the right-hand lane to turn right
- traffic entering the carriageway from the central reservation
- traffic crossing the carriageway
- pedestrians crossing the carriageway
- entrances and exits other than road junctions (for example, to services, petrol stations, restaurants, pubs)
- left-hand junctions with only a short (or no) slip road
- public footpath crossing the carriageway – indicated by an overlap in the central reservation safety barrier.

Human factors in motorway riding

The nature of motorway riding increases a number of human factor risks:

- tiredness or boredom on long journeys, resulting in poor concentration – fatigue is more likely if you're wet or cold
- frustration arising out of stop–start progress in dense traffic

- complacency in low-density traffic making riders less alert to possible hazards
- the behaviour of drivers leaving or joining the motorway from service stations or slip roads.

Stop at the earliest opportunity if you find yourself unable to maintain the high level of concentration needed to ride safely at high speed.

Ask yourself whether your physical state and degree of alertness is optimal for motorway riding before you set off.

Do you have appropriate clothing for the weather conditions?

Have you ever found your concentration flagging on a motorway journey? What do you do to increase your alertness?

Is your approach always effective? How could you manage your fatigue better?

How do feelings of stress affect your motorway riding? Think about whether your brain can deal with the distraction from stress as well as ride safely.

How might dealing with difficult or demanding motorway situations increase your mental workload?

What can you do to reduce the risk of errors and increase your safety in these situations?

See Chapter 1, Becoming a better rider, and Chapter 4, Information, observation and anticipation.

Check your understanding

You should now be able to apply learning from this chapter in your rider training so that you can:

- ☐ show that you can join and leave a motorway or multi-lane carriageway correctly
- ☐ show that you can use the appropriate lane for traffic conditions
- ☐ show that you can safely adapt your position and speed for overtaking, motorway junctions and other hazards, including weather conditions
- ☐ demonstrate correct use of the hard shoulder
- ☐ explain the human factor risks in motorway riding and show how you manage these.

Chapter 13
Emergency response

Learning outcomes

The learning in this chapter, along with rider training, should enable you to:

- list the exemptions in law available to emergency response riders and explain their implications for your riding plan
- explain the importance of going through a process of risk assessment before and during an emergency call
- demonstrate the correct use of your machine's emergency warning equipment
- demonstrate good practice in emergency response riding across a range of traffic situations.

What is an emergency response?

Officers are deemed to be in an emergency response when they're using emergency warning equipment to facilitate progress, at which time they may make use of exemptions afforded to them by legislation.

Drivers who are trained to nationally agreed police driver training programme standards are entitled to make use of legal exemptions. However, it's essential that these are appropriate and used only in circumstances that can be justified. There's no legal definition of what would or would not constitute justification for making use of police exemptions.

Officers who hold a basic driving authority aren't permitted to take advantage of any legal exemptions.

The Road Traffic Regulation Act 1984 and The Traffic Signs Regulations and General Directions 2016 exempt emergency vehicles from:

- observing speed limits
- observing keep left/right signs
- complying with traffic lights (including pedestrian-controlled crossings).

Other exemptions are available under local Traffic Regulation Orders. These will be covered by your instructor.

Use of any of these exemptions must be safe and proportionate to the prevailing circumstances. Remember that you're more vulnerable when you're on response.

Be aware that some motorists over-react or react unpredictably when they encounter emergency response vehicles, for example, by stopping their vehicle in an unsuitable place such as next to traffic islands, on blind hill crests, on the apex of bends or opposite an oncoming vehicle that has also stopped. At busy junctions, motorists are likely to take more time to react to the presence of emergency response vehicles.

Using the national decision model

To help emergency response drivers make decisions and to provide a framework in which decisions can be examined and challenged, both at the time and afterwards, the police service has adopted a national decision model (NDM).

At its centre is the Code of Ethics, the touchstone for all decision-making. Using the model encourages you to act in accordance with the Code and use your discretion where appropriate. It also reduces risk aversion and weighs the balance of resourcing against demand, threat and risk.

See www.college.police.uk/app/national-decision-model/national-decision-model

Risk assessment

Before you begin your response to an emergency call, you should go through a process of risk assessment.

Here are some of the questions you need to ask yourself:

- Does the situation necessitate an emergency response?
- What human factors might increase my risk on response (for example, stress, operational distractions, peer pressure)? How do I manage these effectively?
- Is my machine suitable?
- Am I justified in making use of traffic law exemptions?
- How far will I have to travel?
- Are other units closer?
- Do I need to use lights and sirens?
- What speed is safe and proportionate for the circumstances, including traffic, time of day, lighting, and weather?

An emergency call is an ever-changing environment so continue with this process of risk assessment throughout the response.

While incidents are graded in line with national requirements, as set out in the National Call Handling Standards, riders responding to calls are responsible for assessing the response required. You must decide if the use of legal exemptions and/or the bike's emergency equipment is warranted and you may be called upon to justify your actions at a later stage.

Responding to an emergency

Use of emergency warning equipment

The emergency warning equipment is primarily used to:

- provide advance warning to other road users
- help your progress through traffic
- protect officers at the scene of incidents
- help in stopping motorists, by identifying your machine as a police motorcycle.

Most drivers seeing or hearing the warning of an approaching emergency service motorcycle will try to give way but the use of warning equipment doesn't give you protection or right of way. You may take advantage if other road users and pedestrians give way to you – but only if it's safe to do so. Bear in mind that unwarranted use of emergency warning equipment can undermine its value.

Never assume that your warning will be seen or heard by other road users.

Sirens

Assess when and where to activate your emergency equipment. In normal circumstances, you should activate your emergency lights before using your sirens.

Think carefully before activating your sirens if you're close to other road users, particularly cyclists, pedestrians or animals.

If, in the light of your risk assessment, you decide not to use your emergency warning equipment ('silent approach'), take extra care because other road users may be less aware of your presence.

When using sirens, it's often not noise but a *change* in noise that gets a reaction. It's appropriate to use a long tone between hazards. But changing to a short tone on the approach to a hazard is likely to maximise the benefit of the warning.

Use a different tone to other emergency vehicles when travelling in a multi-vehicle response. The public may see one vehicle, but they may not expect a second or third.

Consider switching off the sound system in stationary traffic. This often takes the tension out of the situation and gives others time to consider what they might do to help.

Headlamp flashers

The automatic headlamp flashers on most emergency vehicles use an alternating flash pattern. This makes it more likely that the vehicle will be seen but also increases the possibility of dazzling other road users.

Automatic headlamp flashers *must not* be used during the hours of darkness.

Blue lights

Strobe lights are particularly effective on multi-lane roads such as motorways, but predominantly show to front or rear. Light-emitting diode (LED) lights do not rotate.

Speed limits

Police riders can use statutory exemptions from speed limits but you must be able to stop within the distance you can see to be clear on your own side of the road. During an emergency response, never compromise safety in order to save time. It is far better to arrive later than not at all.

Keep in mind that members of the public will observe you if you exceed the speed limit or use an inappropriate speed. Inappropriate speed or misuse of exemptions is likely to result in negative public perceptions of response riding.

The following scenario shows why you always need to correctly assess the appropriate speed. The police motorcycle is approaching at 30 mph the rear of a parked lorry which is 9 metres (30 feet) long. As the bike passes the rear of the lorry, a pedestrian steps out from in front of the lorry directly into its path.

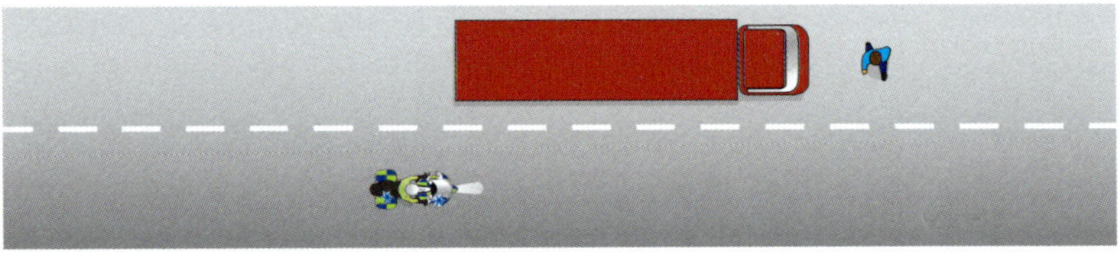

By the time the rider starts braking, the bike will have struck the pedestrian.

Approaching traffic light-controlled junctions

When you pass red signals, you should treat them as STOP and/or GIVE WAY signs. Don't proceed until you're sure that the way is clear, that no other road user will be endangered and that no other road user will be forced to change speed or course to avoid a collision.

When you approach traffic lights, gather information about the road layout and consider the movements of other road users – both those you can see and those you can't.

Your risk assessment must include not only the red phase but also the green phase. This is important. Your speed of approach must enable you to stop if necessary – for example, if the traffic light signals change from green to red, or if another emergency vehicle going to the same incident is using their exemption and entering the junction through a red light.

On the approach to traffic lights, take a position to ensure the best view. Select the least obstructed path with due regard to safety and making yourself as visible as possible to other road users.

Assess the position and movement of all traffic on the approach. When it's safe to do so, move forward at a speed that will allow you to maintain good observation and the ability to stop. Look out especially for the presence of cyclists who are vulnerable and difficult to see among other vehicles.

If your entry speed into the junction is too high other road users may over-react and brake sharply. This could result in a 'shunt' type collision.

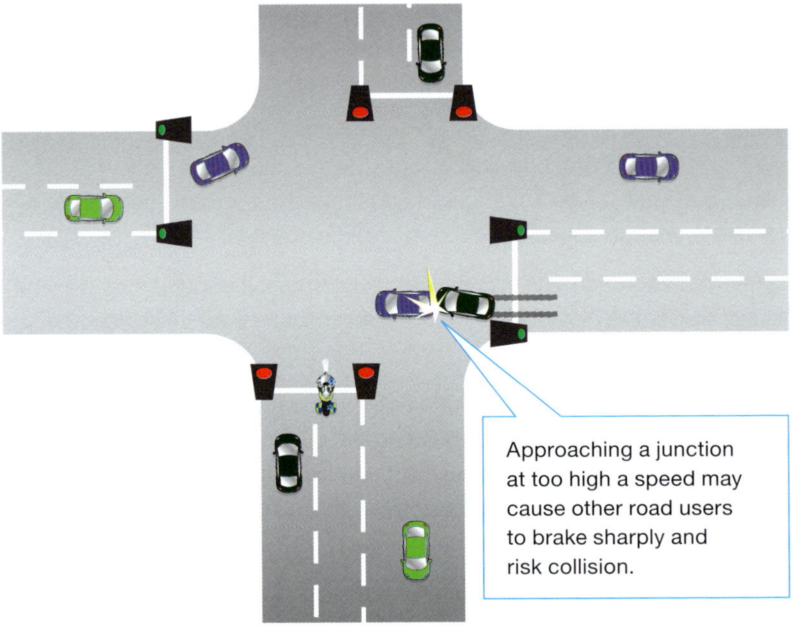

Police riders exercising the exemption to pass a red traffic light must avoid causing a member of the public to contravene the red light.

If vehicles are occupying all the entry lanes at the stop line on your approach to a set of red lights, consider one of the following options:

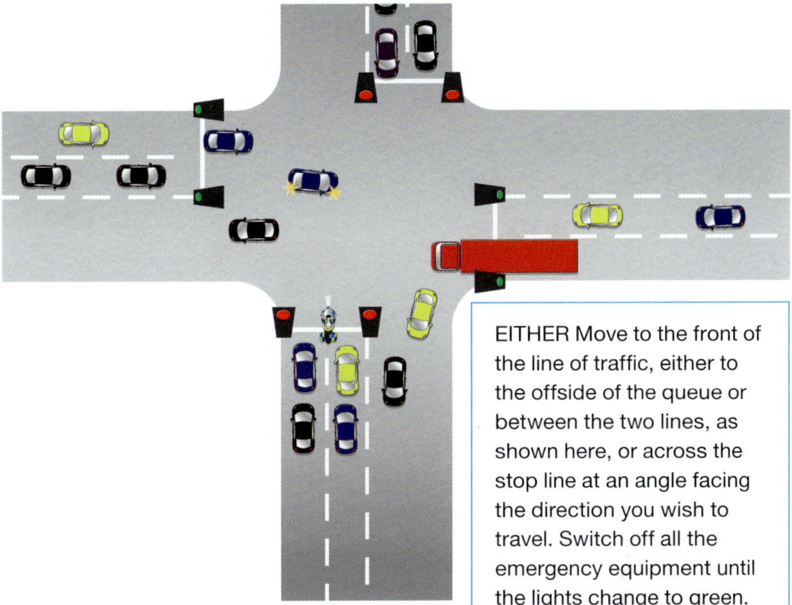

EITHER Move to the front of the line of traffic, either to the offside of the queue or between the two lines, as shown here, or across the stop line at an angle facing the direction you wish to travel. Switch off all the emergency equipment until the lights change to green. (It is unsafe to contravene a red light at a junction where the cross traffic is moving at high speed.)

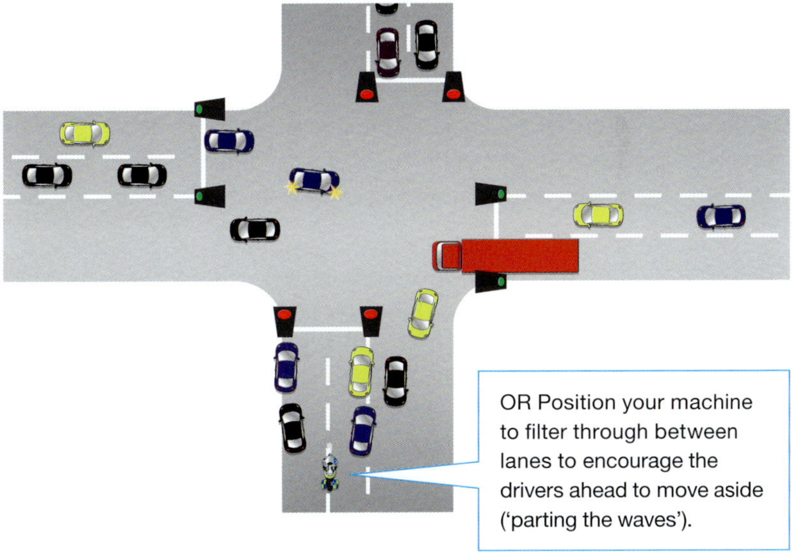

OR Position your machine to filter through between lanes to encourage the drivers ahead to move aside ('parting the waves').

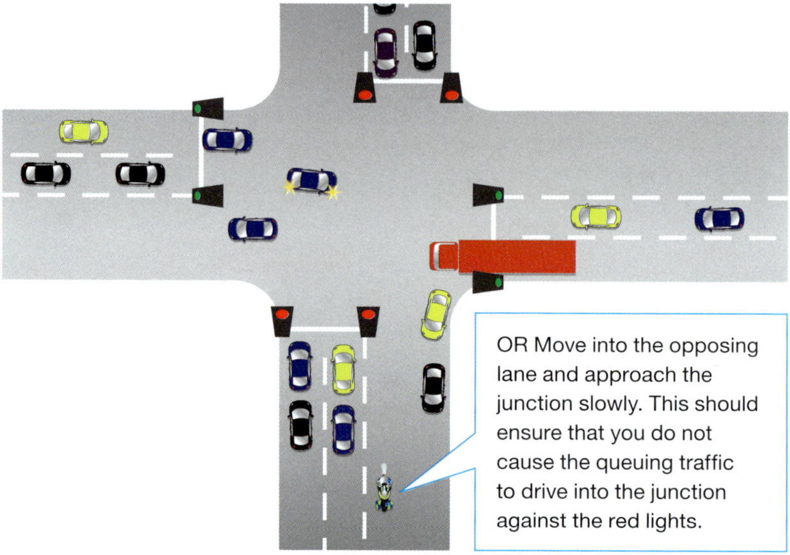

Certain traffic light junctions are too dangerous to cross while the lights are red. These are normally where views are restricted, on multi-lane carriageways or where the speed of cross traffic is high.

Approaching traffic light-controlled pedestrian crossings

The advice on approaching traffic light-controlled junctions also applies to pedestrian crossings. As you approach, gather information about the road layout and the presence and movement of pedestrians.

Your speed of approach should allow you to stop within the distance you can see to be clear. Pedestrians may be hidden by any vehicle on the approach. When a pedestrian has moved onto the crossing, you must give way to them.

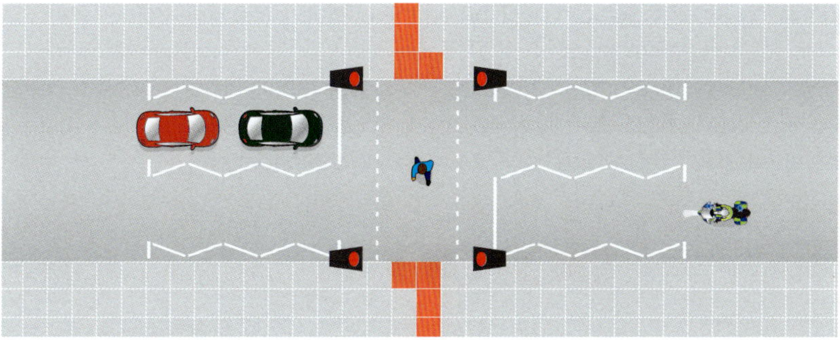

Where a pedestrian has moved onto the crossing, hold back so as not to intimidate them.

Contravening keep left/right signs

If you exercise the exemption to contravene keep left/right signs, you'll be in an unexpected position so you need to be aware of additional hazards.

For example, where there's a central refuge for pedestrians, they may be looking in the other direction as they cross the road and may step out into your path.

Positioning to see and be seen

During daylight, the best visual warning equipment on the approach to other road users is the flashing headlamp/white LED units. To get the greatest advantage, position your bike to make the most of these lights.

Where it's safe to do so, position your bike early towards the offside. This can help you to get early views and it also allows oncoming drivers and drivers ahead of you to spot you earlier.

Be prepared to surrender this position if an oncoming driver doesn't react appropriately.

Adopting an exaggerated position on the offside, as shown below, will help you to keep all hazards at an equal distance. The position shown below also gives a better view of the road and other dangers ahead. The driver of the vehicle directly ahead of the police bike will be aware that it's attempting to overtake rather than requiring them to stop.

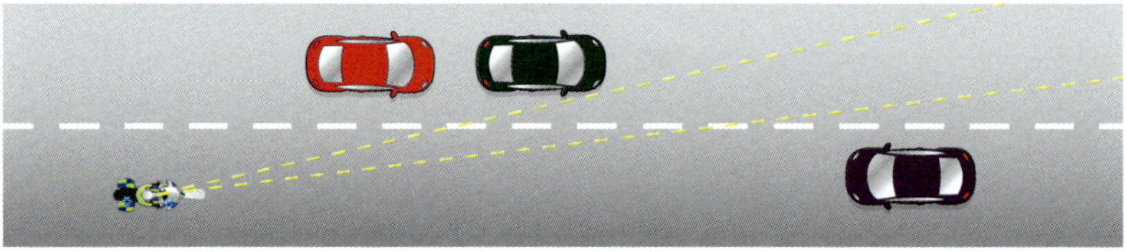

Always ensure that a safe gap is available on the nearside should oncoming drivers not react appropriately.

This position results in a restricted view for both the police rider and the oncoming driver.

Approaching and passing vehicles

Vehicles ahead

When approaching traffic travelling in the same direction, travel at a speed and following position that allows you to respond to heavy or sudden braking by the vehicles ahead. Keep your vision up, look past the vehicle to be overtaken and use your machine's acceleration capability to take opportunities, not chances.

Seek evidence that the drivers ahead are aware of your presence before you attempt to pass them. Look for the nearside indicator operating, vehicle movement into the nearside or offside, a moving wheel getting closer to the white line, and look in the driver's mirror to see the driver's head and body movements. Never assume that other road users have seen and/or heard you.

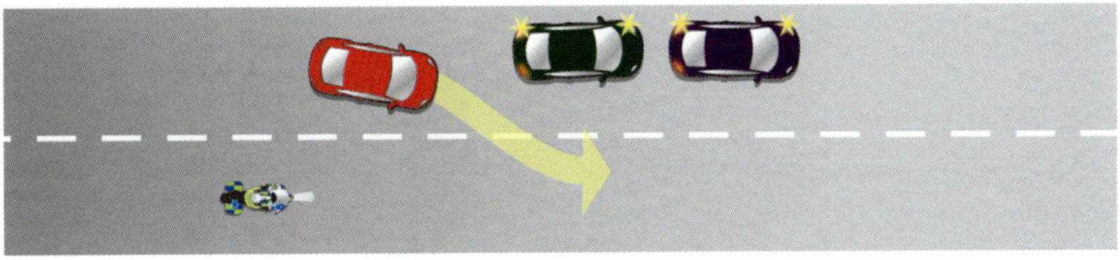

The drivers of the two lead vehicles have slowed down in response to the police motorcycle's presence. The driver of the red vehicle is unaware of the police bike and moves to overtake them, pulling out into its path.

Oncoming vehicles

When the driver of an oncoming vehicle has given way to your approaching motorcycle, always remain vigilant for other oncoming vehicles suddenly pulling out from behind the lead vehicle. Your speed should allow you time to stop should an oncoming vehicle suddenly present itself in your path.

This is especially important if the lead vehicle is large – for example, a large goods vehicle, van or bus.

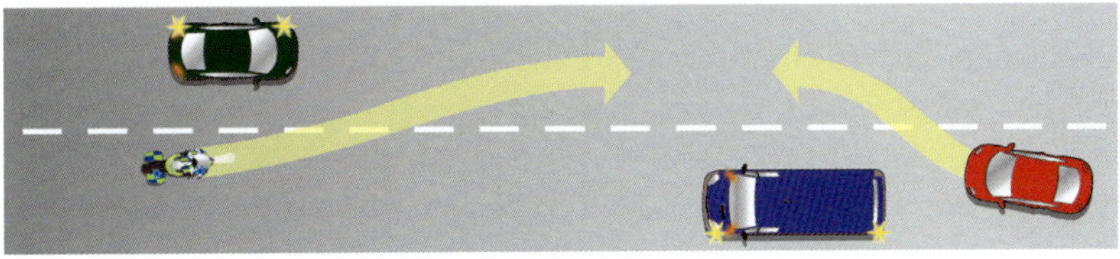

Vehicles behind the lead oncoming vehicle may be unaware of your presence and attempt to overtake the lead vehicle into your path.

Overtaking slow-moving vehicles across junctions

When moving past slow-moving or stationary vehicles, be aware of the additional hazards presented by road junctions and adjust your speed accordingly.

Nearside junctions

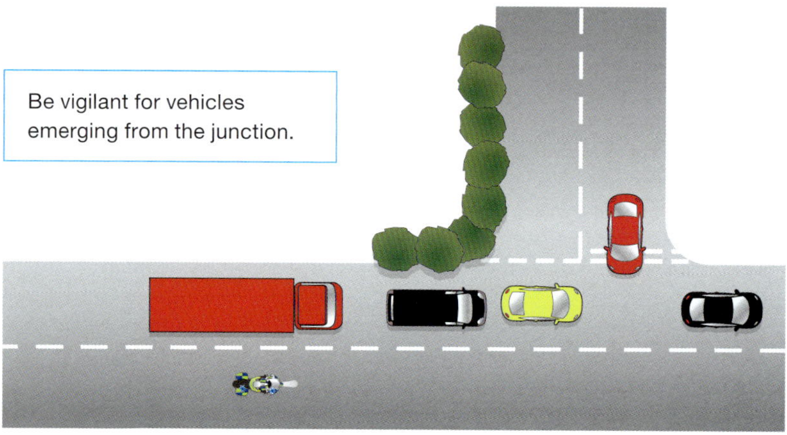

This manoeuvre is particularly hazardous for a rider as you present a smaller approaching profile and will be masked by other traffic until the last moment when the red vehicle emerges. Consider an extended offside position to increase the distance between you and the emerging vehicle. Consider a long horn note or change of two-tone horn note.

Offside junctions

On the approach to offside junctions with limited or no view, take up a position that allows you to stop or regain the correct side of the road. Never assume that the driver of the vehicle waiting to emerge will look to the left before entering the road. Consider the position shown in the diagram.

On the approach to an offside junction, adopt a position that allows you to stop or regain the correct side of the road should a driver turning left fail to spot you.

Interpreting other road users' signals

It's common for motorists to flash their headlights to signal to others their intention to give way in all kinds of driving situations.

In the scenario shown on the next page, there are three drivers who may perceive that the driver of the green car is signalling to them their intention to give way:

- the driver of the red vehicle waiting to emerge from the minor road
- the driver of the black vehicle waiting to turn right
- the police rider.

In situations such as this, take extra care and reduce your speed until you've safely negotiated the hazard.

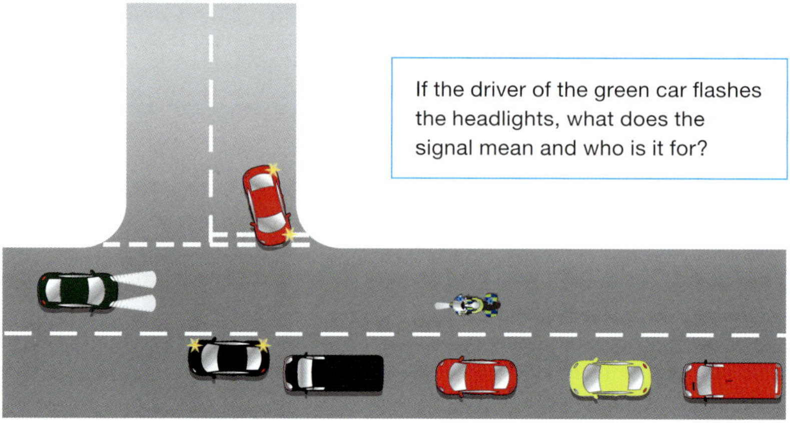

Stationary vehicles at or near an incident

Police riders approaching a scene may become distracted searching for the exact location of the incident. This may mean that their attention is drawn away from the road immediately ahead so increasing risk.

Drivers who have been stationary for some time may try to do a U-turn or leave their vehicle. Pedestrians may also be walking between the stationary vehicles.

Responding on multi-lane roads

On multi-lane roads equipped with central reservations, such as dual carriageways and motorways, your positioning will vary according to the volume and speed of vehicles ahead.

In very congested conditions where vehicles are either stationary or travelling at low speed, it's best practice for police riders to filter through between lanes to allow the traffic ahead to spread left and right. This is often referred to as 'parting of the waves'. Be mindful of cat's eyes unbalancing the machine and the white lines being potentially slippery in bad weather.

Be aware that some of the drivers ahead may not react as expected. Your approach speed must enable you to react to any vehicle crossing your path.

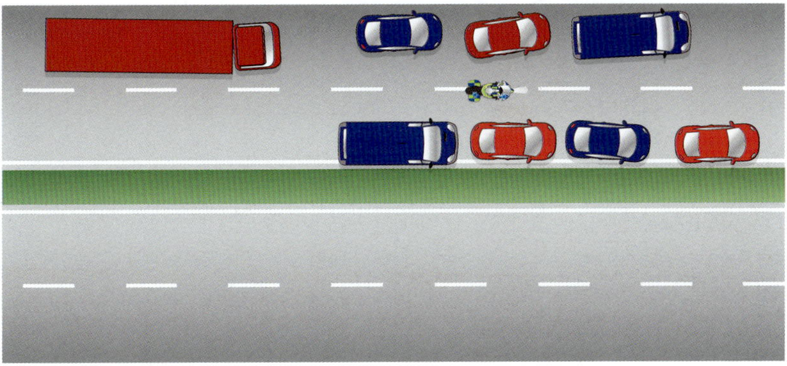

'Parting of the waves'

Where traffic is free-flowing, travel in the outer lane and allow vehicles ahead to move into the nearside lanes – but without placing drivers under undue pressure to do so. Look out for vehicles in lanes on the nearside ahead suddenly moving into the outer lane.

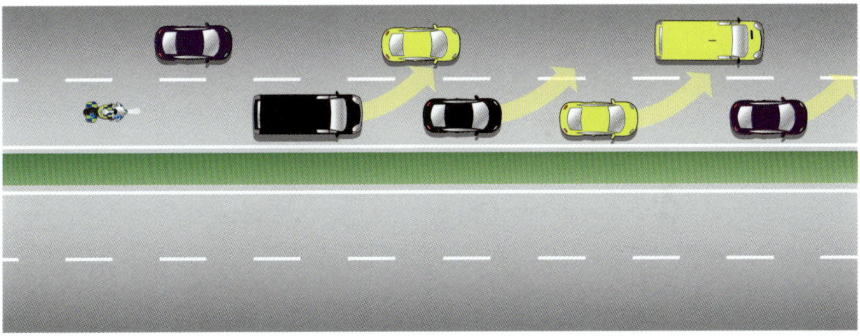

Travel in the outer lane of a multi-lane carriageway if the traffic is flowing freely.

Approaching roundabouts

A roundabout is a one-way system for which there's no exemption.

Approach roundabouts in the same manner as you would red traffic lights. Choose a low approach and entry speed so as not to cause drivers on the roundabout to over-react or brake hard.

If there are vehicles occupying all the approach lanes to the roundabout, use the same procedures as for a traffic light junction. Consider the following options to minimise the risk of drivers ahead entering the roundabout into the path of other vehicles.

Options

- Turn off all the emergency equipment and hold back.
- Straddle the lane markings to cause a 'parting of the waves'.
- Subject to view and safety, use the opposing carriageway. Bear in mind that drivers exiting the roundabout may have a late view of your bike.

A lower approach speed gives other motorists more time to help your progress. Drivers exiting the roundabout may have a late view of your approach.

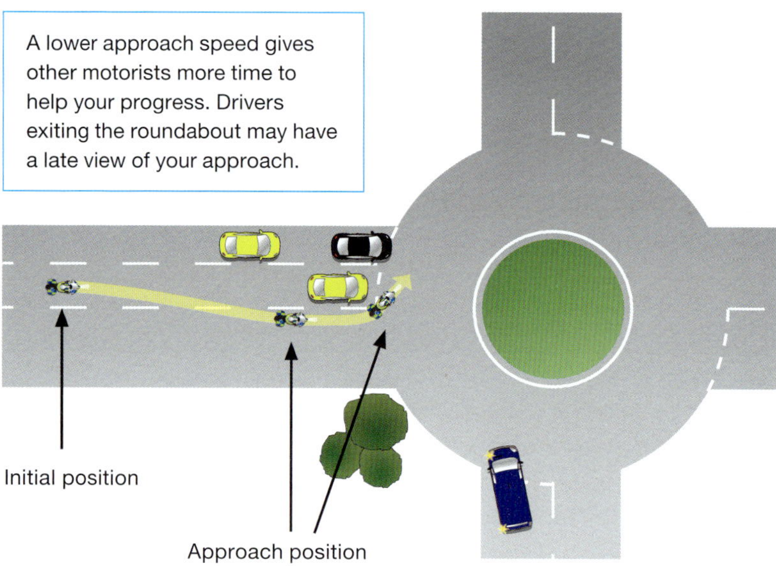

Passing on the nearside of other vehicles

Other drivers may find it hard to visually locate a police bike that is travelling along the nearside of stationary or moving vehicles. The natural response of a driver on hearing a siren is to move to the nearside to help the emergency vehicle's progress. Be aware of this as you formulate your riding plan. Ride at a speed that enables you to stop your bike safely if the vehicle ahead moves to the nearside.

Anticipate by carefully observing the actions of other road users. For example, watch for hand movements on the steering wheel, indicators, brake lights and movement of the wheels. These clues can provide early warning of potential movement to the nearside.

An alternative plan is to travel against the opposing traffic in the opposite lane. Use your narrow width to maximise the distance between you and the vehicles you're passing.

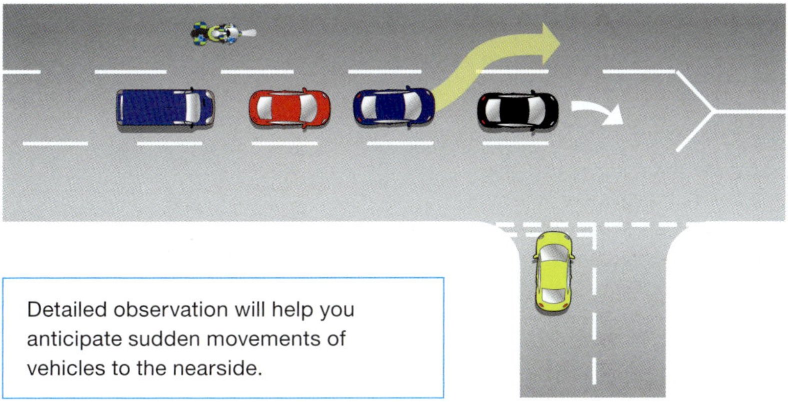

Detailed observation will help you anticipate sudden movements of vehicles to the nearside.

Multi-vehicle response

Multiple vehicles travelling together in response mode are more hazardous than a single vehicle. The public sometimes only react to the lead vehicle, and once it has passed may resume their journey into the path of additional vehicles.

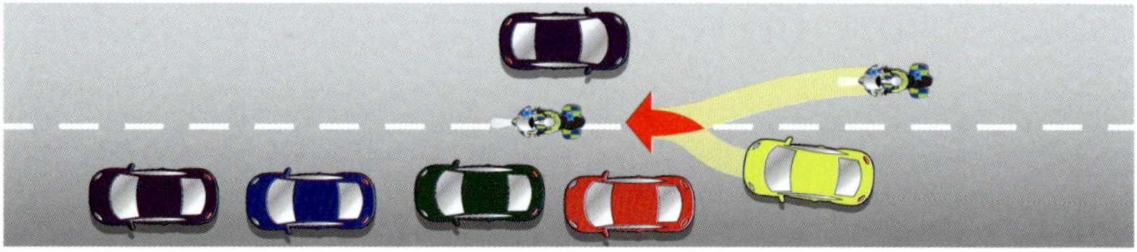

Be aware that other drivers may not anticipate the presence of additional responding emergency vehicles.

Depending on the circumstances, you may need to extend the reactionary gap between emergency vehicles, both to reduce the pressure on the emergency vehicle riders/drivers and to allow members of the public time to realise that there's more than one emergency vehicle approaching. Alternatively, you may choose to close the gap to reduce the risk of traffic pulling out between the two emergency vehicles.

If the vehicles have to remain together (for example, when escorting an ambulance), make sure that each is using a different siren sound.

Even if you're not part of a multi-vehicle response, always be aware of the possible presence of other emergency vehicles attending the same incident or a different one.

Vulnerable road users

Cyclists

Cyclists are very hard to see and may also react unexpectedly when a vehicle on an emergency call is approaching. The natural reaction of a cyclist on hearing the sirens is to look over their shoulder. This can cause wobbling and instability. Make sure you leave an appropriate safety margin when passing cyclists.

Pedestrians

Where pedestrians are present, ride at a speed that enables you to stop if a pedestrian steps into the road. Older people and children find it especially difficult to judge the speed and distance of approaching vehicles.

In bad weather, pedestrians tend to hurry, walking or running on slippery surfaces. Hoods, umbrellas and the use of personal audio equipment may hamper their awareness of your presence.

Horses and other animals

Horses can easily be startled by noise, movement or bright colours and may rear up or bolt, risking injury to the rider or horse. If there's a horse on the road, promptly deactivate all the emergency equipment and reduce your speed. Wait for an opportunity to pass safely. Adopt a slow speed and a position as far away from the animal as possible. Be aware horses may be more startled by a motorcycle than a car.

Don't speed up or reactivate the emergency response equipment until you've achieved a safe distance from the animal.

Be aware of the possible presence of other animals, particularly in rural areas and where animals are being transported in livestock vehicles. Look out for hazard warning signs depicting animals and make use of this information in your riding plan.

Check your understanding

You should now be able to apply learning from this chapter in your rider training so that you can:

- [ ] list the exemptions in law available to emergency response riders and explain their implications for your riding plan
- [ ] explain the importance of going through a process of risk assessment before and during an emergency call
- [ ] demonstrate the correct use of your machine's emergency warning equipment
- [ ] demonstrate good practice in emergency response riding across a range of traffic situations.

Appendices

1 Are you fit to ride?

- I AM SAFE checklist

2 Is your machine fit to ride?

- Roadworthiness/pre-riding checklist
- POWDDERSS checklist
- Testing the brakes

3 Fuel-efficient riding

- Key principles of fuel-efficient riding

4 Goals for Driver Education

Appendix 1 Are you fit to ride?

Even before you get on a bike, you should always assess whether you're fit to ride.

I AM SAFE checklist

Do a self-check using the I AM SAFE* checklist. Ask yourself these questions:

- ☐ **I**llness – Do I have an illness or symptoms that might affect my ability to ride?
- ☐ **A**ttitude – How do I feel about this journey? Am I fully focused on the riding task? What human factors do I need to take account of?
- ☐ **M**edication – Am I taking any medication that might affect my performance?
- ☐ **S**leep – Am I suffering from lack of sleep/fatigue?
- ☐ **A**lcohol – Have I had a drink? Am I still affected by alcohol?
- ☐ **F**ood – Am I hungry or thirsty? Could low blood sugar or dehydration affect my judgement?
- ☐ **E**motion – Am I angry, depressed, or stressed? Could this lead me to take risks?

**There are many versions of this checklist. Follow the one you find most useful.*

Appendix 2 Is your machine fit to ride?

If you haven't ridden the motorcycle before, refer to the machine handbook.

Roadworthiness/pre-riding checklist

Before you start to ride a motorcycle for the first time each day, you should ensure that it's roadworthy. Always carry out the following pre-riding checks.

Identify the type of motorcycle you're going to ride:

- ☐ general patrol/surveillance/specialist (escort group)/lightweight (three wheels)
- ☐ gearbox type (manual/automatic)/number of gears and position
- ☐ safety features – anti-lock braking system (ABS)/combined braking system (CBS)/electronic stability/traction control
- ☐ position of controls and auxiliaries
- ☐ glass/plastic – mirrors and lenses are clean
- ☐ security of carried items – panniers (weight restrictions/balance).

POWDDERSS checklist

Petrol (or charge)

Ensure that you have sufficient fuel or electric charge for your journey:

- Visual check
- Fuel gauge (if fitted)
- Reset trip meter

Oil

Oil levels/type – follow manufacturer's recommendations:

Engine oil

- Dipstick/sight glass – secured/clean
- Secure oil filler cap – top up if required

Brake/clutch fluid

- Levels and colour correct
- No water intrusion/bubbles
- Visual check for leaks on reservoir, hoses and connectors

Water

Radiator water level including coolant/anti-freeze mixture

Visual check for damage to radiator fins/top and bottom hoses

Damage/ Drive

Visual examination of machine:

- Insecure panels and/or damage
- Panniers/luggage – secured and balanced

Visual examination of drive mechanism:

- Chain – oiled and correct tension
- Sprockets – no hooked or missing teeth
- Shaft – no leaks, gaiters in place and not damaged

Electrics Verify operation of electrical systems.

- Lights – mandatory running lights (main and dipped beam)
- Brake light
- Indicators and hazard warning lights
- High-intensity lights front/rear (if fitted)
- Number plate light
- Emergency warning lights (blue, headlight flash, rear red)
- Interior instrument warning lights
- Audible warning systems (horn/two-tone horns)
- Ancillary systems (heated grips/windshield position)

Rubber Wheels – free rotation:

- Tyres – tread depth/free from cuts, bulges, tears/pressure/compatibility
- Valves – caps in place and free from damage
- Handlebar grips – secure
- Throttle (twist and release)
- Footrest rubbers – rider/pillion

Steering/Suspension

- Headrace bearings – free movement lock to lock and self-centring
- Trapped cables (engine tone increase)
- Suspension set for weight – damping/rebound
- Pillion/luggage adjustments
- Fork seals – clean and no leaks

Switch on the ignition. Note the warning lights. Ensure gear is neutral. Neutral light illuminated.

Disengage the clutch. Start the engine. Release the clutch slowly.

- If any checks could not be completed before ignition or start up, do them now
- Carry out a static brake check – front and rear brakes (see next page)
- Visual check of brake discs and pads
- Adjust seat – if required
- Adjust mirrors – when seated
- Visual inspection of all gauges and warning lights
- Remove machine from centre stand – ensure full retraction
- Check operation of side stand
- Emergency engine cut-off switch – check and re-set.

As soon as possible after moving off and in a safe place, carry out a moving brake test (see next page).

Check gauges and warning lights at intervals during all subsequent journeys, taking action if necessary.

Testing the brakes

Brakes are a very important part of the motorcycle. Check the brakes both before you move off and when the bike is moving.

The stationary test

Check that the hand lever and foot pedal move freely and give a firm positive pressure that can be maintained for 3 to 4 seconds.

The moving test

The purpose of the moving brake test is to:

- check that both brakes are working efficiently under running conditions
- learn how much to apply the brakes on that particular bike
- identify any unexpected problems.

A moving brake test is vital when you move off on an unfamiliar machine which you may need to ride in demanding conditions at higher speeds.

Check the brakes at around 30 mph using a non-retarding gear

Test both brakes as soon as possible after moving off. Always consider the safety and convenience of other road users before you do a moving test:

- Choose a flat, level road with good surface conditions.
- Check the road is clear behind you.
- Apply both brakes gradually and progressively, not harshly.
- Feel for anything unusual (for example, a tendency to pull to one side, any vibration or pulsing) and listen for anything unusual (for example, noise from the brakes could mean they are binding).
- Release the lever/pedal before you reach a standstill to check that the brakes release fully and aren't binding.

If you're on the same machine all day and there's no reason to suspect the performance of the brakes, you need to do this test only once in the day.

Appendix 3 Fuel-efficient riding

The emissions produced by vehicles cause damage to the environment and reduce air quality. Riding in a fuel-efficient way benefits not only the environment but also you the rider, other road users and your machine.

Key principles of fuel-efficient riding

- **Enhanced hazard perception and awareness** – looking well ahead and anticipating potential hazards decreases fuel consumption by cutting down on unnecessary acceleration and braking. Maintaining a safe following distance will help you plan your riding.
- **Starting up and riding away** – avoid over-revving the engine when starting up and moving away. Avoid leaving the engine running unnecessarily. If you're stationary for a long time, switch off the engine to reduce noise and air pollution.
- **Selecting gears** – as soon as conditions allow, use the highest gear possible, without making the engine struggle.
- **Select appropriate engine performance mode (if fitted)** – eco sacrifices performance for range.
- **Progressive use of controls** – smooth use of all controls (throttle, brakes, steering) saves fuel. Avoid heavy acceleration or braking. Riding smoothly reduces both fuel consumption and wear and tear on the machine.
- **Compliance with speed limits** – consider reducing your speed where possible to save fuel.
- **Prepare to stop, plan to go** – by using engine braking/torque, using vehicle momentum and avoiding unnecessary stops.
- **Check fuel consumption** – do this regularly to make sure you're getting the most from your machine. Record the amount of fuel you put in against the number of miles you travel.

- **Effective pre-riding checks and motorcycle maintenance** – make sure the motorcycle is serviced in line with the manufacturer's recommendations. Check tyre pressures. Incorrect tyre pressure could result in increased tyre wear, affecting stability and stopping distance. Under-inflation can increase fuel consumption and emissions.
- **Carrying loads/luggage** – consider making additional machine adjustments/checks to account for the increase in weight. Avoid carrying unnecessary luggage. Removing unused boxes/panniers could improve fuel consumption.
- **Use technology** – the manufacturer's handbook will give advice on the correct way to use the technology fitted to the machines within your fleet.

Adapt to changing conditions. Always prioritise safety over fuel efficiency.

For further information, see the DVSA publication, *The Official DVSA Guide to Riding – the essential skills*, Section 17.

Appendix 4 Goals for Driver Education

The European framework Goals for Driver Education (known as the 'GDE matrix') sets out the competences that driver or rider training should focus on to produce the safest possible drivers/riders.

The four levels of competency needed in all riding tasks	Knowledge and skills you have to master	Things that increase risk: be aware of and avoid these	Self-assessment for continuous improvement
4 Human factors before you get on your bike (for example, your personality, confidence, attitudes and mood)	What are your life goals and values? How do you behave on your own and in a group? How do your beliefs and personality affect your riding?	How do you react to peer pressure? In life, do you tend to take risks or avoid them? What personal tendencies or habits could increase your personal riding risk?	Think about yourself, your lifestyle and values. Are you impulsive? Are you always aware of the motives for your actions? What tendencies or attitudes do you need to manage when riding? Are you competitive? Do you find speed exciting? Do you get irritated by other road users?

3 The purpose of the journey	Each journey is different, with a different purpose and set of circumstances. This is about weighing up each journey in context.	What do you need to plan for? What's the purpose of this journey? Is it urgent? Are you under pressure? Or is it routine and tedious? What are the riding conditions likely to be?	Have you planned adequately for this journey? How do you respond to time pressure? What action do you take to manage tedium or monotony? What could you learn from this journey for next time?
2 The traffic situation including road and weather conditions	This is about observing, signalling, reading the road, assessing safety margins, obeying the rules, anticipating danger and positioning your machine to make safe progress.	Be aware of hazards in the specific riding conditions. Are there vulnerable road users? Are you going too fast to stop safely? Are you allowing for weather conditions?	During the ride, ask yourself: are you always in the correct gear and position for your speed? Do you anticipate hazards and deal with them safely? After the ride, assess what you did well, what you did less well and how you could improve.
1 Controlling your machine	This is about the physics of riding: knowing the machines you ride and how to control them (for example, using the throttle, brakes and gears smoothly and safely).	What are the characteristics of the machine you're riding? For example, does it tend to oversteer or understeer? What safety features are fitted? What do they do if activated?	During the ride: can you manoeuvre the machine accurately? After the ride: did it spring any surprises on you? Were you in perfect control throughout? What did you do well, what did you do less well and how could you improve?

For a detailed description of the GDE framework as a theoretical basis for driver education, explaining each competency level, its content and its implications for driver education, see Hatakka *et al.* (2002) and Peräaho *et al.* (2003).

There was a proposal to add a fifth level (social environment) to the GDE framework, but this has not been formally incorporated into the model. For further information, refer to Keskinen *et al.* (2010) in the bibliography. This would focus on cultural and social groups, and their associated values and norms, which impact on the attitudes and behavioural intentions of drivers identifying with a particular group. This in-group mentality may be of particular relevance to emergency services drivers.

Bibliography

This is a selective list of the sources drawn on to compile the advice and statistical information in this edition of *Motorcycle Roadcraft*, and in particular the information presented in Chapters 1 and 4.

Brams, S., Ziv, G., Levin, O., Spitz, J., Wagemans, J., Williams, A.M. and Helsen, W.F. (2019) The relationship between gaze behavior, expertise, and performance: A systematic review. *Psychological Bulletin*, 145 (10), 980–1027.

Brown, L., Morris, A., Thomas, P., Ekambaram, K., Margaritis, D., Davidse, R., Usami, D.S., Robibaro, M., Persia, L., Buttler, I., Apostolos Ziakopoulos, A., Theofilatos, A., Yannis, G., Martin, A. and Wadji, F. (2021) Investigation of accidents involving powered two wheelers and bicycles – A European in-depth study. *Journal of Safety Research*, 76, 135–145.

Chapman, P., Orhan, S. and Moore, L. (2023) Short term memory and peripheral vision at junctions. *Transportation Research Part F: Psychology and Behaviour*, 95, 432–449.

Christmas, S., Young, D., Cookson, R. and Cuerden, R. (2009) *Passion, Performance, Practicality: Motorcyclists' motivations and attitudes to safety*, PPR442, Transport Research Laboratory.

Clarke, D.D., Ward, P., Bartle, C. and Truman, W. (2007) The role of motorcyclist and other driver behaviour in two types of serious accident in the UK, *Accident Analysis and Prevention*, 39(5), 974–981.

College of Policing (2024) *Police Driving: Authorised professional practice*.

Crundall, D., Crundall, E., Clarke, D. and Shahar, A. (2012) Why do car drivers fail to give way to motorcycles at T-junctions? *Accident Analysis and Prevention*, 44(1), 88–96.

de Rome, L., Ivers, R., Fitzharris, M., Du, W., Haworth, N., Heritier, S. and Richardson, D. (2011) Motorcycle protective clothing: Protection from injury or just the weather? *Accident Analysis and Prevention*, 43(6), 1893–1900.

Department for Transport (2023) *Reported Road Casualties Great Britain: 2023 Annual Report*.

Department for Transport (2024) *Reported Road Casualties Great Britain: Motorcyclist factsheet 2023*.

Driver and Vehicles Standards Agency (DVSA) (2013) *National Standard for Riding Mopeds and Motorcycles (category A)*.

Elliott, M.A. (2010) Predicting motorcyclists' intention to speed: Effects of selected cognitions from the theory of planned behaviour, self-identity and social identity, *Accident Analysis and Prevention*, 42(2), 718–725.

Eyssartier, C., Meineri, S. and Gueguen, N. (2017) Motorcyclists' intention to exceed the speed limit on a 90 km/h road: Effect of the type of motorcycles. *Transportation Research Part F: Traffic Psychology and Behaviour*, 45, 183–193.

Hatakka, M., Keskinen, E., Gregersen, N.P., Glad, A. and Hernetkoski, K. (2002) From control of the vehicle to personal self-control: broadening the perspectives to driver education, *Transportation Research Part F*, 5(3), 201–215.

Haule, H. and Dumbaugh, E. (2024) Examining factors contributing to motorcycle collisions with left-turning vehicles at urban intersection locations. *Transportation Research Record*, 2678(11), 1666–1678.

Helman, S., Weare, A., Palmer, M. and Fernandez-Medina, K. (2012) *Literature Review of Interventions to Improve the Conspicuity of Motorcyclists and Help Avoid 'Looked But Failed to See' Accidents*, PPR638, Transport Research Laboratory.

Horberry, T., Hutchins, R. and Tong, R. (2008) *Motorcycle Rider Fatigue: A review*, Road Safety Research Report No. 78, Department for Transport.

Hosking, S.G., Liu, C.C. and Bayly, M. (2010) The visual search patterns of experienced and inexperienced motorcycle riders, *Accident Analysis and Prevention*, 42(1), 196–202.

Keskinen, E., Peräaho, M., Laapotti, S., Katila, A. and Hernetkoski, K. (2010) *Proposal for Driving Instruction in Three Stages to Acquire a B-category Driving Licence*, University of Turku, Finland: Trafi Publications 7/2010.

Kosovicheva, A., Wolfe, J.M. and Wolfe, B. (2023) Taking prevalence effects on the road: Rare hazards are often missed. *Psychonomic Bulletin & Review*, 30, 212–223.

Liu, J., Sun, L. and Li, W. (2025) Video-based hazard prediction and perception tests for Chinese motorcyclists and their associations with crash involvement. *Transportation Research Part F: Psychology and Behaviour*, 109, 1197–1207.

MacKillop, D. (2012) *Single Vehicle Accident on Rural Left-hand Bends*, personal communication.
The 'double apex bend' illustration and caption on page 170 are adapted from this paper with kind permission of the author.

National Police Chiefs' Council (NPCC) (2022) *National Roads Policing Strategy, 2022–2025.*

Peräaho, M., Keskinen, E. and Hatakka, M. (2003) *Driver Competence in a Hierarchical Perspective; Implications for Driver Education*, University of Turku, Traffic Research.

Royal Society for the Prevention of Accidents (RoSPA) (2020) *RoSPA Road Safety Research: Common motorcycle crash causes*.

Sharp, G. (1997) *Human Aspects of Police Driving, Scottish Police College*.

Teoh, E.R. (2023) Left-turn crashes and motorcycle safety, *Traffic Injury Prevention*, 24 (6), 511–512.

Wu, Y., Kihara, K. and Takeda, Y. (2024) Following car reduces motorcycles' size-arrival effect: A study using online experiments. *Applied Ergonomics*, 114, 104153.

Index

Bold page numbers indicate illustrations, *italic* numbers indicate tables.

williams lea | tso
An RRD Company

Published by TSO (The Stationery Office), part of Williams Lea, and available from:

Online
www.tsoshop.co.uk

Mail, telephone & email
TSO
PO Box 29, Norwich, NR3 1GN
Telephone orders/General enquiries: 0333 202 5070
Email: customer.services@tso.co.uk
Textphone: 0333 202 5077